Praise for
THE FUTURE BEGINS WITH Z

"Dr. Tim Elmore is a remarkable thought leader and a valuable resource to anyone who wants to understand and lead younger generations, whether you are a professional or a parent. His evidence-based insights and practical tools have advanced our work at Emory Healthcare as we lead multiple generations. I highly recommend this resource and encourage you to use the fresh ideas he offers to elevate your team."

—POLINA ZLATEV,
Vice President of Talent,
Learning & Culture, Emory Healthcare

"The challenge of leading young team members doesn't get any easier as time marches forward. In fact, the gap seems to be getting wider. Dr. Tim Elmore provides a flashlight to discover the treasure that lies inside Gen Zers but is often hidden. I encourage leaders to read this book and utilize the tools it offers."

—DAYTON MOORE,
Senior Advisor of Baseball Operations, Texas Rangers

"Like most companies, we've seen how today's emerging professionals bring fresh perspectives and new expectations to the workplace. This book opened my eyes to the unique strengths Gen Z contributes to our teams—and how adapting our leadership approach can unlock their full potential. If you're looking to better understand and connect with your youngest team members, this book is a must-read."

—ED HOLMES,
Director of Technical Training
& Development, DN Tanks

"*The Future Begins with Z* is a must-read! Tim Elmore has so eloquently addressed an issue that so often gets neglected. As a Chief People and DEI Officer, I believe we need to focus on all dimensions of inclusion, including the youngest generation joining today's workforce. Tim Elmore has an innate way of cutting through theories about generations to get to the core of what helps a leader empower young team members to operate at their best."

—CAMYE MACKEY,
Chief People, Diversity &
Inclusion Officer, Atlanta Hawks

"If we care about the future, we must focus our attention on helping younger generations learn from our mistakes and successes. The book you're holding is a handbook to connect with and empower Gen Z. Tim Elmore has given his life to helping generations connect. He's the best at equipping leaders to understand the next generation and to know how to lead them."

—DR. JOHN C. MAXWELL,
#1 *New York Times* Bestselling Author,
Founder, Maxwell Leadership

"Tim Elmore has been a mentor and added wisdom to me and everyone who knows him or has read one of his forty-plus books. *The Future Begins with Z* is Tim Elmore's absolute best yet! As a CEO who leads one thousand team members, nothing is more important than culture, and we must understand every generation in order to lead and love them well and give them an opportunity to thrive at work. This book is your tool kit and guide! Thank you, Tim!"

—CHRIS CARNEAL,
Founder and CEO, Booster Enterprises

"Dr. Elmore does a masterful job of providing both insightful learning and actionable direction. Our leadership team has benefited greatly from his guidance in welcoming and leveraging the skills of the next generation."

—SHANE JACKSON,
CEO, Jackson Healthcare

"Our administrators and staff work hard to connect with this new generation of athletes while also onboarding and retaining Gen Zers on the team. Tim has helped us all gain a better understanding on how to lead Generation Z while incorporating all the generations that are in the workforce nowadays. This resource is a textbook on how to succeed at this task. I recommend it to anyone leading young team members."

—JULIE WORK,
Executive Vice President, NACDA
(National Association of Collegiate Directors of Athletics)

"Having known Tim Elmore for years and read many of his books, I continue to be struck by his ability to name what leaders are feeling—and then offer practical, thoughtful ways forward. *The Future Begins with Z* is one of his most timely and important works yet. As an educational leader, I found it both affirming and challenging. Tim doesn't just help us understand Gen Z—he shows us how to lead with empathy, respect, and clarity so we can truly bring out the best in this generation. His voice is as trusted as it is necessary."

—DR. JEFF ROSE,
Three-Time School Superintendent
and Host of *Leader Chat*

THE FUTURE BEGINS WITH Z

INTRODUCING THE JOHN MAXWELL IMPRINT

John C. Maxwell
PUBLISHING

The John Maxwell Imprint is a new leadership-focused division of HarperCollins Publishing that seeks to extend and expand the legacy of leadership expert Dr. John C. Maxwell. Dr. Maxwell has been identified as the #1 leader in business by the American Management Association® and the most influential leadership expert in the world by *Business Insider* and *Inc.* magazine. A recipient of the Horatio Alger Award, as well as the Mother Teresa Prize for Global Peace and Leadership from the Luminary Leadership Network, Dr. Maxwell speaks each year to Fortune 500 companies, presidents of nations, and many of the world's top business leaders.

The mission of the John Maxwell Imprint is to discover and publish books that identify with John Maxwell's personal values and philosophy of leadership. The authors will be men and women of integrity in their personal, business, and spiritual lives, who have demonstrated a desire to add value to leaders who multiply that value to people, whether through their teaching, writing, or business acumen.

THE FUTURE BEGINS WITH Z

Nine Strategies
to Lead Generation Z as
They DISRUPT the Workplace

TIM ELMORE

HarperCollins
Leadership

An Imprint of HarperCollins

The Future Begins with Z
© 2025 by Tim Elmore

All rights reserved. No portion of this book may be reproduced, stored in a retrieval system, or transmitted in any form or by any means—electronic, mechanical, photocopy, recording, scanning, or other—except for brief quotations in critical reviews or articles, without the prior written permission of the publisher.

Published by HarperCollins Leadership,
an imprint of HarperCollins Focus LLC,
501 Nelson Place, Nashville, TN 37214, USA.

Any internet addresses, phone numbers, or company or product information printed in this book are offered as a resource and are not intended in any way to be or to imply an endorsement by HarperCollins Leadership, nor does HarperCollins Leadership vouch for the existence, content, or services of these sites, phone numbers, companies, or products beyond the life of this book.

ISBN 978-1-4002-5605-1 (ePub)
ISBN 978-1-4002-5604-4 (HC)

Without limiting the exclusive rights of any author, contributor, or the publisher of this publication, any unauthorized use of this publication to train generative artificial intelligence (AI) technologies is expressly prohibited. HarperCollins also exercises their rights under Article 4(3) of the Digital Single Market Directive 2019/790 and expressly reserves this publication from the text and data mining exception.

HarperCollins Publishers, Macken House, 39/40 Mayor Street Upper, Dublin 1, D01 C9W8, Ireland (https://www.harpercollins.com)

Library of Congress Cataloging-in-Publication Data
Library of Congress Cataloging-in-Publication application has been submitted.

Art Direction: Ron Huizinga
Cover Design: Thinkpen Design
Interior Design: Neuwirth & Associates, Inc.
Illustrations: Mike Rohde

Printed in the United States of America
25 26 27 28 29 LBC 5 4 3 2 1

CONTENTS

Foreword by John C. Maxwell   *xiii*

Introduction: May I Be Your Interpreter?   *xvii*

PART ONE
Understanding Them Deeply

1. The Peter Pan Paradox   3
2. How We Got to Z   23
3. The Value Generation Z Brings to the Workplace   46
4. The Myths We've Believed About Generation Z   66

PART TWO
Nine Strategies to Turn Land Mines into Gold Mines

5. The Welcome Wagon: Making Them Want to Stay   87

CONTENTS

6 Terms of Engagement: Connect Before You Correct — 107

7 Critical Conversations: Offering Tough Feedback — 127

8 Creating a Safe Place: Helping Them Manage Their Mental Health — 149

9 Rightsizing Their Mindsets: Managing Unrealistic Expectations — 169

10 Awakening Ambition: Motivating and Incentivizing Them — 191

11 Tappers and Listeners: How to Get Through to Them — 213

12 Cultivating Soft Skills: Building Them Into Leaders — 235

13 Building Grit and Fostering Growth — 255

PART THREE
A New You for a New Team Member

14 Upgrading Your Leadership — 275

15 The Big Payoff — 295

Notes — 303
Acknowledgments — 313
Index — 315
About the Author — 323

"Generation Z is the sandpaper on my leadership
I didn't know I needed."

—Renee Walter

FOREWORD

I have always believed in people, sometimes to a fault. When I've hired staff, I had faith in their potential, believing they could do whatever they set their mind to do. It's been the foundation of my leadership. Practicing this, however, has become difficult for many leaders today, especially when it comes to young staff launching their careers.

This new generation of team members entering the workforce today is different. I continually hear from employers and leaders who are frustrated with their attitudes and performance. When I speak at events, I hear managers complain about them, asking me what I think they should do. I usually admit, I too might be a little frustrated at the kind of conduct they describe from those in Generation Z. But then I always encourage them to adapt. That's one of the most important skills leaders can practice today. Adapting doesn't mean you always give in to their requests and give up your values. It means you size up the people in front of you and then adapt your leadership to offer what they need to reach their potential. It's the leader's job to connect, then to direct.

The only way I know to do this is to begin with belief.

We give up too easily. If we want more grit from our Gen Z teammates, why don't we show a little grit ourselves? If we wish they understood our business a little better, why not work to understand them a little better? If we want them to care a little more about their job, what if we first show that we care about them? As Tim Elmore asks in this book: What if we could turn our frustration into fascination with our young employees? When we begin with belief, we assume the best about them, even when they do something that feels illogical. The words of Abraham Lincoln seem appropriate. He once said, "I don't like that man. I must get to know him."

I always benefit from remembering I was once that kid starting my career. I am sure older generations saw me as problematic. As a student, my teacher once gave me an F in conduct because I kept interrupting her by getting up and talking to my classmates. She called my mother in to discuss my behavior. When both asked me why I did this, I explained I was telling them what we should do on the playground at recess. I always wanted to lead and influence others and have built my entire career from doing this. Thank God those caring adults saw my potential and began to channel my energies instead of stifling them.

This book is about seeing the potential in today's newest team member.

I have known Tim Elmore since 1982. I hired Tim right out of college over forty years ago. He was inexperienced, but I was able to see past that and identify his potential. I chose to invest in him, and it was well worth the effort. He became an effective leader and communicator and launched his own organization in 2003. Along the way, he's written forty books, most of them about how to lead the emerging generation. This book may be his most important one yet. In a time when we feel the generational divide more than ever, we need a guide to help us build bridges instead of walls. This book is a road map for that journey. In this resource, you will understand young people better, you'll discover how to motivate them, how to offer feedback when they seem fragile, how to connect with them and keep them on the team, and even how to develop them into leaders.

FOREWORD

Consider this. Because this book is about leading our young people, it's about the future. If we care about the future, we must care about preparing them well. Forget for a moment how you feel about their mannerisms, tattoos, piercings, or opinions. Like it or not, they represent tomorrow's world. They represent tomorrow's consumer. They represent tomorrow's leaders. Ready or not, they will take over someday.

I encourage you to absorb this book. In a sense, it can serve as an encyclopedia, offering information you need to know about your young team members, your nephews and nieces, your grandkids or maybe even your own kids. Additionally, it can be a reference guide, where you go straight to a certain chapter for help with a particular need. Recently, Tim and I spent some time together and discussed the ideas in this book. Those conversations were very intriguing to me. I believe this content will be to you as well.

Your friend,
John C. Maxwell
2025

INTRODUCTION

May I Be Your Interpreter?

This book is the accumulation of forty-five years of work with younger generations. Yes, you read that correctly. I began teaching and leading young people when I myself was a young person. I studied how they learn and communicate and get motivated. Even then, I recognized a growing gap between teachers and students, employers and their young staff. I began to see them growing frustrated, rather than fascinated with each other. Two very different mindsets were forming, each misunderstanding the other, and creating a divide that, frankly, some couldn't get past. Young people would quit on the older ones, and older leaders would give up on the young.

This was obviously no way to move forward.

So, I decided I'd do the work of a translator between old and young. I soon realized that wasn't enough. Translating words was insufficient. Both young and old needed an interpreter—who not only explained values but interpreted why they existed. A translator puts foreign words in your language. An interpreter explains their meaning. I have hosted countless focus groups over

INTRODUCTION

the years and taken loads of surveys to gather both qualitative and quantitative data on the young. More recently, on the old as well. Along the way, I found myself playing the role of interpreter for each demographic. I would say to baby boomers, "Yes, I know that decision Austin made seemed illogical—but let me share what he told me that drove him to make it." Or, I'd be with young staff, who were confused by the stubborn and skeptical mindsets of colleagues over fifty years old. I'd empathize with them but then explain the logic of people my age. Even if the two groups didn't agree right away, at least they understood one another. And that was a beginning.

I hope this book becomes an encyclopedia for you. I trust it will explain the mind and heart of a Generation Z member. We've heard the phrase for years, "Don't put the cart before the horse." In this volume, I put the heart before the course. I begin the chapters helping you see why Gen Z has become the people they are, then provide a mini-course on leading through these challenges. As I studied and wrote, I learned so much. My compassion for them grew deeper. My understanding of them expanded. Along the way, I realized they are products of our making. If we don't like how they've turned out—we need to look in the mirror. Today, I can honestly say to anyone who reads my words: *I believe in Generation Z.* And I believe they will disrupt the workplace as they eventually take it over. How that plays out is chiefly up to us. The outcomes are in the hands of leaders. We must learn how to lead them so they can make all of us better. So they can prepare us for the future.

I have a confession to make. I need to acknowledge that I changed as I studied Gen Z. I had been frustrated with them, even furious with them at times because of how they acted. But getting up close, I began to see the why behind their words and behaviors. Now, I am a fan. I believe in these young people. And I'm more convinced that if we lead them well, they will stand on our shoulders and one day lead better than we did. They will be

INTRODUCTION

the source of inventions and discoveries that we only imagined in our day. Our job is to turn our frustration into fascination. We must not get furious but get curious about them so we can lead them well. Their success may well be up to us.

I heard a story of a young boy who held a bird in his hand. The bird was so small, he could cup his hand around it, so you couldn't tell if that bird was living or not. The boy asked an elderly man seated on a park bench if he would guess whether the bird was dead or alive. The old man stared at it for a moment, then smiled and replied: "If I say the bird is dead, you can release it and prove I was wrong. If I say it's alive, you could crush it and prove me wrong. The truth is—the answer is in your hands."

So it is with us, and these young team members. My friend Bob Taylor once told me, "Always invest in the inevitable." May I remind you—it is inevitable that Generation Z will one day rule our world. It's to everyone's advantage that we invest in them.

Tim Elmore
2025

THE FUTURE BEGINS WITH Z

PART

1

UNDERSTANDING THEM DEEPLY

In this opening portion, I want to help you step into the minds and hearts of Generation Z, understanding how they think, what they value, and why they do what they do. In knowing these realities, you'll be prepared to lead them in a more relevant way.

1

THE PETER PAN PARADOX

In 2018, Colin Webb graduated from the Massachusetts Institute of Technology. While at MIT, he served four terms as class council president and now serves his alma mater as a member of the MIT corporation, the school's board of trustees. I can vouch for him—this guy is a sharp young man. I'd hire him in a New York minute if I could afford him.

A few years back, Colin told me his career had taken a sharp turn.

Upon graduation, he was offered a job by General Motors. Colin was asked to be a design, release, and development engineer with their Cruise autonomous vehicle program. At twenty-two, Colin Webb was helping to design smart cars for one of the Big Three in Detroit. Not a bad gig. He quickly realized, however, he was part of an old industry with a traditional style of getting things done. Obviously, he and his young teammates brought some new ideas, but when he bounced them off his direct supervisor, he was told to keep his head down, his mouth shut, and his nose to the grindstone. In short, don't make any waves. Instead, Colin did something audacious. He wrote Mary Barra, the CEO of GM. In his email, he suggested some ideas for improving the company and developing the employees. Mary replied, saying she felt his ideas were good and that she would put him in touch with her executive team. The executive team was open, but when the ideas made their way down the org chart to the managers, they got stuck. At that middle level of leadership, the managers expect you to be in the industry for eight years before you earn the right to lead. It was hard for them to listen to an idea from a "kid." Further, his ideas were different from the way they did things. Within a matter of weeks, those ideas died on the vine.

Before the year was out, Colin chose to leave the company and launch out on his own.

Colin Webb is now an entrepreneur. He cofounded Sauce Pricing, where his team created data-driven pricing strategies for restaurants. Using artificial intelligence, he's leveraging it in more relevant ways than many other companies led by older generations. After a couple of years, he sold the company, and it's now called Linked Eats. He'll be on to new ventures soon. He holds no resentment toward his former employer, and he remains optimistic about Gen Z contributing to today's workforce. When I shared how many employers are frustrated by the way Generation Z approaches work, he smiled and replied, "Young people will figure out a way to succeed."

Colin's path makes sense. He said, "Being a small part of a large organization seemed like a predictable path, yet what I could build on my own seemed limitless. I knew that if I worked hard to solve a real problem for people, not only could I make a huge impact, but each year was potentially worth millions. My biggest fear? What if I didn't take that chance?"

Different versions of Colin's story are being lived out every day around the world.

I drew a couple of conclusions after listening to his story. First, the challenge for leaders and companies may not lie at the C-suite level. Mary Barra welcomed new ideas and opportunities to improve General Motors. The problem rested at the supervisor level, those who worked directly with a new generation of very different team members, the ones who've grown up in this new world in which we live today, those who have an intuition on where our culture is going and are not stuck in past paradigms.

My second conclusion is that neither the old nor the young may be patient enough to stick with the other. Three in four managers find Generation Z the most difficult population to work with as employees, according to a 2024 survey by ResumeBuilder.com. Three in ten managers report they avoid hiring Gen Z employees. Thirty percent of managers report firing a Gen Z employee within a month of their start date.[1] The results of a 2024 *Forbes* "Gen Z Workers Report" found that just as boomers had concerns about millennials, Gen Z now encounters similar criticism. Even 45 percent of Gen Z hiring managers share the same sentiment about their peers.[2] Sadly, the average Gen Z employee stays on the job two years and three months, according to a report by CareerBuilder.com.[3] The data show that Generation Z and younger millennials are disengaging and quitting companies at fast rates.

I believe we can shift our approach to keep the best Gen Zers on our team.

THE TRANSFORMATION THAT'S ON ITS WAY

If we don't face what's happening, learn how to lead young generations, and leverage what they bring to the team, Gen Z's tenure with us may be short-lived, just like Colin Webb. Mark my words: we are staring at a transformation coming in the workplace. For some, it will be a *revolution*, where your industry and workplace change rapidly, even abruptly. For others, it will feel more like an *evolution*, taking place over several years. But it is coming. Unlike past generations when fresh graduates joined a team with no experience and needed to learn the ropes from seasoned veterans and pay their dues over time, these "new kids on the block" recognize that past experience in our day can work against you. It's why so many young adults become entrepreneurs. They'd rather start something than join something. Those over forty-five years old may have work experience that's built on the past. Generation Z has personal, portable-device experience that's built on the future.

REFLECT AND RESPOND

Have you noticed any similar shifts in your workplace?

SEASONED VETERANS	YOUNG ROOKIES
1. Bring perspective from the past	1. Bring perspective based on the future
2. Have visibility on their former years	2. Have visibility on where the future is going
3. Possess insights based on their career	3. Possess intuition based on their culture
4. Battle habits or ruts from former routines	4. Have few habits or ruts to combat
5. Prefer to tweak what's happening now	5. Prefer to overhaul what's happening now
6. Can be coaches teaching timeless skills	6. Can be creators building timely offerings

We must recognize that our job as leaders may be changing as well. What they bring to the table will require us to do *more listening* and *more coaching*. Did you catch that? Taking time to listen to young employees more than we did in the past and to coach young employees more than we did in the past. We're staring at the Peter Pan Paradox.

NAVIGATING THE PETER PAN PARADOX

Business managers and employers face a paradox today. While it's been emerging slowly for years, this paradox is now the top reason for frustration between young team members and older generations at work. I call it the "Peter Pan Paradox" for a reason.

You may recall the fictional character Peter Pan, created by novelist and playwright J. M. Barrie. If you haven't read the book or seen the stage play, perhaps you've seen the 1953 animated movie created by Walt Disney, *Peter Pan*. Over the years, several other versions have been released. Much has been written comparing millennials and Generation Z to Peter Pan and his refusal to grow up. This book is different. It offers ideas on managing this downside of Gen Z but also furnishes ideas for how to capitalize on the upside, namely, that they bring something new and captivating to our workplaces.

This vivid metaphor helps us understand the two sides to Gen Z today.

First, Peter Pan is a winsome character who brings magical qualities with him. He doesn't seem to have a care in the world, he can fly anywhere, he mysteriously plays musical instruments, he can outsmart pirates, and he possesses hidden talents that help him navigate a complex world. This is what makes the story fun. Call it pixie dust.

Second, Peter Pan refuses to grow up; hence, he wants to reside in Neverland, where you can remain a child forever. While the innocence of this choice is attractive, he comes to recognize this lack of maturity can lead to problems. With autonomy, we learn in this story, comes responsibility. It naturally surfaces as time marches on.

I first wrote about this in my book *Generation iY: Our Last Chance to Save Their Future*, published in 2010, which became a bestseller. Fifteen years ago, we began to see a growing population of young adults who appeared much like Peter Pan.[4] While this sounds insulting, the data proved it to be true, and it's not all bad. There were two sides to the coin inside this new population of employees, and it's only become more vivid since then.

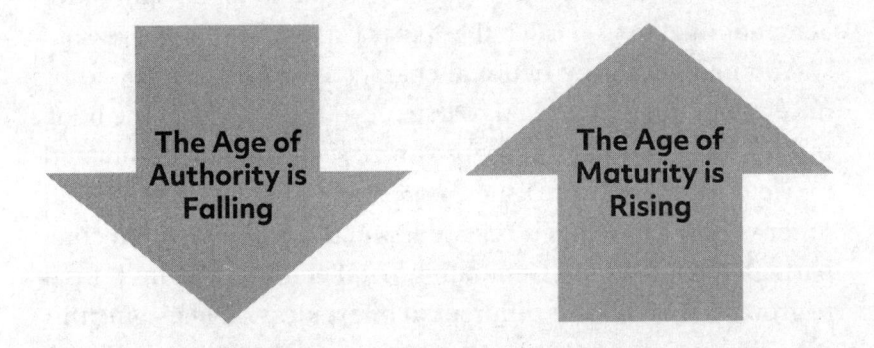

> The Age of Authority is Falling

> The Age of Maturity is Rising

THE AGE OF AUTHORITY IS FALLING

An increasing number of employers have told me their Gen Z employees came up with an idea to reach customers through off-beat social media sites, using an odd strategy, and it worked. Sales leads went through the roof. These young entrepreneurial minds join a team with little to no *experience* but lots of *experiments*. In their youth they have experimented on various platforms, and it's informed their interactions in public spaces. They know things we don't know. They hear things we don't hear. They see things we don't see. With or without a leadership title, young professionals often bring with them an intuition about the future. They have clearer visibility on where culture is heading and what consumers will want in the future. Why? They represent the future.

I witnessed this when I launched a nonprofit organization, Growing Leaders, in 2003 and hired young team members fresh out of college. We offered curriculum to teach life skills, leadership, and social and emotional learning for students in schools. By 2005, we'd already sold thousands of books, and our potential looked unlimited. That year, however, David, a recent grad from Pepperdine University, said, "You know, we probably need to look into a digital offering of our content, right?" I replied, "A digital offering?" He smiled and said, "This may sound crazy, but since the internet is the future, I think one day, more schools will want our Habitudes on an online platform."

He was right. The Blockbuster mindset was giving way to the Netflix mindset. It took years, but we created HabitudesOnline, and today, far more administrators purchase a license and passwords to get our content than buy books. My younger teammates continue to give us a jump start on the future. Call it pixie dust.

Organizational psychologist Adam Grant confirms this notion that the traditional age of authority is decreasing as young professionals bring fresh ideas, valuable insights, and "next gen" knowledge into the workplace. This is accelerated by both technological advances and Gen Z's widespread access to information that allows them to make quick and significant contributions to a team. In short, *the "boss" may have experience, but they have exposure.* You have the position, but they have the perspective.

In 2015, Maggie Grout was a fifteen-year-old high school student, dreaming of ways she could improve the world. As an adopted Chinese girl, she realized how education completely transformed her life. That year, she got an idea and launched Thinking Huts. This nonprofit organization combines technology and humanitarian-driven goals to support quality education. What do they do? Maggie and Thinking Huts create school buildings with 3D printers. Yes, you read that correctly. They've begun to fill the need for schools all over the world, in the most needed places, believing that education is a universal solvent that can prevent health epidemics, tackle environmental issues, lift economies, and empower communities in every corner of the world. These 3D printed schools can be run by solar power in remote parts of the earth. Maggie is a member of Gen Z who saw and did something older folks didn't. I love that pixie dust.

This generation is rethinking what it means to enter the workforce. WP Engine found that 62 percent of Gen Z members plan to start their own business someday. A majority, 70 percent, are currently freelancing or plan to in the future, according to a February 2024 Fiverr survey of 10,033 Gen Zers from around the world. More recent research by Square puts the number even higher, saying 84 percent of Gen Zers want to own their own company in the future.

I discovered why in a focus group I hosted with members of Gen Z. They were keenly aware that the economy is uncertain today, and they feel that working for someone who may not have their best interests in mind puts time, housing, and income out of their control. Their trust in traditional institutions, including corporate America, is low right now. When they join a company and leaders don't listen to them, it only reinforces their notions.

In my book *A New Kind of Diversity: Making the Different Generations on Your Team a Competitive Advantage,* I share Tony Piloseno's story.[5] During his senior year of college, he took a part-time job at a paint store. He loved his work so much that he started a TikTok account to post all the amazing colors he'd created by mixing the paints at the store. People loved Tony's posts so much that he attracted a massive following. By 2020, he had 1.4 million followers and twenty-four million "likes." Having gone viral, Tony decided to share what he'd done with the executives of the paint brand. Maybe they could monetize it. He was surprised, however, when he didn't get one leader who was open to meet with him. He never got one set of eyeballs to look at his slide deck on how they could monetize his social media following.

Instead, he got something he didn't expect. He got fired. So after graduation, Tony moved to Florida, now has 2.1 million followers on TikTok, he's got 3.8 million followers across TikTok, Instagram, and YouTube, and he started his own paint store. He ships out thousands of gallons of paint from Tonester Paints. While I admit we don't have all the details on his career journey, I do know one thing: that paint store in Ohio missed out on an opportunity to grow if they'd only listened to a kid.

Keep in mind, this population of young professionals grew up in a digital world from the beginning, immersed in screens, smart technology that has rewired their brains. Farhan Hidayat, CEO of HRConsol, writes, "A growing discourse suggests that Generation Z is endowed with higher cognitive abilities compared to their predecessors, the millennials. This assertion prompts an exploration into the unique characteristics and experiences that might contribute to the perception of heightened intelligence within Gen Z." This rewiring of their cognitive abilities has pros and cons, according to NYU professor and author Jonathan Haidt. Twenty-first-century kids have matured in a "phone-based" rather than a "play-based" childhood, which affected how they approach life. The downside is they endure high anxiety and lower social and emotional development. The upside is they don't have to unlearn many things my generation has had to unlearn.

ONE ANTHROPOLOGIST SAW THIS COMING

Margaret Mead was arguably the most famous anthropologist of the twentieth century. I recall being intrigued and amused by her words when I was in college. More than fifty years ago, not long before she died, Margaret saw something coming that we are now experiencing. I am amazed at her foresight and insight. She predicted that for the first time in history, young people would know more than their elders about the world in which they live. In her book *Culture and Commitment: A Study of the Generation Gap*, Mead clarifies three stages of human history:

1. **The Postfigurative Society.** This era continued for thousands of years. It was strongly past oriented,

where older generations dictated how life would be for their young. Family names were important, ancestors were honored, and traditions were followed for centuries. The young learned nearly everything from elders and from the time-honored customs of the past. In short, older adults taught the young.

2. The Cofigurative Society. This era emerged as reason became predominant in Western culture. The printing press and the Enlightenment moved society into one in which the old and the young began figuring out life together. The world changed more rapidly when both old and young could read and reason. For the first time, the young got to participate in choosing their mate, their career, and their lifestyle.

3. The Prefigurative Society. This era has begun in our day. Margaret Mead envisioned this new social order that's future oriented, and cultural transmission is increasingly from the youth to their elders. Mead predicted, "I believe we are on the verge of developing a new kind of culture . . . I call this new style *prefigurative* because in this new culture it will be the child—and not the parent or grandparent—that represents what is to come."[6]

Culture critic Neil Postman explains further why we see this reality. He says genuine childhood can be maintained only when adults manage the information coming at our kids. In times past, adults ensured sequential learning for kids—limiting what children consumed intellectually.[7]

Walk back in time with me. Centuries ago, the life experience of kids was limited (they were either illiterate or they didn't have much to read). The experience they did have was sequenced (as they were ready) and real (not virtual) as they worked the farm and understood how to manage risk and energy. Today, a young teen likely has unlimited exposure to information, even adult information, mostly on a screen. Information is instant access, on demand, and usually free on television, computers, tablets, and smartphones. The hierarchy has collapsed.

I chuckled when my baby boomer friend Derric Johnson mused, "I hate it when I can't figure out how to operate my iPad and my tech support guy is asleep. He's five and it's way past his bedtime."

Add all of this to the fact that younger brains enjoy "fluid intelligence," which enables them to learn and adapt more quickly than older brains, and you have the recipe for this Peter Pan Paradox.

This means that millions from Gen Z enjoy "rookie smarts." Although they don't have any *positional authority*, they might just have *intuitive authority*. Rookie smarts often stem from rookie ignorance regarding how things have been done. In past generations, having experience was a feather in your cap; it gave you authority. Today it may be the opposite. Your experience may reflect the past, not the future, and may be seen as a liability to Gen Z, not an asset.[8] Having tenure may or may not work in your favor. One Gen Zer, Blake, put it this way: "A boss may accuse us of not knowing how things have been done in the past because we have no job experience. But past experience could be detrimental to seeing the future clearly. Someone with lots of experience may have blinders on. They could have limits to the scope of their vision."

Hannah Herbst enjoys rookie smarts. She's the young scientist who created a device to help bleeding victims. As a twenty-three-year-old Florida Atlantic University graduate, she was on a mission to save lives with an automated version of a tourniquet device. While older generations were busy tweaking the current, manual version of a tourniquet, this member of Generation Z looked at the issue completely out of the box. Access to tourniquets is a huge problem for minimally trained people to treat those who are bleeding. She calls her solution AutoTQ, and it's now registered with the FDA. One Florida city is inserting the new device in all their paramedic units and has seen it save lives. Why? The person applying it to a bleeding victim needs no training at all.[9] Hannah is just one more example of how the age of authority is dropping.

In the Land of Tomorrow, we are the immigrants, they are the natives.

THE AGE OF MATURITY IS RISING

What makes this Peter Pan Paradox so challenging is not merely that Gen Z enters the workplace with a sense of audacity but that millions enter unready for the workplace. Certainly not all of them, but millions graduate and arrive for a job interview ill prepared, or they show up for day one late or dressed inappropriately or use language that is unprofessional. I've already mentioned the 2024 survey by ResumeBuilder.com, reporting that 30 percent of managers avoid hiring Generation Z candidates, and the same number report firing a Gen Z employee within a month of their start date. Why is this? Their interpersonal skills are missing. Their work ethic appears absent. They don't seem to care about the work. And they just approach their job . . . so differently. Their GPA was high, but their EQ is low. These are objections I've heard from hiring managers. It feels like too much work to get them up to speed. I have spoken to focus groups of human resources executives who've told me their CEO has instructed them to not hire any young person right out of college. They hire them only after they've had at least one full-time job to avoid the chasm between college and career. These leaders want to avoid the "first-job hassles" with recent graduates. I don't blame them.

My friend Sangram Vajre launched his company, GTM (Go To Market), a few years ago. They hired a young lady who interviewed well, but when it came to the job, she left something to be desired. She meandered into work about 10:00 a.m., an hour and a half past their start time. This happened for several days. When her supervisor questioned her, she'd reply that she was out late the night before at a party and needed to sleep in. This didn't seem to bother her, but it did bother her supervisor. He said he never felt like she took him or her job seriously. Within weeks, she sent an email to everyone (not just her supervisor) and nonchalantly announced she was quitting. She never spoke to her boss directly. She didn't give a two-week notice. She simply said that that day was her last day. Surprisingly, she didn't have another job lined up; in fact, she didn't know what she was going to do except that she was moving back home with her parents.

Years ago, I began hearing university deans mourn the same problem. The phrase they used was "twenty-six is the new eighteen." These higher-ed leaders were no longer expecting an eighteen-year-old to act like an adult, to demonstrate responsibility or initiative. Students' social and emotional maturation was missing. Consider what's happened in our culture today. Adolescence is expanding on both sides. Kids are being nudged into it in elementary school, getting on teen websites, being exposed to adult information, getting a piercing or tattoo early on. Yet many remain in adolescence emotionally into their mid-twenties. So if you've hired a young twenty-something, you may see teen behavior even though they're adults. I recognize this sounds cruel. Throwing any young professional under the bus is not my intent. Yet the positive elements these young team members bring to work can be sabotaged by their own immaturity.

One attorney CEO told me he recently interviewed an intelligent young woman for his law firm. She had recently graduated from a top tier university, with a 4.0 grade point average. She dressed to the nines and entered the conversation confidently. In fact, maybe a bit too confidently. Less than fifteen minutes into the interview, she smiled at this CEO and said, "I'm gonna have your job in eighteen months."

I am sure she meant to come across confident and self-assured. Instead, it revealed her low self-awareness, coming across as arrogant and self-centered. This is a common aspect of Generation Z's demeanor. Growing up with a smartphone and a Google reflex has provided them with a deep sense of self-sufficiency. A post on social media a year ago illustrated this truth beautifully:

> Gen Z will drink one medium caramel latte, not eat a single meal till 4 pm, verbally abuse a racist, crack a joke about their mental health and pick up a tear gas canister with their bare hands, but get nervous when they have to call to make a doctor's appointment.

In our own office, Vance interviewed well and got a tour of the place when our vice president decided to hire him. As they strolled through the workspace, Vance asked a question, with a straight face: "When is spring break?"

Our vice president was stunned for a moment, but then realized Vance was serious. She smiled and replied, "Uh, we don't have a spring break here. You can certainly take PTO or vacation time, but we work all year round, every weekday."

Vance appeared troubled by this and inquired, "How many hours do you all work?"

She responded, "Eight hours a day, five days a week."

It was at this point the interview ended. With a serious look on his face, Vance revealed, "I'm just not an eight-hour-a-day sort of guy."

In early 2025, the *Wall Street Journal* published an article titled "What Happens When a Whole Generation Never Grows Up?" It mourned, "As American 30-somethings increasingly bypass the traditional milestones of adulthood, economists are warning that what seemed like a lag may in fact be a permanent state of arrested development. In many ways, this age group is in a better place financially, on average, than their parents were at this age. The problem is that they don't seem to know it." In February 2025, *Psychology Today*'s cover article was titled "The New Grown-Up" and posed the question: When does adulthood begin? That number is measurably higher than in the past five generations. Just when we need them to enter the workforce creative, energetic, and prepared—millions stall.

Sometimes, I am not sure whether to laugh or cry. These stories are not anomalies. They've become quite common. A December 2023 survey of eight hundred employers and hiring managers in the US from Intelligent.com found more than half of employers thought Gen Zers were unprepared for the workforce and displayed unprofessional behavior during job interviews. One recent study from ResumeTemplates.com revealed that 25 percent of Generation Z members bring their parents with them to their job interview.[10] We are in a new day, with an entirely new generation of candidates and parents. I would have been absolutely embarrassed had my mom or dad accompanied me.

Our consolation on this issue is that members of Gen Z admit this. Many acknowledge their lack of interpersonal communication skills needed in the workplace. In a recent US Harris Poll, 65 percent of them said they struggle to make conversation with colleagues. This delayed maturity is an issue we must face right now. Too much is at stake.

ADVANCED AND BEHIND

How do we explain this combined brilliance and delayed maturation in Generation Z? First, let me say again, there are many exceptions to the rule. But—this data seems to be the rule. Millions of Gen Zers endure a condition I describe as "artificial maturity." I released a book more than a decade ago by this title. I noticed today's young adults are:

1. Overexposed to information earlier than they were ready.
2. Underexposed to first-hand experiences later than they were ready.

This gave teens and young adults a facsimile of maturation; after all, they know so much at such young ages. Yet, digging a bit deeper, it's clear that knowledge is based on consuming information on a screen, not from real-life experience. When you meet a ten-year-old boy who knows all his math tables, who can download the latest software on his tablet, and who can navigate an app on his smartphone, you'll be tempted to say, "Wow, what a mature kid!" Maybe, but maybe not. That same boy at sixteen years old might not be able to look an adult in the eye and enjoy a conversation. He is ahead in some categories but behind in others. Here is what I've concluded about Generation Z:

Millions Are Advanced
- Cognitively. They process more information and ideas younger than ever.
- Biologically. They are developing earlier, entering puberty earlier, and living longer.

Millions Are Behind
- Socially. Their interpersonal skills are developing later in their lives.
- Emotionally. Their self-awareness and self-management is lower.

WHERE DO WE GO FROM HERE?

If there is a kernel of truth in what I've shared in this chapter, we have our work cut out for us. This book is all about how to lead in such conditions. How do we diminish the downside of this young generation while capitalizing on the upside they bring to us? The truth be told, leaders today are likely going to need to adjust and meet them in the middle on many issues. The chapters ahead will talk about how to onboard them in such a way as to retain them, to equip them in such a way that they increase their value to the team, to provide feedback that elicits better effort from them, and to lead them in a way that motivates them to give their very best effort, time, and talent. For now, let's begin with two challenges:

1. Leaders will need to listen more than we used to listen.
When I began my career, it was a time when new employees were to be seen more than heard, like children back in the day. Today is different. I dare you to push pause and hear them out. Even when some of their ideas may sound ridiculous, they're born out of an idea or foresight that prompted that young staff person to share it. They long to be heard, and sometimes they will give you a competitive advantage in your industry.

2. Leaders will need to coach more than we used to coach.
Younger team members have always needed coaching as they entered their careers. Because of today's culture, Gen Z will need even more. The classroom did not prepare them for the workroom. I challenge you to prepare to push pause and coach them more than you used to do. Take pains to provide wisdom they need, to offer insights and skills they need, even if you believe they should already possess them. They need mentors.

I am part of the baby boomer generation. There was a day we needed older generations to believe in us and to mentor us. I recall listening to a fascinating podcast called *Kids in Control.* It was about Apollo 11, the NASA mission that landed on the moon in 1969. Many assumed it was an impossible mission—and most of those doubters were older people. Many associated with the project said Apollo 11 was successful because young people were placed in key leadership roles. I'd always assumed it was veteran engineers and operators who did the heavy lifting at NASA. Do you know how old those NASA operators were who put Neil Armstrong and Buzz Aldrin on the moon?

The average age of the control center operators was twenty-seven years old. Many were even younger. In fact, the team member who saved them from aborting in the final minutes was twenty-three. A few of them had started as interns just a few years earlier. Their job was to give tours of NASA, and they said it forced them to know the function of each department precisely. Being young and familiar with new technology seemed to help them succeed. Many of them assumed this was how careers worked: you get a big job with an important objective, and you do it. Their age helped them achieve the mission. One operator recalled he'd caught a vision to work at NASA by watching a special Walt Disney program on television where Walt said, "One day, we just may land a man on the moon."

What those young engineers needed were mentors.

Enter the Simulation Supervisors, or "SimSups," as they were called. They were the older, more experienced engineers who oversaw the young operators at the control center. They offered wisdom, ideas, and supervision, but they let those young "kids" do the work. And boy did they come through.

OBSERVATIONS ON THE LUNAR LANDING

Fifty years after Apollo 11, some of the team members were tracked down and interviewed. I loved their observations and reflections on what sparked their success:

1. We didn't know what we didn't know. We were just naive enough to believe we could pull it off.

Experience might have thwarted some of our ideas. Many were fearless. Audacity worked in our favor.

2. We were intelligent yet young enough to prevent doubts from stopping us. While seasoned veteran engineers became skeptical over the likelihood of our success, we avoided being cynical through idealism, trust, and teamwork. It was rookie smarts.

3. We bought into our president's vision to put a man on the moon. In 1961, President Kennedy had begun talking about putting a man on the moon by the end of the decade. We didn't have the technology, but we were determined to get it.

4. Older staff didn't fit in well because of all the reasons why it couldn't work. They likely had too much experience with past technology, which had been improved. They were suspect of what could go wrong. We were current and hopeful.

5. NASA pushed decisions to the lowest level possible. Why? Young staff adapted to the new technology we used for the landing faster than the older staff. They chose to build the mission from the ground up, not the top down.

6. Nothing pulls out the best in people like a big goal with high stakes. Apollo 11 challenged a bunch of twenty-somethings with the highest stakes of any project we'd ever seen. With high stakes, people engage at their highest capacity.

Just thirteen minutes before the landing, they almost aborted the mission. "We didn't want to lose Neil Armstrong and his crew. It was the toughest period of the mission: the landing." It was a twenty-three-year-old, Jack Garman, who played the key role in those vital minutes and kept them from aborting. "When most assumed we should stop, he said we should finish. He was cool as a cucumber." Those young operators pulled off a feat that in today's dollars was worth $153 billion. I'm so grateful the SimSups prepared them and trusted them.

In the chapters ahead, we'll talk about how we can enjoy that same experience.

TALK IT OVER

1. Have you witnessed this Peter Pan Paradox on your team anywhere?

2. This chapter highlights the need for leaders to listen and coach more. How can you balance empowering younger employees while maintaining team productivity and cohesion? What strategies have worked for you or others in leading Gen Z?

3. The chapter discusses both the pixie dust and challenges of Gen Z employees. How can your team capitalize on their tech savviness and creativity while addressing issues like delayed maturity or lack of interpersonal skills?

2

HOW WE GOT TO Z

My wife was at the Atlanta airport recently and decided to grab a coffee before her flight. She stepped into a long line and noticed a staff person at this coffee shop taking the orders and then making the drinks each customer ordered. She was alone. When my wife asked why she was a "one-person show" that day, the woman smiled and explained that both of her colleagues had called in to say they "wouldn't be able to work today." The reason? Both had been at a party the night before, and they were tired. They would not be their "best self," and they felt it was best for them to stay home.

I can't imagine giving this excuse for my absence as a young employee.

I'm not going to lie to you. As I hear more employers tell me this absentee or tardy conduct has become normalized, I grow frustrated. Where did these young people get the idea that they could excuse themselves from work so easily? Outside of being sick, people should show up at work, even if they're not their "best self."

Years ago, a manager's recourse would be to simply fire the failing employee. Today, it's not that simple. Many tell me they can't find young job candidates to replace them, especially in service jobs. Or they tell me they can't afford the salary the young candidates require. Organizational psychologist Adam Grant says we're experiencing a "democratization of the workforce." It's a power shift between the organization and the employee. For many, the power gap is closing. When several companies requested staff to not bring up political issues that weren't part of their mission while at work, employees balked. Google employees protested at work for the Pentagon to change a military policy. Whole Foods employees sued their company for not being allowed to wear Black Lives Matter masks to work. Hundreds of Amazon staff chose to risk their jobs by violating company policy. Wayfair employees walked out to protest sales to migrant detention camps. Baffled leaders are asking: Who is the real boss? Is it the employer, or is it the court of public opinion?

Truth be told, the shift going on aims to flatten the organizational chart, to shorten the distance between supervisor and team member, to give everyone a voice, even to experience multiple check-ins daily. Employees feel empowered, and it's only been enhanced by tech tools like Slack, Microsoft Teams, Zoom, and others. Because employees see that they're not alone in their opinions, they're creating a new psychological contract at work between management and labor. Some are crafting a new ideological agreement that believes their social causes deserve their dedication as much as the work they do on the job. What's more, many now feel emboldened to choose their terms for work. New language has become popular:

> "I'm putting up boundaries."
> "I'm taking a personal day."

> "I am not working past 4:00 p.m."
> "I am not my best self today."

To be honest, these shifts are not all bad. The two oldest generations on the job today have built a reputation for workaholism. Generation Z members often say to their elders: "You live to work. I work to live." Further, Generation Z has seen greed in corporate America where the pay gap between executives and employees is disproportionate. Following the pandemic, millions were laid off. Their response to employers? "You didn't look out for me, so why should I look out for you?" It's clear why we see a divide between management and labor. Social media platforms offer a voice to everyone, including our young team members. Sadly, in such a context, both the leader and the staff person can feel like a victim, as if they must defend themselves against the other, often perceiving one another as adversaries rather than allies. Loads of leaders keep the poorly performing team member and merely kick the can down the road. It's time we make a pivotal change.

What if I told you that changing the way you lead young team members could be a game changer? What if I told you that there are better strategies to lead them that are healthier and more sustainable than our former, "old-school" methods? What if I told you that adapting your approach could lead to better results? But this shift will require an internal change.

Until 2016, baby boomers made up the largest population in our US workforce. That year, millennials surpassed them as the largest and now make up more than 50 percent of our workforce. According to the Bureau of Labor Statistics, the number of Gen Zers in the workplace today has now exceeded that of the boomers. The workforce is getting younger. According to the United Nations, half of the world's population is under thirty. They are a growing force that we cannot ignore. We can get mad—or we can get busy.

Instead of getting furious, let's get curious.

COMMON MENTAL DISORDERS

It won't surprise you that the top reason Gen Z calls in to request a personal day away from work is mental health issues. They're even comfortable requesting time off for this reason. A report from *Business Insider* highlighted that Generation Z is driving a significant increase in workers calling out sick and taking mental health days. Sick leave rose by 55 percent in 2023 compared to 2019, with younger workers under thirty-five taking more days off than their older colleagues. Some are taking sabbaticals in their twenties. What's up with that? I began to investigate the pattern of Gen Zers calling in for personal days, PTO, and mental health breaks. The *New York Post* carried a report saying, "Due to the rise of Gen Zers with 'common mental disorders' (CMD), such as anxiety and depression—spurred by everyday issues like breakups, meeting deadlines and the pressures of social media—employees in their early 20s are far more likely to call out of work for a 'mental health day' than Millennials and Gen Xers."[1] Further, did you know that *anxiety and depressive disorders affect nearly 50 percent of those aged eighteen to twenty-four*, according to the Kaiser Family Foundation?[2]

In fact, a growing number are remaining jobless because of poor mental health. "Youth worklessness due to ill health is a real and growing trend," said analysts from Resolution Foundation, an economic and social policy hub in the UK. "In the past decade, the number of young people aged 18 to 24 who were out of work due to ill health has more than doubled, rising from 93,000 to 190,000," noted the clinicians. "Between 2020 and 2023, two in five young people (42%) who were workless due to ill health stated that a mental health problem was their main health problem."[3] My experience tells me these CMDs are the top reason why a young teammate might just ghost you or not show up for work at all and neglect to tell you. Many feel they don't have it in them to face the issue with their boss.

The struggle is especially difficult for zillennials, who are late millennials and early Gen Zers. These "tweeners," born between 1996 and 2006, seem to be most susceptible to this challenge. Experts believe zillennials will continue valuing mental health over work in years to come, but researchers warn young people against taking too many privileges in the trend. One employer acknowledged their rationale is smart. "It's like a trump card. How can you say 'no' to someone who says they need to work on their mental health? We would appear insensitive if we require them to come in."[4]

Some years ago, our organization had several young team members who called to take "personal days" simultaneously. This happened more than once. At the time, we had an unlimited PTO policy, so they weren't breaking any rules; it just hindered our productivity and morale. When our department heads asked them about their timing, immediately the staff members got defensive, as if to say: "How could you dare question my mental health decision? Don't you prioritize self-care?" It was a difficult issue for weeks until I met with them, along with their department head, and asked them what they would do if they were in my shoes facing this issue. A productive debate ensued helping them to see what it feels like to be on the management side of the dilemma, where teammates felt cheated and resented their requests being questioned. Only then did we resolve the issue. For two of them the solution was helping them find jobs someplace else.

THE WORLD IN WHICH THEY'VE GROWN UP

There were numerous culture-shaping events that created the population we call Generation Z. When we uncover them, we have a chance at becoming wiser and more empathetic leaders for them. Let's first look at the generations that led to Gen Z and the qualities that define their demographic. We'll peek behind the curtain on what formed them, learning the "why" of their development, so we can practice an effective "how" as it relates to leading them. Some of the most significant challenges are from their early years:

> A culture of uncertainty has only deepened their mental illness.
> A culture of distrust of authority has only deepened their cynicism.
> A culture of portable devices has only deepened their addictions.

In short, you're likely going to see a difference in today's young employee. While there are certain aspects that always define young adults (because their brains aren't fully developed), there are other aspects which set them apart from their millennial counterparts. Because the brain's neural pathways are developing in the first twenty to twenty-five years of our lives, people are shaped a little like wet concrete. The plasticity is at its highest and is forged by experiences and inputs in our earliest years. Let's look at what shaped Generation Z so far.

TEN TERMS THAT SUMMARIZE THEIR WORLD

1. Instant Access (They have a Google reflex and want immediate answers.)
2. New Normal (They grew up with terrorism, inflation, and overwhelming content.)
3. On Demand (They expect entertainment when they want it and hate boredom.)
4. Multicultural (They're a mix of ethnic races; the most diverse in US history.)
5. Immediate Feedback (They prefer fast replies on social media, games, or texts.)

6. **Cancel Culture** (They know the easiest way to face adverse opinions is to cancel them.)
7. **Constant Contact** (They're connected all the time, with little margin for solitude.)
8. **Blended Family** (They've adopted new norms of family, marriage, and sexuality.)
9. **Anything Goes** (They grew up in an era when traditional morals are being questioned.)
10. **Virtual Reality** (Much of their life has included screens and artificial experiences.)

> **PAUSE AND REFLECT**
>
> Have you seen evidence of this list? Would you add anything to it?

For years, I've worked with professional sports teams from the NFL, NBA, and MLB, teaching leadership or life skills to young players. Teams held discussions based on our Habitudes curriculum, which imparts soft skills via images. I recall one year a minor league baseball player approached me after my session in spring training and said, "My life has been split into two parts: baseball and portable devices. I have never learned these skills in my twenty years of life—is there any way to fast-track learning these principles?"

I smiled and suggested anything worthwhile in life usually feels like a marathon not a sprint. But I went on to advise him to identify all the transferable work skills he's learned from the game of baseball. (There are loads of them.) The game requires patience, focus, discipline, continual improvement, resilience, and more. Then I suggested he do a detox from all the "on-demand, instant access" technology in his life. I spoke to him about the inverse relationship between technology and emotional intelligence. To his credit, he implemented everything I said and later transitioned

FIVE GENERATIONS COMING OF AGE

GENERATIONS	BUILDERS Silent Generation	BOOMERS Pig in Python Generation
Birth years	1929–1945	1946–1964
Narrative as they began career	Be grateful you have a job	I want better
Sense of identity	I am humble	I am valuable
Attitude toward authority	Respect them	Replace them
Role of work	Means for a living	Central focus
Role of relationships	Significant	Useful
Technology	Hope to outlive it	Master it
Consumer expectations	Goods	Services
View of the future	Seek to stabilize	Create it!
Managing feedback	I give it to you not vice versa	Annual, full documentation
Motivation	Strong work ethic	Bonus, corner office
Work-life balance	What's that?	I live to work
Handling change	Slow and steady	It worked fine in the past
Communication preferences	Face-to-face	Formal email, professional
Respect	Normalized	You earn it
Philanthropy	I give to programs	I give to productivity

BUSTERS Generation X	MILLENNIALS Generation Y	HOMELANDERS Generation Z
1965–1982	1983–1999	2000–2015
Keep it real	Life is a cafeteria	I'm coping and hoping
I am self-sufficient	I am awesome	I am fluid
Endure them	Choose them	Not sure I need them
Necessity	Place to serve	It's my hobby
Central; caring	Global	Superficial
Employ it	Enjoy it	Hack it
Experiences	Transformations	I consume & create
Skeptical	YOLO	FOMO
Be honest, offer practical steps	Frequent, be nice about it	Listen and empathize daily
Flexibility, work on my terms	Money, autonomy, meaningful work	Work my way, on a screen
Balance ebbs and flows	I want work-life blending	I work to live, not vice versa
I love change if it's my idea	I want change, every few months	My attention span is 8 seconds
Authentic, either digital or in person	Texts, Slack, interactive apps	Digital, abbreviate
Reciprocal	You owe me	Equity for all
I give to people	I give to passions	I give to projects (short-term)

from professional baseball to corporate America beautifully. It was an intentional effort, however, on his part.

LET'S COMPARE AND CONTRAST

If you're like me, it helps to examine older and younger generations, comparing them to mine, noting where we are alike and different based on the conditions that shaped us. People are formed in their first two decades or so, based on shared technology, media, economies, music, tragedies, societal issues, and tone in the culture. In the chart, check out the topics on the left of each row and notice the perspective of each generation as they entered their careers. Obviously, people do change over time, but certain mindsets were born as they transitioned from backpack (school) to briefcase (career). Having spent time in focus groups with more than two thousand representatives from all the generations, I summarized my findings in the table on the previous pages.

It's wise to note that Generation Z has been influenced by each of the four generations before them, as grandparents, parents, uncles and aunts, and, of course, colleagues at work. Yet Gen Z has been deeply influenced by culture, as much as anything, having been exposed to notifications, social media platforms, and especially TikTok, where millions get their news. Consider the world that shaped them over the last twenty years: a volatile economy (three economic downturns since 2000), conspiracy theories, smartphones, social media, AI, mass shootings, a pandemic, and political polarization all make for a dark and anxious backdrop preceding their first full-time job.

On top of these various perspectives, we have the common fears that each age group naturally faces. Leaders often neglect to recognize these fears as factors in employee behavior. For example, while there are exceptions to each of these fears, my research demonstrates common generational fears are:

- > Builders fear they are no longer relevant and aren't valued for the wisdom they bring.
- > Boomers fear their jobs could be taken away by younger, faster, and savvier generations.
- > Gen Xers fear reduced profitability and the high turnover rate of younger team members.
- > Millennials fear disapproval from older colleagues and feel unprepared to lead older staff.
- > Gen Zers fear not being taken seriously, not feeling respected, or not having status on the team.

REFLECT

How do these perspectives and fears inform you and make you a better leader?

DRUNK ON DOPAMINE

All leaders face a new challenge with teams at work. Our people are living in what I call a "binge culture." Behavioral scientists call it a "dopamine culture." We can control our pleasure by swiping and bingeing on anything that prompts happy chemicals inside us. This is where it affects us at work. Our brain rewards these brief bursts of distraction with dopamine. This chemical is released and makes us feel good, so we want to repeat the stimulus. Pleasure feels great, certainly better than the job we have in front of us. This reality has pushed us past art, entertainment, and distraction, and is manipulating us into a culture of addiction. Stanford research psychologist Anna Lembke reminds us our brains are always seeking balance between two outcomes:

- > Pleasure: our appetite for comfortable, satisfying, happy feelings

> Pain: the physical or mental suffering or discomfort due to illness or struggle

When we feel pain, our brain sends happy chemicals to offset it, hence the runner's high we enjoy after jogging for miles and feeling pain. Chemicals like dopamine, serotonin, and oxytocin help us stay balanced. The bad news? Our bingeing sends pleasure into our systems, causing our brains to counterbalance. They can sense too much pleasure, from social media, porn, opioids, nicotine, alcohol, or prescription drugs.[5] For the first time in history, we can binge on almost anything. It is not a stretch to wonder: Are some of our mental health problems due to our binge lifestyles messing with our natural brain chemicals? This creates a poor Gen Z employee who may have little resilience. More on this in the chapter on grit.

REFLECT

What have you observed on your team? Do you spot any symptoms of bingeing?

LOW STAKES, DEEP FAKES

In this often-artificial world, the stakes are low, and emerging adults must learn to navigate high stakes, not fake ones. They may master virtual reality, but many bosses wonder: How about reality? The world of facsimiles imitates the high stakes of the real world, but they're not genuine. Sometimes these artificial experiences have played a role in delivering an unready employee to the workforce. In other words, the step into the real world can be a giant leap.

One of the greatest ironies of Generation Z is that they value authenticity highly yet have lived in such an artificial world—full of filtered photos online, fake news, hyperbolic messages, doctored up selfies, emoji, and GIFs. The world they grew up in provides so many artificial versions of life: artificial sweeteners, artificial Christmas trees, artificial turf, artificial hearts, artificial plants, and now, artificial intelligence. I don't blame them for this; it's a world most of us are born into. Yet our only hope to find real solutions is to begin with the raw truth. The genuine over the virtual. The authentic over the artificial.

We talk today about how much people wear "masks." It's a figure of speech describing those who are hiding something or pretending to be someone else. Like past youth generations, Gen Z hates masks yet lives among them all the time, even with peers. The term *mask* is short for masquerade. It's about pretense, a false representation that looks real. Let's examine three of them that can confuse us all, even at work.

THREE MASQUERADES FROM GEN Z'S EARLY YEARS

Information has masqueraded as experience.
Generation Z is the most informed population of youth to date. Most of them have been on screens all through their childhood, and millions got a smartphone by middle school if not before. They have consumed content. Lots of it. Consequently, they may enter a job or even an interview and come across experienced, answering questions with an air of confidence. Yet it may be born only from information. We all know if you ask someone if they understand skydiving, and they reply, "I sure do. I've watched several YouTube videos on skydiving," that means little compared to the person who says, "I sure do. I've been skydiving several times in my life." The person who's read something or watched a video is informed but not experienced. Millions of kids are over-informed and under experienced by the time they launch their careers. It's led therapists to diagnose some with high arrogance, low self-esteem. There's a veneer of confidence, but it crumbles quickly as underneath they recognize they've applied little of their

knowledge. I don't blame the young adult with this diagnosis. They grew up in a world that gave them confidence because they know so much yet may have experienced little. We must help them recognize this and cultivate humility.

Portable devices have masqueraded as community.
When smartphones and social media were normalized some fifteen years ago, many of us were idealistic about it. It was all about connection with others: old friends from college, colleagues across the nation, and extended family. Today, it's mostly about performance. Social media platforms are loaded with people competing for views, likes, and shares. It's millions of amateurs performing for one another. Further, connections are not genuine. So far, the screen has failed to replace face-to-face interactions. In my interviews with Gen Zers, they reveal that most of their connections are *superficial*, yet they remain if the connections are *beneficial* to their tribe's growth. While I admit there's nothing criminal about this, it doesn't come close to meeting our real need to participate in a community. We all know we can be technologically connected and socially disconnected at the same time. We are innately social creatures, needing support and accountability, yet our population today is the loneliest one in recorded history, according to social scientist Robert Putnam (author of *Bowling Alone*), and Generation Z is the loneliest demographic, according to the Ballard Brief, from Brigham Young University.[6]

In fact, loneliness is a greater problem for Gen Z than anxiety. (We'll discuss this later in the book.) We must help them find their people at work and belong to a community.

PAUSE AND REFLECT
How can you offer Gen Z experience through experimentation?

Intelligence has masqueraded as maturity.
As a generation of kids who've grown up consuming content, they can appear as mature, as if they are ahead of their time. Yet it can be a mask they wear. I mentioned earlier the ten-year-old boy who's savvy with a screen, enabling him to download the latest software, to know his math tables, and to navigate the latest apps on his portable device. He can even fix your portable device! It would be easy to assume that kid is so mature. After all, look how advanced he is! Yet that same kid at sixteen years old may not be able to look you in the eye and have a conversation. He may be unable to interact with you intelligently or fluently. His maturity might be categorical, as I've suggested already, advanced cognitively but behind socially or emotionally. "Artificial maturity"[7] is a state that millions of Gen Zers have become victim to, having been left to their own devices, quite literally. It looks real yet is a facsimile of maturation. Missing might be interpersonal skills, humility, or professional language. Employers, beware: you may need to separate their strengths from their ability to be a good teammate. Cheer them on in their strengths, but coach them up in their EQ.

> **PAUSE AND REFLECT**
> How can you help Gen Z deepen their community on the team?

Here's my point. Millions have been satisfied with this artificial world. Virtual experiences are "good enough." Consider the twenty-first-century culture in which Generation Z grew up. They enjoy virtual reality with goggles. They make virtual connections with social media. They take virtual risks playing video games. They relish virtual thrills on a roller coaster. They celebrate virtual success with multiple-choice tests in school. (Circling a letter on a paper is not the same as applying an insight in

> **PAUSE AND REFLECT**
> Where have you seen and responded to this masquerade?

our lives.) They delight in virtual creativity with AI. They experience virtual conversations with text messages. They enjoy virtual dating with online apps. They revel in virtual intimacy with porn. And far too often, my research has found, they are satisfied with the artificial. Their world is more prone to ask them to "fake a risk" instead of "take a risk." Several young adults in our focus groups said they were "good enough." The *Hidden Brain* podcast aired an episode in 2019 called "Close Enough: Living Through Others." It was about the growing number of young adults who appeared to be content with getting close to reality but not requiring it. It was about the dangers and delights of vicariously living through others. Some young women, for instance, will grab a bag of chips, lie on their bed at night, and watch a video of another woman doing her nightly routine (removing makeup, moisturizer, washing her face, and so on) instead of doing it herself.[8] It boggles my mind. I now teach my young community:

> Information is usually not enough. You need experience.
> Virtual connections are usually not enough. You need face-to-face contact.
> Test scores are usually not enough. You need to show me what you learned.
> Video games are usually not enough. You need to take genuine risks.
> Screen messaging is usually not enough. You need in-person conversation.

So, how has this cultural landscape affected their thinking?

GENERATION Z CHARACTERISTICS

For decades, I've attempted to stay on top of realities within the youngest populations entering the workforce and entering the marketplace as customers. There was a different cultural tone and economy for each one as they entered adulthood. In the generational chart you saw earlier, I offered the narratives each population brought into their careers. These narratives are summaries from research by Gallup, McKinsey, and the Pew Research Center, as well as the focus groups I hosted with members of each generation. Examine their mindsets as young professionals:

1. The Silent Generation, 1929–45 (Builders): *Be grateful you have a job.*
2. The Baby Boom Generation, 1946–64 (Boomers): *I want better.*
3. The Baby Buster Generation, 1965–82 (Gen Xers): *Keep it real.*
4. The Millennial Generation, 1983–1999 (Gen Yers): *Life is a cafeteria.*
5. The Homeland Generation, 2000–15 (Gen Zers): *I'm coping and hoping.*

"I'M COPING AND HOPING"

They're "hopeful" because they're young, but feel they're "coping" with current, depressing realities. This may help you climb into their brain to understand them as consumers and teammates. To make this memorable for you, their characteristics spell the word: COPING.

THEY TEND TO BE:

C—Cynical

This is a shift from millennials at the same age. Gen Z watched adult leaders argue over how to handle a pandemic and be uncivil over most political issues. McKinsey reports Gen Z has "less-than-positive outlooks, with lower levels of emotional and social well-being than older generations." Looking ahead, they see an unstable economy, mass shootings, low wages that don't keep up with inflation, endless wars, volumes of bad news coming at them on a smartphone, and aging leaders in Washington, DC. They use words like *skeptical* and *pessimistic* to describe their outlook. This may explain their distrust in leaders or suspicion of plans that feel like they benefit the establishment not the people.

O—Overwhelmed

Almost every member of Generation Z we interviewed agreed this word best describes their life. Nine in ten say it's the number one word they use to define themselves. Both Gallup and McKinsey studies report Gen Z has the "least positive outlook and the highest prevalence of mental illness of any generation." Their angst has many sources: global unrest, climate anxiety, educational interruptions leaving them feeling "postponed" and with reduced economic opportunity. Further, 58 percent of Gen Z report not having a basic social need met in their life. This may explain an inability to "pull their weight" or their need for lots of PTO for mental health reasons, as I mentioned earlier.

P—Pragmatic

They're much more pragmatic than millennials were at the same age. The comparison is not unlike the boomers and Gen X. The mood in culture migrated from confidence to caution. As young professionals, their pragmatism is a mix of complicated idealism and worry about the future. Gen Z dreams of personal career satisfaction but anticipates economic struggles. This nudges them to be more private, individualistic, and more realistic in their choices than millennials were at their age. They hope to avoid many of the traps and debt millennials faced. This may explain their apprehension to jump on board with projects or their need for support when making decisions.

I—Inclusive

More than previous generations, Gen Z deeply values racial justice, environmental justice, social equality, and building a sense of belonging in their community. Even consumption for Gen Z is more about access than ownership. (Think movies, music, rides, and travel stays.) It's a community feel. Ironically, Gen Z is individualistic yet inclusive. Belonging isn't about changing themselves to "fit in" but about being themselves and yet "belonging." Gen Zers are progressive: most see the growing ethnic diversity in the US as a positive thing and are less likely than elders to see the US as superior to other nations. They care about those who are marginalized (minorities, LGBTQ+ folks), and they want to see equity at work.

N—Nuanced

Whatever you do, don't pigeonhole Generation Z. Even these characteristics are meant to help you to understand them, not stereotype them. They are nuanced and shifting about their preferences. Because Gen Zers are more likely to engage in educational endeavors, according to Pew Research Center, and because new information is always available, Gen Z is fluid in their beliefs, sense of identity, and gender and has cyclical preferences on goods and services. McKinsey research reveals they have an ever-changing sense of style, from retro to postmodern. This may explain their unpredictability and their avoidance of embracing absolute facts in deference to relativism.

G—Globally savvy

Gen Z has been the most well-informed generation of youth because adults left them to their own devices, namely portable devices in their hands since middle school. This has given them a high sense of empowerment and agency, according to Australian researcher Mark McCrindle.[9] They are instantly aware of what's occurring on the Gaza Strip or Ukraine. They follow K-pop in Asia and the climate movement centered in Europe. But globally savvy isn't the same as tech savvy. For many, tech is about entertainment. Three in four managers find the new generation difficult to work with, and according to ResumeBuilder, the top three reasons are lack of effort, motivation, and technological skills that are useful for work.[10]

PAUSE AND REFLECT
How should these characteristics inform your leadership?

HOW DO WE LEAD THEM?

1. Earn their trust
Although you have a title and tenure, earn their trust through connecting. Ask questions, listen, empathize, and then guide them. You may have to slow down to accelerate later. Earning trust requires time, but once established, it speeds up productivity.

2. Build their incentive
While older staff see their jobs as a large part of their identity, Gen Z sees their job more as a hobby. Since your voice competes with so many others, offer a "why" before your "what." This can motivate them to give more than their job description requires.

3. Give them ownership
All through their school years, Gen Z was told what to think but not always how to think. They've been led prescriptively. We now must lead descriptively, describing a goal then letting them determine how to reach it. They will support what they help create.

4. Invest in their future
Gen Z doesn't want to be managed; they want to be mentored. Why not approach supervisory roles by offering tips to succeed and coaching them to get ahead on the job? This strategy communicates you are for them and want them to thrive in whatever they do.

5. Offer them hope
Since their perspective is cynical, choose your words and actions well. Provide hope for them as you lead them. Communicate faith in them and their future on the team. This may be the most important leadership gift you provide for them.

Zach Thomas is a friend of mine who is a Chick-fil-A restaurant franchisee outside of Atlanta. He has a hundred employees, ranging from age fifteen to seventy-five. I love how he navigates the relationships between old and young on his team. Don Tanner retired from the Marines and later from General Motors, then joined Zach's team at seventy-five years old. He worked more than four years at the restaurant and never missed a single day of work. He's disciplined, punctual, and has struggled with younger team members who seemed fragile and inconsistent. Don was raised with a strong work ethic and often labors to show patience with the teens. He'll admit he just doesn't understand them. It went both ways: young team members felt Don was a grouch, and he thought they were flakes. In response, Zach chose to teach everyone how to connect with empathy. Several times, over the course of a year, Zach sat down with Don and several of his younger team members and played the role of mediator. This was a feat, as some of his staff were sixty years younger than Don.

Zach would begin the conversations with "Let's start with common ground: we are all human and we all want to accomplish something great." Then, Zach launched a dialogue that former Facebook COO Sheryl Sandberg created years ago: "What's It Like to Be on the Other Side of Me?" Zach let Don tell stories about how he was brought up, what he learned in the Marines and later at General Motors. His journey helped the young employees understand him better. Don needed to be heard.

Then Zach asked Don to listen to the young staff. They shared the overwhelming world they lived in with smart technology, absent parents, and anxiety disorders. Zach then asked them to share how they experienced Don and his attitude, his nonverbal communication, his tone, and even his gaslighting. These roundtables struck at the heart of the issue, deepened their connections, and provided breakthroughs for this team. They now have bridges of communication where there once were walls between them.

Are you ready to have this conversation?

TALK IT OVER

1. Generation Z is described as living in a "dopamine culture," influenced by instant gratification and bingeing habits. How can leaders balance encouraging productivity while addressing the potential negative effects of this culture on Gen Z employees in the workplace?
2. The chapter highlights a shift in workplace dynamics, with younger employees demanding greater autonomy and emphasizing mental health. How can organizations adapt their leadership

styles and policies to accommodate these changes without compromising productivity?

3. The "masks" worn by Generation Z, such as intelligence masquerading as maturity and portable devices masquerading as community, can create challenges in the workplace. What strategies can leaders implement to foster authentic relationships and genuine skill development among Gen Z team members?

3

THE VALUE GENERATION Z BRINGS TO THE WORKPLACE

In 2017, a New Hampshire woman wandered into a local thrift shop searching for an old picture frame to restore. Browsing the secondhand store, the woman picked up an antique white frame with an old painting inside. Nothing about it appeared extraordinary, yet she figured even if she couldn't restore it, the price was negligible. She eventually bought the old frame, spending a grand total of four dollars.

When she showed the frame to friends and family, someone suggested the frame was nice enough, but the painting looked like the style of a famous artist. Others agreed that it might be worth investigating. This is where her story got interesting. While the shopper was originally interested in the frame, she soon became fascinated by the painting it held. No one had any idea it was a rare work by a renowned American artist from a century ago.

When a conservator named Lauren Lewis examined it, her eyes grew wide. This four-dollar thrift store purchase turned out to be an original N. C. Wyeth piece of art called *Ramona*, which later sold for $191,000 during Bonhams Skinner's American Art auction.

Did you catch that? A four-dollar investment turned out to have a $191,000 value. Not a bad day.

"It's everybody's dream," said Lewis, describing how astounding it is to discover something so valuable and rare. I agree, and I bet you're like me. We love hearing stories like this for a simple reason. It's exhilarating to stumble upon something and later realize it's far more precious than you expected. This unassuming antique customer thought she was buying the frame, but it was what's inside the frame that proved to be worthwhile. I'm no different. I love making a small investment only to discover it's worth more than I expected.

THE VALUE GENERATION Z BRINGS

Please forgive me if I'm getting too cheesy for you—but I think this is a vivid analogy for us. It's a picture of Generation Z. (Pun intended.) At first, nothing about them may appear extraordinary. Perhaps they're even a bit odd. We're willing to pay a little for them, hope to restore them for work, and later discover it's what's inside the frame that offers their true benefit. In the end, we stumble upon a treasure.

This has been my experience. Oh sure, there have been some bad eggs along the way. There are bad eggs in every young generation, including mine. Yet over the years, I've found treasure in young hires. I think of Jim, Andrew, and of Chloe. Then there's J. T. and Tyler. Matt was pure gold when we hired him, and he's only gotten better. And I can't forget Alysse. I think of Sara Grace and Selah, and of course, Shingi. And I think of Sam, Lila, Palmer, and my man, Cam. (I love him like a son.) The list goes on. As I mentioned earlier, they can come with some deep needs or wounds. They needed help navigating some mental health issues. But along the way, they were hidden treasure, well worth finding.

A man once asked a prospector why he was kneeling near a stream. He replied that he was panning for gold. To this observer, it looked like he was collecting dirt. So the man inquired how the prospector could wade through the dirt and mud for hours searching for it. The prospector smiled and replied, "The key is to focus on the gold, not the dirt." This explains my forty-five-year journey with young teammates. I keep my eye on the gold inside them.

A QUICK READ ON GENERATION Z

In the US, there are approximately fifty-nine million members of Generation Z,[1] the first batch of kids who have grown up in the twenty-first century.[2] (Right behind them is a younger population called Generation Alpha.) To summarize who they are, let me reiterate what I touched on earlier in this book. The two mega-characteristics they bring with them are:

> A high sense of agency. They grew up with smartphones and feel they know a lot.
> A high sense of anxiety. Having grown up with smartphones, they're overwhelmed and often suffer from mental health issues, like stress, anxiety, and depression.

They are unique from former generations, including the millennials before them, who are now in their late twenties all the way up to midlife.[3] Below is a quick look at the data on Generation Z, which I curated from multiple sources, including the Pew Research Center,[4] Higher Ed Dive, the Barna Research Group, the Chronicle of Higher Education, Deloitte, the Gallup organization, and the J. Walter Thompson Innovation Group. Here's what we know about Generation Z and work:

THE VALUE GENERATION Z BRINGS TO THE WORKPLACE

1. They're the most diverse population at work: 48 percent are not white.
2. They own smartphones (96 percent) and multitask on up to five screens a day.
3. They're smart consumers: 35 percent plan to save for retirement in their twenties.
4. Salary is a high motivator (70 percent); and health insurance is a must (70 percent).
5. Almost six in ten say they would work weekends for higher pay.
6. Unlike millennials, only 38 percent consider work-life balance important.
7. More than 90 percent prefer to have human interaction at work, not just screens.
8. Less than half identified as purely heterosexual, meaning their attractions are fluid.
9. They tend to be fiscally conservative, and their top concern is income.
10. Forty percent want daily interactions with their boss and feel they've done something wrong if they don't get a touch point. Sixty percent want multiple check-ins daily.

> **REFLECT**
>
> How does knowing these characteristics help you modify the way you lead them?

These days, it's easy for managers to focus so much on Generation Z's differences and weaknesses that we miss the strengths they bring to our teams. While there are similarities in every young generation (due to their age), previous generations did not experience what they've experienced at such a young age, nor do they provide what Gen Z brings. In this chapter, I want to help you climb into their brains and understand their perspective. We'll summarize the attributes of their sociological group and examine the chief contribution they'll likely make to your team. I have found they can be prophetic.

GENERATION Z PREDICTIONS FOR WORK IN THE FUTURE

In chapter 1, I suggested Gen Zers have a keen intuition of the future. So I asked them: What do you see coming? What's your intuition tell you? Here are some of the best answers I received from Generation Z members in my focus groups. After I reviewed a LinkedIn article about future predictions, I found it uncanny how the responses I got from young adults reflected the experts, even before the article was released. I hosted thirteen focus groups, with a total of more than a hundred members of Gen Z. Fasten your seat belt. I've taken the liberty to translate some of their language, and here's what the Gen Zers said:

The new work ethic will be shortcuts.
As a society, what "smart" looks like is changing; what hard work looks like is shifting. Many from my generation will work harder to not work hard and find "life hacks." We will be more efficient at creating shortcuts and innovating old, antiquated habits. We need a work ethic, but our generation may change its definition. We will be the epitome of "work smarter, not harder" because we've grown up in a world of googling and instant access to information. Bosses may not like this, but hey, if we get the job done efficiently, isn't that what matters?

THE VALUE GENERATION Z BRINGS TO THE WORKPLACE

We will enjoy a four-day workweek, thanks to AI.
We've heard about shorter workweeks for years now, but AI will make it possible. We will get more done in less time and choose to cram our workweek into four days so we can enjoy a longer weekend. The integration of AI into our daily routines has become less of a novelty and more of a cultural norm. Soon it will be a necessity—a thing people will begin to expect from their resources at work—and will spark a productivity revolution. We won't feel weird about a shorter workweek because we never got used to a longer one.

In-person commerce will return in a new way.
Our generation is known for being on our screens all the time. That's made us hungry for face-to-face interaction. We may not be good at it, but I think our craving for human contact will push us all toward returning to human connection. We know we have mental health issues, including anxiety and loneliness. Maybe fewer transaction screens and long lines and more open meeting spaces, informal workshops, and freshly brewed lattes will help. For a lot of us, it's the way to build social capital after the pandemic sent us home. So we need workplaces that know how to help us do this, on our teams and with our clients.

There will be a new employee on the team: an office influencer.
This probably sounds crazy to employers, but soon, they'll see the value of a full-time influencer for their brand. Just like NFL teams once didn't pay for a full-time kicker and now can't live without them, this role will involve hiring a social media influencer and paying them to create content, inject humor, and push the product or service of that company. With our relentless demand for brand authenticity and personal connection, more bosses will hire in-house office influencers to coach them and to give their

online presence a relatable touch. We'll listen to this person over a celebrity reading a script.

Women will take most of the leadership roles.
This is already taking place. Guys can feel the rise of educated women taking on key roles in the office and leading differently than traditional leaders from the past. It's old news that males are falling behind in school and work and females are surging ahead. It's shaken up the dating scene, and we're trying to figure that out. There's a bigger divide between guys and girls in our generation, socially and politically.[5] Ultimately, we will be fine with following a woman as a supervisor, but the egos of older generations may struggle with it.

Our generation will usher in a new era of leaders.
One thing we agree on: our generation feels we must welcome a new type of leader, different from the stale, greedy, ego-driven CEOs of the past. Both millennials and Gen Zers will be a new kind of leader, if for no other reason than to replace an old style. "I think companies will change for the better with millennial CEOs at the helm," one young professional said. "I think we have a better tenor for listening and communicating in a multigenerational way where we can connect the dots for folks." This new era may take a while, since Xers and boomers are staying longer and don't want to let go of the reins. But it will happen eventually.

Internships will include a broad spectrum of ages.
More nontraditional realities will surface, including both young and old interns at work. We think it's kind of cool. It's okay for young people to lead and for old people to be interns. In recent years, we've seen a boatload of retired people head back to work, driven by both economic pressures and a search for personal fulfillment. (The share of baby boomers who returned to the workforce in 2023 after retiring was almost 24 percent higher than

2022, according to recent research from LinkedIn's Economic Graph.[6]) We know the more experienced staff bring valuable qualities, and it opens the door for reverse mentoring, where the old and young both pour into each other.

Robots will make unwanted hands-on jobs irrelevant.
We don't want to do some of the work that past generations of young people did, like retail or construction work. We see AI stepping into many of those undesired roles and doing it better than a human can. For example, AI could solve the housing crisis in the world. As the labor shortage in construction deepens, AI-powered robots could be key to building homes faster and more efficiently. One young professional said, "I read that the global rise of robots in home building will grow almost 20 percent by 2030. I think that's awesome." Just like past innovations moved people from working with horses to working on cars, people will find new, relevant ways to use their skills, and technology will take care of the other jobs.

Virtual and augmented reality will transform traditional work and leisure.
One interesting but sad prediction is that the "virtual" may just substitute for the real in our generation. For many of us, VR will revolutionize tourism, offering a sneak peek at vacation spots. For others, if you have VR tech at your house, you can take a vacation and see the world for free in your den. This immersive technology is transforming the travel industry, with virtual tourism expected to reach more than $24 billion by 2027, according to Statista. (We will see if people are going to be satisfied with the artificial because it's cheaper.)

Food at work will bring teams together.
Community and mental health are mammoth issues for employees. Coming back together in the office is a huge issue for

employers. Food might just be the key. Offering us free lunches and snacks, believe it or not, may just foster the community we all need. Work catering services are already seeing an uptick in business. "Research suggests that it's very powerful when we eat together," says Tracy Brower, PhD, a sociologist and the author of *The Secrets to Happiness at Work*. "Eating together is tied to increases in acceptance, trust, sense of community, and even better enjoyment in life." Brower adds that team meals are also tied to better outcomes, performance, and retention.

Employees will continue to increase in power at work.
We don't believe our generation will put up with the cr*p older generations did, and we will demand change. Already, we saw employees push for change as they realized it wasn't just the boss who had power. One larger change—the pharmaceutical industry will be pushed to change by everyday employees who realize their influence as they band together. The 2024 shooting of UnitedHealthcare CEO Brian Thompson by twenty-six-year-old Luigi Mangione is a violent but vivid example of how young generations are fed up with the broken health care system the US endures. (While I do not condone the murder, it was a young man's reaction to a failed system. Get ready for change.)

> **REFLECT**
> If there's any truth to them, how can you utilize these Gen Z predictions?

FIVE UPSIDES OF GENERATION Z

When we survey the data on this new population of workers, we immediately notice a handful of positive traits they bring with them into their careers. Some are significant qualities and others are smaller—but each can be used to build a great team member. Here are six attributes the newest generation possesses:

THE VALUE GENERATION Z BRINGS TO THE WORKPLACE

1. They have a high interest in entrepreneurship.
As I mentioned already, Generation Z has an entrepreneurial bias. Research from ZenBusiness shows a staggering 93 percent of Gen Zers have already "explored" business ownership.[7] And it's not a passing trend; 75 percent of them have their sights set on becoming full-time entrepreneurs, as the allure of traditional careers continues to fade. Eight in ten say they're more suited for start-ups than their parent's generation. They see the rules of commerce are changing, and they are digital natives. More than seven in ten teens plan to start something rather than join something in their careers. Because they grew up with a smartphone in their hand, they were conditioned to figure out how to leverage that device for their benefit.

Companies that can pivot and create entrepreneurial zones inside their teams will benefit from this bias in Gen Zers and be more likely to keep them. According to a 2024 Deloitte survey, more than 50 percent of Gen Z lives paycheck to paycheck.[8] Year over year their financial concerns have only grown. Economic uncertainty nudges them to postpone big life decisions. Joining an organization that provides them with a secure income yet also furnishes projects and places to act like an entrepreneur could help them thrive going forward.

> **REFLECT**
> How could this entrepreneurial bias add energy to your team?

Just ask Ann Makosinski, who's been in the news since she was a teen a decade ago. She was on Facebook interacting with a friend in the Philippines when she discovered her buddy was failing a school course. When Ann asked why, her friend admitted she had no electricity in her house, so when the sun went down she couldn't do her homework. How did Ann respond? By inventing a flashlight powered by human body heat. She sent it to her Filipino friend, and the rest is history. Her friend began passing her classes again. This was only the beginning. Ann is a driven inventor who in addition to her unique flashlight created a coffee mug that can charge a phone and even toys that run on green energy. That's when established businesses made room for her in their world. Ann has worked with major brands including Maybelline and Uniqlo and loves locking arms with them.

2. Their focus is social justice for the marginalized.
Both Generation Z and Generation Alpha, the younger kids coming after them, display higher levels of empathy and compassion than previous generations at the same age.

Generation Z has sought to challenge stereotypes and dismantle barriers that hinder equal opportunities for all employees at work. They value authenticity and the ability to be their true selves. This should not be surprising because Gen Z is the most diverse generation in US history and more aware of minorities and marginalized populations. Data shows that they are keenly interested in helping those who've been discriminated against and in issues like climate change, gun violence, animal rights, bullying and cyberbullying, criminal justice reform, immigration and refugee activism, and income inequality.

Research from United Way of the National Capital Area reveals "nearly one-third of Gen Zers (32%) are regularly engaged in activism or social justice work (compared to 24% of millennials)."[9] These two cohorts include more activists than all other generations. I have vivid memories of the 2020 Black Lives Matter marches. Most of the protestors were young adults, made up of teens and twenty-somethings. And most of those genuine activists led peaceful protests hoping to spark positive change. When Gen Z sees a group of people, they are drawn to those on the fringes who need

---

REFLECT

How could this focus on the underserved play an important role on your team?

---

extra help and who are often left in the shadows. Marginalized people could be refugees, minorities, immigrants, the disabled, abused women, unborn babies, or anyone else who appears to be disadvantaged.

3. They possess a higher sense of agency than past youth did.
I want to revisit this reality with you: I've mentioned that Gen Z can come across as arrogant and disrespectful to colleagues. I believe they'll need to cultivate emotional intelligence to become good team players. At the same time, the culture they grew up in has conditioned them to feel empowered. Their Google reflex has provided answers to their questions in seconds, they talk to smart software agents like Alexa, Siri, Cortana, and Google Assistant without missing a beat, and nearly every decision they make can be tested and improved instantly. As students, they've adjusted to AI quickly, which can make them feel invincible by the time they reach their careers. It's like they have a virtual team assisting them in whatever they want to do. (I certainly didn't enjoy that upon college graduation!)

> **REFLECT**
> How could this high sense of agency speed up improvement on your team?

You probably remember the dirty water problem in Flint, Michigan, back in 2016. Water and wastewater treatment plant operators and other professionals had allowed elevated levels of lead into Flint's drinking water, and it was harming consumers, especially kids. While stakeholders debated whose fault it was, a student named Gitanjali Rao began working on a response to stop the bleeding. In just three and a half months, she came up with a solution: a portable device that could detect the levels of lead in water faster and at a lower cost than what was currently available. I'm not sure if locals felt grateful or embarrassed. These kinds of stories surface all the time, but we seldom hear about them on the news, perhaps because we are, indeed, embarrassed that a young person solved a problem faster than we did.

Millions see young people as a problem. I see them as a solution. A solution to our world's many problems. Organizations need to harness this innovation and leverage it.

4. They are natural hackers and can dig into and discover how things work.

Hacker is a term that's no longer limited to the world of technology. While it often does apply to someone who gains access to information on a computer system and tampers with it, the definition now involves someone getting behind a system, discovering how it works, and using it for their advantage. This person may or may not be experienced, but they are intuitive. Generation Z is a DIY population. In 2020, with classes held virtually, millions of us realized students were savvier with technology than their teachers or parents. Students were quick to both help their teachers with their Zoom meeting and cheat on exams since they knew they could get away with it. Gen Z considered these elementary hacking skills. No big deal. In my focus groups, several expressed they felt they deserved to get a better grade by cheating because they demonstrated such skills.

> **REFLECT**
> How could this hacker, DIY mindset make your team better?

I launched a nonprofit organization called Growing Leaders in 2003. We are dedicated to developing the next generation of leaders, hence the purpose of this book. Today, everyone who serves on our team is younger than me, some of them three or four decades younger. I believe our team members have great hearts and minds, and I often feel I'm on a team of "hackers." Whenever I ask someone to help me with a project, some research, or an initiative, I see them go after it and figure it out. Melissa is a quick learner, amazing at each project I throw at her; Matt is intuitive at

THE VALUE GENERATION Z BRINGS TO THE WORKPLACE

finding how things work and how to solve problems; Meme won't stop until she resolves whatever challenge I give her; and Andrew and Patrick are very quick at solving my problems, even the ones I create. This is why I believe in reverse mentoring. We don't hire slackers; we hire hackers.

5. They have a keener interest in leadership globally than previous generations.
Universum is a global leader in employer branding. They published the results of a huge survey called *Generation Z Grows Up*. According to the study of fifty thousand young people across forty-six countries, Gen Z is not only interested in starting their own company but shows a keener interest in leadership than the previous two generations.[10] Why is this? I think it's because they look around the world and see incompetent or corrupt leaders and wonder if they could do better. The good news is more than half of the world's population is under thirty, according to the United Nations. (The median age on the continent of Africa is nineteen.) These are members of Gen Z and Gen Alpha. The bad news is only 2.6 percent of members of government globally are a part of Generation Z. It's no wonder they feel underrepresented and desire to have a voice in where our world is heading.

> **REFLECT**
> How could you capitalize on cultivating this interest in leadership?

In Florida's 10th Congressional District, Maxwell Frost became the first member of Gen Z ever elected to Congress a few years ago. Frost, a twenty-five-year-old Democrat, ran on a platform of change. Earlier, an ailing city in Arkansas elected Jaylen Smith, an eighteen-year-old, to lead them as mayor. Back in 2005, voters in Hillsdale, Michigan, elected eighteen-year-old Michael Sessions to be their next mayor. Sam Juhl was elected mayor of Roland, Iowa, days after his eighteenth birthday, and at the ripe old age of twenty, he ran for a second term and won. In 2018, Ben Simons was elected as mayor of Yoncalla, Oregon. He was eighteen at the time. This is now becoming more and more common. Gen Z wants to have a say. We'll talk more about developing your Gen Zers into effective leaders later in this book.

WHAT YOU NEED TO KNOW

The age of influence is upon us. I am not talking about influencer marketing. Instead, I'm talking about workplace influencers. According to new research by McKinsey senior partner John Parsons and his coauthors, these employee influencers are key factors in making—or breaking—change in the workplace.[11]

Why do I think Gen Z could be poised to do this?

First, they're true digital natives: from earliest youth, they have been exposed to the internet, to social networks, to smart technology, and to mobile systems. That context has produced a hypercognitive generation very comfortable with collecting and cross-referencing many sources of information and with integrating virtual and offline experiences, according to McKinsey and Company research. All they have consumed cognitively furnishes them with an intuition, a sort of sixth sense about what the future looks like and where our culture is heading. Yet our tight grip on the past can prevent us from reaching for the future. "A bird in the hand is worth two in the bush," we say.

What we've learned from the past, however, begs us to reach forward, not backward. Do you remember the name Steven Sasson? Shortly after graduating from college in 1973, Steve went to work for Eastman Kodak, a leading company producing cameras and film. Just two years later, when he was twenty-five years old, Steven had invented something that would change the world of photography for everyday people like you and me. He invented the first digital camera in 1975. It was archaic. That first iteration weighed about eight pounds and was roughly the size of a toaster.

But he was excited to show his new creation to his employer. This young engineer saw where the future was heading and got ahead of the curve.

How did Kodak respond?

They felt threatened, knowing this invention could cannibalize their current products. Not unlike Blockbuster Video stores who turned down Reed Hastings's idea for Netflix, and later paid dearly for it, Kodak decided to patent Sasson's idea in 1977 but not to seize the day. It was for the purposes of preventing anyone else from utilizing it. In Steven's own words, they "never let it see the light of day."

While Kodak had been given a sneak peek into the future by one of their very own, they couldn't see the forest for the trees. Steve Sasson was a young engineer. He didn't really understand their industry. He had no real work experience. And he seemed a bit too confident. So they kicked the can down the road. And we all know how this story ended for them. Kodak forgot its roots. Launched in 1888, the Kodak camera had just been invented by its founder, George Eastman. It was all about innovation and risk-taking, and leading their industry. But less than a century later, this lean and mean company had grown fat and sassy. Competitors seized the day, and by the turn of the twenty-first century, Kodak was a fraction of what it once was. They were in trouble by the 1990s and desperately attempted to jump into the digital world. Even though one of their own had given them a chance to lead the field, they struggled to break even. Kodak filed for bankruptcy in January 2012. They're still around—but no one perceives them as a leader.

ONE SHIFT YOU CAN MAKE TO CAPITALIZE ON GENERATION Z ATTRIBUTES

I hired Blake after his senior year of college. He served as a summer intern the year before, and we quickly recognized that he was our kind of team member.

He worked in the shipping room, filling orders for books and traveling with me on road trips to do events. He told me he deeply appreciated the opportunity, but I noticed a slow leak in his enthusiasm after six months. When we met to discuss how he was doing, he confessed he had mixed emotions. On one hand, he felt guilty for expressing anything but gratitude for the job, but on the other, he had begun to feel "unmotivated."

At first, I chalked it up to the wake-up call that most graduates experience. They enter jobs as idealists and quickly realize it's not what they assumed it would be. For Blake, however, there was something deeper going on. He's a member of Generation Z, and like many, he began to feel like a commodity. He was offered the lowest job available, given a small wage, and told to "pay his dues." While this is the way we'd always done it, I realized I needed to manage Blake differently. I needed to change my mind about rookies and power.

I'd like to suggest a better approach to Gen Z employees so you can not only retain them but empower them to make a significant contribution to your team. Let me be blunt. Employers need to stop treating Gen Zers as "property rentals." When I entered my career, it was normal to treat recent grads this way. We were cheap workers who had the chance to prove we were worth keeping. This rarely works today. A growing number of Gen Z staff are asking about their career path in their job interview. To be frank, I would have never asked a hiring manager that question; my career path was up to me. Today Gen Zers want to see if their boss views them as valuable enough to offer a growth plan. They want to know they're more than cheap labor.

THE VALUE GENERATION Z BRINGS TO THE WORKPLACE

One reason Gen Zers stay at a job for only two years and three months on average (according to CareerBuilder) is that they feel like objects. LinkedIn reports they are switching jobs at a faster rate than previous generations, 134 percent faster than they did in 2019. Employers seem utilitarian, and young staff feel they're treated like "commodities." Brianna used this term in a Gen Z focus group. Let me remind you, commodities are raw materials used to make products to own or consume. We can unwittingly make them feel like consumables.

We've done the same thing with our power. We act as if our power is something we own and can use however we wish. Over the last fifty years, as economist Milton Friedman's theory on business became popular, we've turned so many business elements into commodities. In 1970, Friedman wrote a *New York Times* essay titled "A Friedman Doctrine: The Social Responsibility of Business Is to Increase Its Profits." His theory argues that the main duty of a company is to maximize its revenue and increase returns to shareholders. While this is not criminal, you can see how every resource, including human resources, can become a commodity. We'd never admit it, but people can be objects to be used to generate income. Throughout history, we've seen the commodification of humans in various contexts, including surrogacy and, at their very worst, slavery and human trafficking.

SHIFTING FROM COMMODITY TO CURRENCY

What if we changed our mental framework? What if we treated both our people and our power more like currency? We perceive currency as valuable and often treat it as an investment. Because its value grows over time, we tend to manage it well. In fact, currency is something we exchange between people. It is only valuable as it is passed along. A hundred-dollar bill isn't valuable because of the paper it's printed on but because of the value it represents. This makes us perceive the paper differently. We possess currency for a season and then pass it along. In between, we hope to multiply its value.

Today, as we onboard members of Generation Z, I treat my power as a currency. One day, I won't be the leader of the organization I founded, but for now, I have some currency I can loan to our young staff. I can let them borrow some of my influence and vouch for them in meetings; I can invite them to the stage for an interview when I speak at an event. I can give them significant projects and serve them as a consultant more than a commander. So, I have shifted my mental framework about young teammates:

> I will treat my people as currency in which to invest and multiply their value.
> I will treat my power as currency in which to invest in others to multiply its value.

Too often, we invite Gen Z onto our teams as fresh graduates but don't expect much from them early on. After all, they have little to no job experience, we pay them less, and we perceive them as cheap property to leverage to generate revenue. Going forward, this is no longer a helpful way to manage them or to multiply their value. I've witnessed a better perspective.

Drew joined our team when he was twenty-one years old. Soon after, Brad, our director of operations, told me Drew wanted to be part of a meeting that was normally limited to our leaders. It seemed strange, but I thought it might be good for Drew. Even though we'd never had a rookie attend, I agreed. During that meeting Drew took notes, asked great questions, and even suggested an idea that sent the discussion in a better direction. When we ended, I had to decide on who would run point on a new project. Our leaders all agreed—we should let Drew run with it. Essentially, we treated him like currency, not a commodity; we invested in him. I loaned him my influence and authority to pull it off. It was the right call. He rose to the occasion and multiplied his value. It didn't surprise me that Drew became a college president in his thirties. I felt a little like I stumbled into a thrift shop, found a picture frame . . . and later discovered a masterpiece painting inside.

TALK IT OVER

1. Reflecting on the analogy of "finding hidden treasure," what strategies can leaders adopt to identify and nurture the potential within Generation Z employees? How can this approach be balanced with addressing their challenges, such as anxiety or lack of experience?

2. Generation Z is characterized by a high sense of agency but also high levels of anxiety. How might these contrasting traits affect their role in the workplace? What leadership approaches would best leverage their strengths while supporting their mental well-being?

3. Given Generation Z's entrepreneurial mindset and interest in social justice, how can organizations create an environment that fosters innovation and inclusivity? How might these traits influence team dynamics and organizational goals?

4

THE MYTHS WE'VE BELIEVED ABOUT GENERATION Z

On October 30, 1938, millions of Americans were listening to the radio when the broadcast was interrupted by what seemed like a news bulletin: "I'm speaking from the roof of the broadcasting building," the announcer said. He then described an alien spaceship landing on a farm in New Jersey. Martian invaders soon emerged from the spaceship and started taking over the United States. Bells rang over the airwaves to warn listeners to evacuate the city as the Martians approached. "Estimated in the last two hours, three million people have moved out along the roads to the north. . . . All communication with Jersey Shore closed ten minutes ago. No more defenses, our army wiped out . . . artillery, air force, everything wiped out. This may be the last broadcast."

For years, this story has intrigued me. It was Orson Welles's broadcast of "The War of the Worlds" airing that Sunday in New York, causing national panic when the program vividly described this invasion. The massive hysteria was mostly caused by the listeners who tuned in to the broadcast late and missed the introduction that provided the context for it. Welles had little idea the chaos his hoax would cause. Call it the original "fake news" broadcast. It was all a fabrication. And it became mythical because the story of that night has been told repeatedly through the years and grown bigger over time. That's how myths survive.

HOW DO MYTHS CATCH ON?

When a widespread panic is created among people, psychologists call it an "emotion contagion." No one has any details, and panic thrives when there's ambiguity. No one has ever experienced a Martian attack, so folks can only imagine what to do if it happened. Without full information, emotion contagion causes people to adopt the emotions of their social surrounding. People mistake emotions for facts. We fill in the gaps in our minds with distorted narratives when we don't have accurate information.

Further, myths can catch on as people become guilty of "fundamental attribution error." In Orson Welles's story, people heard a few headlines and assumed Martians were all evil and destructive. No one had ever seen one before—so the assumption was imaginary. But millions attributed these characteristics to the aliens based on a radio story.

Truth be told, even with higher levels of education, we still buy into myths today for the same reasons. Myths become sacred tales that explain the world and our experience. Because they elicit emotion, they are as prevalent in the modern world as they were in ancient cultures. In the early 1900s, people believed that radioactive items could help with rheumatism, arthritis, and aging. Doctors once promoted cigarettes as "good for you" from the 1930s through the 1950s, in advertising campaigns. And today, despite the existence of fact-checking, it's stunning the fake news people believe. I suppose we believe what we want to believe.

Unfortunately, this happens to us every day, often with our young teammates. For example, someone from an older generation witnesses a Gen Zer doing something they don't understand. Because they possess a different paradigm for how things get done, they're limited. They assume the Gen Zer is wrong and that all of Gen Z is guilty of the same "wrong." Fundamental attribution error is a cognitive bias that causes people to overemphasize a person's traits when judging their behavior, while underemphasizing situational factors. Without full information, we fill in the gaps in our minds with what could be a faulty narrative. For example, if someone cuts you off while driving, you might assume they're a jerk, but you might not consider that they're rushing to the hospital.

My research shows it's been common for us to be guilty of fundamental attribution error and emotion contagion when it comes to Generation Z. We draw conclusions quickly, we don't take the time to uncover who they really are, and then we become frustrated with them. Next we begin to stereotype. Stereotypes are mental shortcuts. We determine their "type," throw all of them into a category, and spread the story. While none of us who are older want to be stereotyped, we quickly do this to our youngest generation. And what has it done? It's driven different generations apart. My friend and fellow author Ryan Jenkins says when people from various generations don't connect:

> They are seven times more likely to disengage on the job.
> They are five times more likely to miss work.
> They are three times more likely to quit their job.[1]

Further, a study by *Fortune* magazine and LinkedIn revealed that one in five Gen Z workers have not even had one conversation with someone over fifty in their workplace. Somehow the myths we hold about those young people prevent us from connecting.

Let's examine six common myths that hinder our ability to lead them.

THE MOST COMMON MYTHS WE'VE BELIEVED ABOUT GEN Z

In every generation of young people—even young professionals on a job—older adults will spot a rookie error and assume it's typical for that generation: "They're going to ruin the company!" Assuming young people are disrespectful and lazy dates back to Socrates. We often talk in dark and despairing terms about Gen Zers, and thanks to social media, they see what we're saying. They can feel we don't believe in them. In 2018, Growing Leaders, the nonprofit organization I founded to train a new generation of leaders, partnered with Harris Poll Interactive and surveyed more than two thousand adults, asking them how they felt about Generation Z. The results were revealing:

> A full 66 percent of older adults experienced a negative emotion first, not a positive one, when they thought of Generation Z. That's two out of three. The top word was *concerned*, and others included *frustrating*, *afraid*, *uncertain*, *angry*, *sad*, and so on.

> A full 64 percent believed that Generation Z will not be ready for adulthood when they enter it. Adults reported kids will fall short of expectations and responsibilities required of them when it's time to launch their careers. They'll be unprepared.

Let me ask you a question: How do you think it feels to be led by someone who doesn't really believe you're ready for what's coming and who feels a negative emotion first when you come up in a conversation? Gen Z can sense it: our verbal, nonverbal, and paraverbal communication are difficult to hide. No wonder we endure a generational divide right now in our world. It's a wide gap to cross for millions of employers, teachers, coaches, and parents. So, let's evaluate the biggest myths many of us have embraced and see if we can turn the tide toward hope, positivity, and belief. These myths surfaced in my focus groups with hundreds of members of Gen Z (all employees) in 2024.

Myth One: They don't listen because they don't care.
This is an easy assumption to make for us who are over forty-five years old. To be clear, I'm sure there are Gen Zers who are guilty of not listening to us because they don't care. But focus groups with dozens of Gen Z members reveal there's a more prominent reason. My meetings with Gen Z employees reveal they "do care, but [they] care about different things than older generations do." One Gen Zer, twenty-one years old, put it this way: "My life is so different from my manager's. He thinks I'm apathetic, but I care deeply about a world he doesn't understand." Gen Zers told me they feel older generations "care about things that really don't matter." One told me: "It depends on circumstance; I do care about certain things but not always to the degree older team members do. Some of what they care about seems irrelevant. We live in two different worlds. We value different things."

Truth: Gen Zers are all unique, but there is a collective focus on correcting the mistakes that older generations have made about work-life balance, mismanaging finances, and broken families. Many Gen Zers say older generations are "workaholics who no longer have healthy lives or families." So they often enter their careers with boundaries, deliberately thinking differently than their older counterparts. Gen Z perceives the mistakes that boomers and Xers made as a black eye on their generation. They are demanding more from employers. Clarifying the why behind a task or project needs to be a priority for managers. This communicates your awareness and your trustworthiness.

Myth Two: They're lazy and entitled because they have no clue about life's hardships.
There's no doubt about it—managers across the US have observed Gen Z's high sense of entitlement and agency as they enter the workplace. Gen Z feels empowered and comes across as arrogant at times. When this is true, remember all behavior has a reason. First, most of them have grown up with smartphones and feel they know a lot as they launch their careers. Certainly, they'll have to keep learning, but Gen Xers and boomers frequently treat them as "incompetent" (expressed in a focus group), and Gen Z feels they must help their older colleagues see they do know a thing or two.

Truth: In reality, every age group today feels more entitled than previous generations. My grandparents' generation never expected high speed internet, air-conditioning, convenient searches online, smartphones, or meals delivered to their door. We all do now. Gen Z just happens to be the youngest among the entitled. Gen Z may look lazy or disengaged, but it's partly because they observe workplaces operating in a style that is fading. I call it the "gatekeeper" style where authorities are power brokers of all that happens. Gen Z intuitively knows that gatekeepers are disappearing. Songwriters no longer need a record label to distribute their music. Authors no longer require a traditional publisher to distribute their content. Even start-ups and social entrepreneurs can use digital means to raise the money they need, without depending on venture capital. And before we assume Gen Zers have no clue about hardships, why not get to know them? In focus groups, I consistently heard from Gen Zers who revealed some mammoth challenges they were facing, but I had no idea. Natalie told me how she's taking care of her mom with stage four cancer, going to college, and holding down a job. She's barely making enough to live on. She admits she's set a lot of boundaries, but she believes she's working as hard as anyone on her staff.

Myth Three: They don't trust authorities because they consume fake news.
Each of these myths contains a kernel of truth; many Gen Zers possess a jaded view of traditional institutions because they've digested unreliable news on social media feeds. I discovered, however, their distrust of authority (and the establishment in general) is because they've heard of so much *real news* of corruption among leaders. Consider the headlines we've all seen over the last decade: embezzlement among corporate executives, lobbyists paying off greedy politicians, performance enhancing drugs among athletes, child abuse in the Catholic church, and sexual scandals in the evangelical church. While these perpetrators are a minority, headlines report these stories as if they're normalized. It's given the establishment quite a horrific reputation.

Truth: Consider Gen Z's point of view: they see elders failing to practice what they preach. Millions have watched older generations, including parents, overspend, requiring them to work past retirement age; they've witnessed divorce rates climb; they've seen authorities fail to embody ethical leadership and instead display moral corruption including business, religious, and political leaders. They've also seen universities charge ludicrous tuition fees for a degree that doesn't equate to a job. This is why Gen Z finds it hard to trust us. The media and social media platforms have dirt on everyone. Gen Z is looking for authentic and moral leaders, ones who model the way. Forget positional authority. Just because a boss wears a badge doesn't automatically earn them the respect of a Gen Zer. They will follow us when we lead better; they'll listen better when we do so as well.

THE MYTHS WE'VE BELIEVED ABOUT GENERATION Z

Myth Four: They are fragile because of social media's influence on them.

Research from Jonathan Haidt and Greg Lukianoff proves we have raised a generation of fragile kids. In fact, cancel culture and the need for trigger warnings have cultivated fragility across our culture today. Becoming fragile is not in question; the question is why? The *New York Times* carried an article in the fall of 2024 unveiling a new trend in parenting these days. Instead of letting kids go to a neighbor's house for a sleepover, they now limit these outings to a "sleep under."[2] What's that? It's an outing where a parent won't allow their child to spend the night but rather only part of the night. They want their child to call or text them when it's time for bed, even if it's 2:00 a.m., so Mom or Dad can come pick them up. These anxious parents fear for their child's safety and want to limit their risk. When Gen Z was growing up, adults risked too little, rescued too quickly, and rewarded too easily. Now many require extra caution to not be triggered. I met a new friend who spent seven years in the Navy. When I asked how it was, he replied, "Well it was different than I expected." When I inquired why, he explained, "Well, in boot camp, our drill sergeant gave us all cards to hold up in the air if he said anything that made us feel uncomfortable." It's a new day.

Truth: I would argue it's not solely social media's fault that young people are fragile. It is culture at large that older adults created. Gen Z grew up in a world that we made, one that focused more on protecting them than preparing them. They are victims of our making. In fact, I meet people of all ages who are pitifully fragile—and are often miserable because the world won't cater to their every whim. It's time for change. We must now lead them into a realistic perspective, away from the mistaken expectations of our culture. With some genuine relationship building and some good training, I've seen Gen Zers develop grit and resilience, especially as they come to love and value the work they've been given to do. It's a matter of the heart. When we connect with them, they can move from fragile to agile.

Myth Five: They are not loyal and won't do grunt work.
I've heard dozens of employers say this to me over the last five years. Leaders see Gen Zers hedge their bets at work and won't display the loyalty or commitment past generations did. It's easy to assume that Gen Z is unwilling to do the "small tasks" we ask of them. They seem different. I've even heard some recent graduates echo the idea, saying: "I hate the term 'pay your dues.'" Yet we all know, that's how you get ahead, right? Anyone over forty-five years old has heard that term when they were younger. So, what's changed? Gen Zers were raised in the shadow of the global financial crisis of 2008, an event that's had long-lasting impacts on the nature of employment. "It used to be that people went to work for big companies thinking they'd be there their entire career and that the company would watch out for them: providing health insurance, and so on," according to Roberta Katz, a former senior research scholar at Stanford's Center for Advanced Study in the Behavioral Sciences (CASBS). "But after the 2008 recession, and even more recently following the COVID-19 pandemic, companies have cut back labor costs and implemented other cost-saving measures, like reducing perks and benefits. Meanwhile, mass layoffs have also been rampant." Gen Z is only reciprocating and protecting themselves from these realities.

Truth: The organization I launched in 2003 employs several Gen Zers, and they've shown deep loyalty—but a different kind than baby boomers. Gen Zers don't exhibit the loyalty you find in a hierarchy or a monarchy, a blind loyalty to a "king" or a "personality," one that adheres to strict protocols or regulations. It's the kind of loyalty you find in a free market. It's more transactional, one that you negotiate, the kind of loyalty you exchange with your customers or clients. Leaders often spend loads of time pleasing customers. What if we did the same thing building loyal staff:

investing in them, growing them and their skills, and rewarding them? This kind of loyalty deepens when *transactional* interactions at work become *transformational* ones, where leaders make emotional connections with their staff. When I do this, Gen Zers are happy to do whatever it takes, even grunt work, because they're emotionally connected to the people and work. Like anyone, however, they must know we notice their grunt work and know it will lead to rewards and recognition. Vague promises about the future aren't enough. They want an exchange of loyalty.

Myth Six: They're not serious about work like Gen Xers and boomers.
This one is important for older generations to understand, including me. When I began my career, I was completely committed to my work and to getting tasks done and pleasing my boss (who happened to be John C. Maxwell). When I reflect on it, however, I was being paid a wage that enabled me to get ahead; it inspired me to work harder because I was saving to buy a house soon. And my wife and I did get that home by the time I was twenty-five years old. Today, Gen Zers wonder if hard work and commitment even matters as their salary does not give them hope to purchase a home in the foreseeable future. Perhaps never. The gap is much larger today between their wage and the cost of living. I felt hopeful at twenty-five years old; many of them feel hopeless. One Gen Zer told me in a focus group: "I feel like a commodity. I am being used and could get fired at any time."

Truth: I've found Gen Z wants to work hard at something they care about, but at the same time they want balance and boundaries, along with a fair wage. They want to enjoy a healthy, sustainable, balanced life. Surveys show they are willing to work extra hours and even work on weekends when the pay matches the task and time they provide. My friend J. J. had several Gen Zers on his team who left their job each day the minute the clock struck 5:00 p.m. He assumed they just didn't like work but later learned the truth. They all had two to three side hustles they had to get to so they could make enough money to pay the bills.

They're part of today's "gig economy." This term describes the free market system where organizations and independent workers engage in short-term work arrangements. Think Uber drivers. Think contract workers. Think freelancers. Think temp workers. It's estimated that 36 percent of US workers take part in the gig economy, and 33 percent of companies extensively use gig workers. The word *gig* refers to the transient nature of the job itself. About 44 percent of gig workers say their gig work is now their primary source of income.[3]

WHAT YOU SHOULD KNOW ABOUT GEN Z

Gen Z feels empowered by their smart devices. While it's causing anxiety, it's also liberating them to seize control of their future. Fewer see themselves as a servant to a boss or a climber on a corporate ladder. They are "hackers" who are savvy enough to decode the normal protocols or systems. They'll find a way to make options work for them. A growing percentage are not doing the typical four-year, liberal arts college experience. It's a track they may not want to go down, and today there are other viable options for a smart kid.

To keep them in your workplace, you'll want to know something about them.

Research from David Yeager, at the University of Texas, reveals that in this stage of their career, young adults have some internal objectives. I've added to his list and believe employers do well to recognize Gen Z is preoccupied by three pursuits:

1. Status on the team. Am I esteemed for who I am and what I bring to the team?
2. Respect from colleagues. Do I have the respect of others even when I'm young?

3. **Recognition of value added.** Why am I here and what difference do I make?

Every young team member desires to possess and perceive status, respect, and value, and any interaction that feels like they have little status or are disrespected or don't bring real value may draw a negative response from them. On the other hand, recognizing their added value and treating them with respect goes a long way. It could be a game changer. They are the ones who will connect what's new to what's old. Remember, Gen Z staff doesn't need us for information; they need us for interpretation. We must offer context to the content they consume. This means leading differently. Adam Grant said, "The hallmark of expertise is no longer how much you know. It's how well you synthesize. Information scarcity rewarded knowledge acquisition. Information abundance requires pattern recognition. It's not enough to collect facts. The future belongs to those who connect dots."

Too often, older generations assume young people are flawed, entitled, or just exhausting. We say one thing; they hear another. The new research on Gen Z, however, argues that the source of young people's frustrating behavior comes from their normal and even positive developmental needs, says Yeager. According to neuroscientist Ron Dahl, "We shouldn't fear this adolescent sensitivity to social status and respect; instead, we should help youth harness it for good." When young professionals have their status or respect questioned, a barrier of mistrust is formed. *They long for status and respect.*[4] (We did too at their age.) It makes them read between the lines of each comment a manager makes trying to discern if the older colleague is disrespecting them or not. They may just focus on the unsaid part more than what was said. Gen Z needs us

> Have you been guilty of believing any of these myths? What beliefs should you change?

to show both high belief in them and high expectations for them. Without these two, progress may stall. Yeager calls this the "mentor mindset." Mentor leaders don't buy into the myths; they buy into the beliefs that Gen Z has great value to bring to a team and that we must, therefore, believe in them and expect much of them.

THEIR THREE LOOMING QUESTIONS AS YOUNG PROFESSIONALS

Kara Powell is the executive director of the Fuller Youth Institute.[5] (I love the fact that this institute's initials are FYI.) Powell wisely points out that young adults are striving to discover the answers to three paramount questions, whether they know it or not. The work they do, the people they get to know, and the content they consume will all help them answer these three huge questions. I believe supervisors will lead more wisely if we recognize young team members are figuring these questions out for themselves.

1. Who am I?

This is about their identity. Their career will play a major part in answering this question. The sooner we realize that their hours working for us are about more than mere time, that it's about helping them establish a clear sense of identity, the better leaders we will be for them. The problem is—our brains are not yet fully formed until twenty-five to twenty-eight years old according to the National Institute of Mental Health. Few young adults have established their identities yet; in fact, millions say it is still fluid. The problem with fluidity is it can lack congruency. We all must eventually come into our own, knowing who we are and what we have to offer the world.

A few years ago, I visited West Point, the military academy of the US Army. I was impressed with the leadership and the facility, but I was most impressed with the cadets. They are in a pursuit of figuring out who they are. I enjoyed breakfast with Trey Grindley, who was in his final year at West Point. Naturally, I asked him what he wanted to do with his life. His answer was both brilliant and stunning. He replied, "Dr. Elmore, my answer to that question comes later. I am working on who I want to be. And once I determine the man I want to become, I'll work on what I will do, why I will do it, and where I will go. In that order."

This is all about the first objective: *status on the team.* Am I valued for what I bring?

Now, I recognize you hired your young employees to do a job and to generate revenue. If you could approach your managerial role in their life differently, however, you could both keep them and bring out the best in them. They'd become better workers. What if your supervisors met with young staff and assumed the role of a mentor, not just a manager? What if you discussed how the tasks they perform can help them answer this big question? What if you could help them see any overlap between your company's mission and their personal mission in life? This could be a game changer.

2. Where do I belong?

This is a question the Gen Zers I've surveyed are more aware of than the first question. Members of this young generation experience a higher sense of loneliness than they do anxiety. They desperately want to enjoy community but often don't know how to experience it. The portable screens they've spent thousands of hours on have not equipped them to grow in their emotional intelligence. While I'm not suggesting their workplace will supply all of their BFFs (best friends forever), I do know that most of their day is spent at work (if they work full time), and they tell me they'd love to spend those hours with those they consider friends. One even said to me, "I want work-life blending more than work-life balance."

Keep in mind, however, the difference between belonging and fitting in. University of Houston psychologist Brené Brown explains these two. *Fitting in* means a person sees who they are and that they must change a little to have a role on the team. They can't genuinely be themselves; they must change to stay. *Belonging* means a person can be completely who they are but do so on behalf of the larger mission. The unique personality, talent, and passion they bring isn't just about them. It is about expressing it for the purpose of making the team better.

This is all about *respect from colleagues*. Do I have the respect of others even when I'm young and different? They want to enjoy a unique place on the team, a place others don't have. They want to know their differences are not only tolerated but welcomed.

Alan had just graduated and taken a role at a catering company near his home. His days as a student were spotty. He didn't make great grades, nor did he stand out in any extracurricular activity. He never played a sport or an instrument or joined a club. In fact, Alan would say he was lonely during his high school and college years. At this catering company, however, he got to enjoy his passion, which was culinary arts. He loved preparing food for events. This came from his hours watching the Food Network in his earlier years. I met him when I spoke at an event hosted by this catering company. I admired his work ethic afterward, seeing him sweat as he removed the plates and cleaned up the tables. I wondered if he hated his job. When I asked him, he smiled and said, "I love this job. I belong at this company. Today was the best day of my life."

3. What difference do I make?

This one is usually addressed after the first two questions. Once a young professional knows who they are and enjoys the role they play with peers, they become the best version of themselves when they're convinced they make a huge difference in the mission. Great supervisors help them connect the dots between the (often) menial tasks they must perform with the overall vision of the organization. This helps them answer the why question. Any teammate spirals downward into trouble when they forget their why or, worse, when they never knew it in the first place. When I talk to Gen Z members, the majority of them tell me they feel like a "cog in the wheel." As I said before, many feel like a commodity that can be bought and sold. This does not energize them. Too many managers have failed to cast a compelling vision and show them how they fit into the overall mission.

This question ultimately answers: *Why am I here?* It's about purpose. In chapter 1, I told the story of those young engineers at NASA, the operators who put Neil Armstrong and Buzz Aldrin on the moon in July of 1969. It wasn't until President Kennedy cast the vision for this big goal that many of those young, recent college grads shifted into high gear. In fact, before the vision was clear, many of those young men and women said they "felt like a piece of furniture" around NASA. Just taking up space. The big goal, however, turned everything around.

Suddenly, new technology was required for the big mission, and young MIT graduates understood how to operate that technology better than their seasoned counterparts. So the older engineers became mentors, "SimSups," and the twenty-somethings were positioned as the operators who actually completed the task of landing a space capsule on the moon. The veterans provided the wisdom and experience; the younger generation provided the technical know-how. It was a perfect blend. But knowing their why provided the energy.

> How are you helping your young team members answer these questions on your team?

ROOKIE SMARTS AND OLD FARTS

Young people are so in touch with what's trending and where culture is going, they often don't take us seriously because our information and experience seems antiquated. Many of us feel "so twentieth century" to them. Believe it or not, we crossed a milestone in 2024. There are now more people from Generation Z in the workplace than baby boomers. The old are departing, and the new are entering the marketplace in droves.[6]

Sarah is one of them, and her story is a case study for all of us. Less than a year on the job, she made a costly mistake at work, to the tune of an $800,000 expense. Her manager asked to meet with her the following Monday, and she told her roommate she was sure she'd get fired. Her previous experience with leaders predicted that. She had been treated with suspicion and caution; her previous bosses didn't trust anyone under thirty. On Monday, however, her direct supervisor asked her how she was doing then suggested they talk about what had just happened. Instead of letting her go, he said, "That was an expensive mistake. Let's make sure we all learn from it before I turn you loose on your next project."

Needless to say, her manager's belief in her deepened her loyalty to that team.

One of our organization's core values is "Begin with belief." That means we show respect and trust from day one, both to old and to young. I've found they tend to reciprocate with the same quality. Gen Z is a unique generation of young people, having matured in a unique period of history. Let's rise to this occasion, not assuming they are like us but that they will complement us, as a generation.

During the economic downturn of 2020–21, I interviewed a dozen "Great Depression Kids" who are now ninety to ninety-four years old. They are senior citizens who grew up during the Great Depression and World War II. I asked them what adults did as they grew up that enabled them to mature into adulthood with such grit and resilience. Their answers were fascinating. Collectively, they responded by saying that adults did not allow them to feel like victims. In fact, most admitted they didn't even know they were in an economic depression. They said their parents, teachers, coaches, and employers expected the best out of them and believed they had it in them to succeed even in difficult times. And they did. That generation grew up with a gritty, resourceful attitude. What if we could do the same for Generation Z in our organizations? Let's begin with belief, not myth.

TALK IT OVER

1. How do common myths about Generation Z, such as their perceived laziness or lack of loyalty, affect the way leaders approach managing this generation? How can leaders shift from these misconceptions to a mindset of belief and support?

2. The chapter highlights the importance of addressing the three key questions young professionals ask themselves: *Who am I?*, *Where do I belong?*, and *What difference do I make?* How can leaders create an environment that helps Generation Z answer these questions while aligning with organizational goals?

3. The concept of "beginning with belief" encourages leaders to show respect and trust in Generation Z from the start. How can this approach foster resilience and loyalty in young professionals, and what practical steps can leaders take to implement it?

PART

2

NINE STRATEGIES TO TURN LAND MINES INTO GOLD MINES

In this second portion of the book, I provide you a guidebook on leading through nine of the most challenging situations leaders face with Generation Z. They will help you turn land mines into gold mines. Each chapter will define the pain point, offer research on the issue, then furnish practical steps to address it.

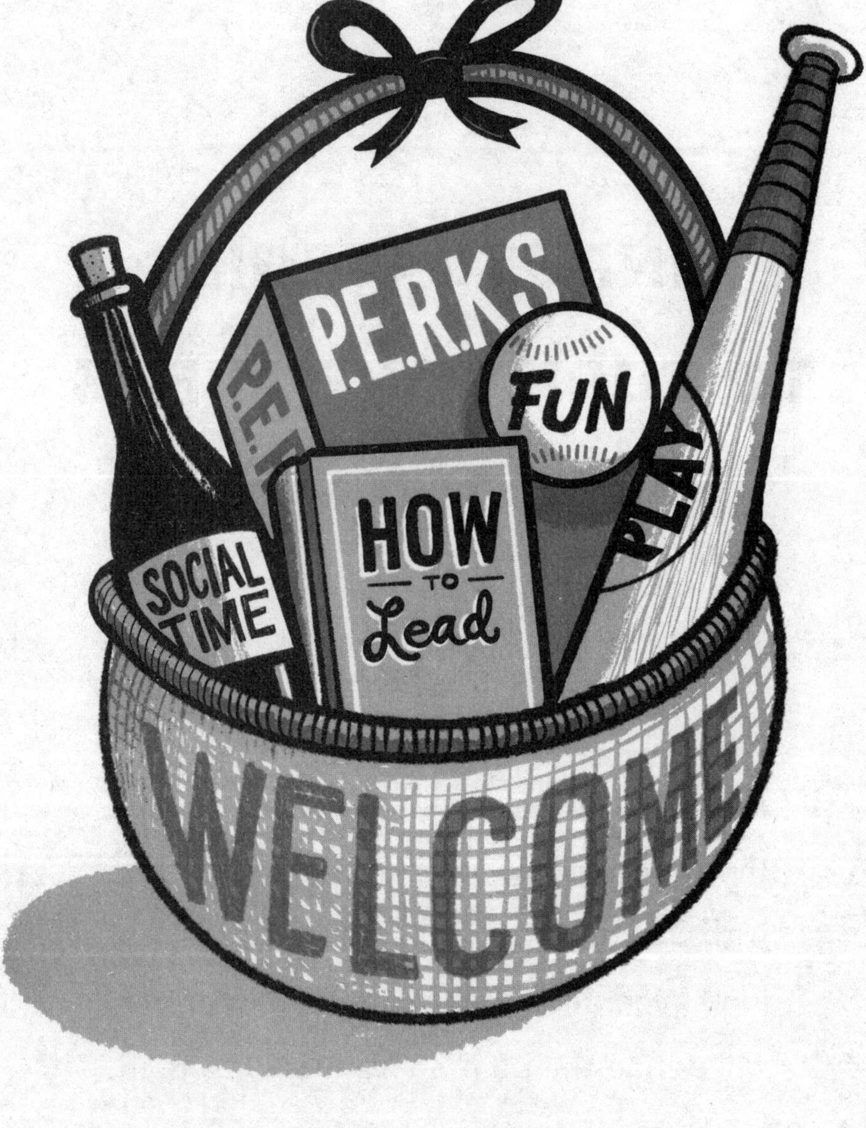
P.E.R.K.S
P.E.R.
FUN
PLAY
SOCIAL TIME
HOW TO Lead
WELCOME

5

THE WELCOME WAGON

MAKING THEM WANT TO STAY

Nate and Stuart launched their careers following college graduation. Both did well in school, both served in summer internships, and both had jobs lined up upon graduating from their respective universities. After that, however, their stories are very different.

Stuart started at Enterprise car rental and was quickly moved up the organizational chart. The company is keen on finding sharp, ambitious young men and women and offering opportunities to make progress, get promoted, and earn more income. In fact, Enterprise seeks them out. Enterprise car rental is widely recognized as one of the top companies for hiring recent graduates, consistently ranking as the number one entry-level employer, according to CollegeGrad.com. This means they hire a significantly higher proportion of recent graduates compared to other companies in the industry. They hired eighty-five hundred management trainees last year alone. Stuart still works there four years later.

Nate, on the other hand, has taken the typical route of most Gen Zers. Over the last four years, he's worked at three companies, averaging about a year and a half at each one. At these jobs, he started fine but within weeks had made up his mind on how long he could endure at that place. One job was in retail, another was at a corporate office (where he worked in a cubicle), and the other was at a bank. Each one felt stale before the year was out. He was proud of himself for staying longer than twelve months at a job.

Research shows members of Generation Z are job-hoppers. This trend began with millennials, but so far Gen Z is remaining at one job an even shorter amount of time. A recent study by CareerBuilder revealed a startling commitment gap between working generations.[1] The average length of stay in a job varies greatly according to age. Baby boomers last eight years and three months, Gen X for five years and two months, millennials for two years and nine months. For Gen Z, it's two years and three months. A recent Gallup poll rated Gen Z as the least engaged group of these generations.[2] My research says Gen Z leaves for four big reasons:

1. I got bored.
2. I need more money.
3. I don't fit here.
4. I have a bad boss.

You've probably heard that these young professionals have short attention spans, they get bored quickly, they expect a lot out of their leaders (supervisors), they assume they'll be promoted rapidly (just like in school), and more of them have ADHD than any other generation globally. These alone may explain their short tenure. One CEO remarked to me that the corporate ladder has become the corporate "lily pad," where Gen Zers hop from lily pad to lily pad like frogs in a pond.

I would argue, however, it doesn't have to be this way.

THE CHALLENGE IN A NUTSHELL

Because Generation Z has built a track record of hopping from job to job and gig to gig, this chapter examines the art of onboarding and welcoming them well. The first impression should be the right impression if you want to retain them. All's well that begins well. We'll examine their interview, their first week, their onboarding experience, and setting them up to win.

This may be enough to combat the circular mindset so many of them have about work. They belong to the gig economy. For example, Bo, a Gen Zer in his twenties, sells expensive gems for a jewelry outlet, oversees a studio recording songs for artists, and rents two Airbnbs on the side. He has three gigs. They are all different, so Bo never gets bored, and life is never dull since he's multitasking in three different hobbies. (Do you remember the generational chart in chapter 2? Work is like a hobby.) This prevents Gen Zers from falling prey to the poor mindsets we often have in established organizations.

This is one reason millions of Gen Zers are choosing this journey. David Yeager, author and cofounder of the Texas Behavioral Science and Policy Institute, explains that many leaders suffer from a perspective he calls the "neurobiological-incompetence model." We see young people as flawed and deficient thinkers who can't comprehend the future consequences of their actions. The problem is, young people sense this, and they don't want to be around it. Who wants to follow a leader who doesn't believe in you? Yeager believes we must experience a revolution of thought. We must believe that young people are not "a problem to be managed but a resource to be cultivated." Another study from the UCLA Center for the Developing Adolescent reminds us: *young people want status and respect from both peers and leaders, earned by making meaningful contributions.*[3]

Another member of Gen Z put it this way: our views on work focus on output, not hours. We prioritize work-life balance above almost everything else. According to Deloitte, less than half (49 percent) of Gen Zers say work is central to their identity, compared to 62 percent of millennials. Instead, Gen Z admires people whose top trait is work-life balance rather than a passion for work, job title, or seniority.[4] Knowing this will help us onboard them better.

STEPS TO WIN AND KEEP GENERATION Z

I discovered some organizations that have learned how to keep Generation Z employees by managing staff in a new and different way. They make employment attractive to young adults. Take Enterprise car rental, where Stuart works. Although the industry usually endures high staff turnover rates, Enterprise has recently seen record retention, with double-digit tenures for senior leadership and management. Enterprise's retention strategy includes promoting employees, celebrating employees' development, and closely tracking internal advancement. They don't seem to be threatened by Gen Z but rather want their young team members to stay and climb.

Let's begin with a benchmark. Two industries where young adults have typically found employment over the decades are retail and quick-service restaurants. When I grew up, I worked in both industries between the ages of sixteen and twenty-two. It was common. Today, fewer teens and twenty-somethings even take such jobs, often feeling those jobs are beneath them. For those who take a job at a fast-food restaurant, the stay is usually short.

The average tenure of a young staff member at a quick-service restaurant (QSR) is stunning.

Only 54 percent of QSR employees reached ninety days of work before quitting in 2022, according to an HourWork report revealed in the publication *Restaurant Dive*, and based on employee surveys at more than eight thousand QSRs.[5] At McDonald's, a recent report suggested the restaurant chain experienced 100 percent turnover rate each year. Sounds like a revolving door to me.

Others handle young team members differently and have managed to keep them longer. The turnover among Chick-fil-A operators (franchisees) is a low 5 percent a year. Among hourly workers, turnover is 60 percent, compared with 107 percent for the industry that same year. They employ loads of Gen Zers, more than a hundred thousand of them at their restaurants. According to Comparably.com, Chick-fil-A's retention score has remained steady at 65/100. Chick-fil-A ranks first versus five industry competitors, which include KFC, McDonald's, Wendy's, Taco Bell, and Fogo de Chão. So, what are they doing?[6]

In my focus groups with Gen Z team members at Chick-fil-A, they were candid about what made them stay. I heard remarks like:

> They care for me here and offer me a college scholarship.
> They train me for various positions, which makes me more marketable.
> They have a "second-mile service" culture that makes emotional connections.
> They lead by their values, which match with mine.
> They are preparing me to lead my own restaurant in the future.

On the other hand, Chick-fil-A is like a magnet, attracting some workers and repelling others. Zach Thomas, a Chick-fil-A operator, once told me he hired a young woman who soon afterward quit and took a job at another quick-service restaurant because she "wouldn't have to work so hard."

WHAT GENERATION Z WISHES YOU KNEW WHEN YOU INTERVIEW THEM FOR A JOB

Does this scenario sound familiar? You've had a job opening for six weeks, and young candidates continue dropping out of your pipeline. Some want only virtual or hybrid work. Others show up late. Still others ghost you and never show up. What's going on? Sadly, Gen Zers are picky, and they're not choosing jobs that young people once found attractive.

Then you notice a pattern that you know you can fix.

It's the interview process. Several candidates interview with your company and decide to say no before having a second meeting. Was it something in the initial meeting that was a turnoff? Was it language a manager used? Was it the "old-school" environment? I spoke to a physician who told me she hired a young doctor after he finished his residency—and on day one, he failed to show up. He was one of several who ghosted the employer, failing to get back to the HR director that they had changed their minds. Another employer invested lots of time interviewing and conceding on several issues to make the job offer more attractive. On the day of the offer, the candidate chose not to work after all.

I believe every situation we face as leaders falls into one of three buckets:

1. It's in my control. In response, I must take responsibility and own it.
2. It's out of my control. In response, I must trust the process and not lose any sleep.
3. It's within my influence. In response, I must approach scenarios wisely and adapt.

Let me offer some ideas that will enable you to connect with young job candidates and wisely manage that third bucket in your leadership, specifically in Gen Z job interviews.

1. Shift your approach from gatekeeper to guide.
I mentioned this in our last chapter. Gen Z intuitively knows our world no longer needs gatekeepers to succeed. Musicians don't need a record label, and authors don't need a publisher to distribute their content. Older generations typically approach interviews with young job seekers from a position of power. Great hiring managers today no longer approach them as a gatekeeper (from a power stance) but rather as a guide or coach (from a relational stance). We must hire for talent but convey that we want the best for the candidate, not just our company. As I've said before, organizational psychologist Adam Grant wisely observes we're experiencing "the democratization of the workplace." The ground is more level, and this begins with the interview. Reduce the power gap as much as you can with your approach. It can lubricate potential differences between old and young.

2. Be warm and clear in your communication, using simple language.
Often Gen Zers admit to me that they don't fully understand professional language and are not familiar with business terms. Be warm and personal yet professional in your correspondence, using digital means to message them early on. Review your language and procedures to see if they need updating. This lets them know they're not a number and they will be more likely to respond similarly. Nearly 60 percent said clear communication from the recruiter would improve their experience and be more attractive. If they don't understand a term, share that you didn't understand it either as you began, making them feel at home.

3. Utilize various leaders and team members in the interview process.

One step our nonprofit organization took five years ago was to include a team in the interview process, involving a director, colleagues that the candidate would work with, and a manager. It was a three-step process that we tried to complete within seven to ten days. Seventy-five percent of Gen Zers said they value the opportunity to meet directly with employees they'd work with, and 63 percent said they'd like to meet with a leader while interviewing. Be sure to include people who are warm, relational, and can identify with the job candidate's interests and qualities.

4. Keep the interview process to two weeks or less.

You already know their attention spans are shorter. When companies take too long to complete the interview journey, they'll likely move on to someone who's more interested in them. More than 70 percent of Gen Z respondents ranked a quick interview process (two weeks or less) as a factor that would improve their likelihood of taking the job. One reason that ghosting happens is that a candidate will accept another offer because they don't know when to expect a decision. Set expectations up front about how long it typically takes to move through the interview process, and try to keep it to two weeks or less for Gen Zers.

5. Invite them to ask questions about the organization.

They'll often walk into the interview a little nervous, just like you were back in the day. Set them at ease, letting them know that once you finish your questions, you'd like to hear what questions they have for you. You will learn a lot about them by listening to their questions and interests. In short, make interviews a two-way street. Companies that are patronizing and have a command-and-control interview style are failing to recognize the "democratization" of the job interview these days and will therefore feel old school to Gen Zers.

THE WELCOME WAGON

6. Extend the interview process into the onboard experience.
Truth be told, 86 percent of Gen Z respondents to a Handshake survey say they want to remain engaged leading up to their start date.[7] This means they want connection and relationship. Three in every four said they want to stay in touch with their hiring manager over email, and two in three said they want to form connections with current team members. More than half said they want to attend new hire events to get familiar with the workplace. This encourages us to go the extra mile by extending the interview process seamlessly into the onboarding experience and to help these young professionals get ready and be excited they chose you.

7. Address their issues using their language.
You don't have to utilize words that Gen Z uses on TikTok. That can come across as disingenuous. Instead, be real using words you're sure they'll recognize. Prior to the interview, search for language that conveys your big ideas but that they'd recognize as familiar and common. Their terms change all the time, so do an online search a day before the interview. This relays you're relevant and that you care. Next, let them know your company isn't merely about generating revenue for stakeholders. Share how you make the community and environment better, and how you add value to the world they live in. Gen Zers say they'll choose one job over another if the organization is altruistic.

INTERVIEW TO DISCOVER PERKS

Beware of terms that Gen Xers and boomers use that are a turnoff for Gen Z. It doesn't mean you cave to cancel culture. It just means you want to dodge biases that put a wall between you, terms that prevent you both from really getting acquainted. Avoid formal jargon, and use conversational language. On the other hand, you'll want to figure out who they are before you offer a job. Hiring managers report Generation Z often enters a job with demands or expectations that past generations would not have expressed in an interview. Because of this high sense of agency they bring, I recommend you use a template I call PERKS. It's an acronym that enables you to discuss important issues up front and discover who they are. I will cover these in detail later in this book, but these issues (PERKS) should be addressed before you get too far down the road:

> **Preferences.** Ask them about what they prefer to be the reality on the job, such as breaks, PTO, community building, policies, and so on. These are not deal-breaker issues, just ones to know before they begin on the team. Ask them if these opinions are, indeed, preferences not requirements. This will help you lead them better if they're hired.

> **Expectations.** Ask them what they expect at your workplace. Conflict expands based on the distance between expectations and reality. Unmet expectations frequently come from unspoken expectations. Managers can fail to cover these and later find disgruntled staff who didn't voice them up front. Get them out on the table.

> **Requirements.** Gen Z frequently voices demands about the conditions of their job, having little employment experience. Sometimes these demands are only preferences that are best to distinguish early on. If their demands don't match your culture or values, it's good to know before you hire them. It's best to show them the door and avoid wasted time.

> **Keys.** Often these issues pop up too late. What are the keys to understanding who they are and helping them flourish? I've heard comments like,

"Well, you need to know I'm not a hugger!" Or "I'm an introvert and don't do well in social situations." Job candidates may clarify traits, qualities, or "love language" to help you grasp what motivates them.

> **Salary.** This one is obvious, but as you discover who they are, this is a natural place to discuss compensation requirements or desires. Clearly, this should be an issue they've already observed when you posted the job opening, but all too often, the interview becomes a place to discover wants and needs on their part. Clarity is king.

How could these suggestions improve your interview process with Gen Z?

I hear more human resource officers complain about miserable Gen Z job interview experiences than any other. Some say it feels like a cross-cultural interaction. This is partly because parents or colleges did not prepare their students for it. It's also because Gen Zers bring with them their own terms and vernacular.

IF GENERATION Z HAD A PERFECT WORK ENVIRONMENT

I met a young employee at Toyota who told me what he loved most about his workplace. Believe it or not, he wasn't in a white-collar position. He worked on the assembly line, but he was satisfied nonetheless. To be honest, I was surprised. He did not fit the typical profile of a twenty-something who wants to begin a career with a six-digit income and enjoy dictating the terms of their day-to-day tasks. He was doing hard work, even monotonous work. How could this graduate enjoy his job?

I was curious, so I asked him.

He replied, "I love this place." When I smiled and replied how little I hear that comment from a young professional, he went on. "I had planned on staying at this job for a year or so, then moving on, thinking I would get bored or disinterested. But I found comradery and authority and mentors who were willing to both teach and listen—and I didn't want to leave. Like I said, 'I love this place.'"

He continued to describe what Toyota calls an "Andon Cord." It's a cable that any team member can pull when they spot an error on the conveyor belt. Immediately, a supervisor approaches the teammate and asks about what they spotted. They explore the situation and determine what needs to happen. In short, they problem-solve together. Often, nothing needs changing, but if it does, the line stops and the correction is made, even if it's by a rookie staff person. Toyota doesn't see this as an expense but as an investment. Problems are solved, avoiding long-term, big-time problems.

This kind of authority and listening was magnetic to my new young friend.

Having gathered information on these young adults from meeting with hundreds of them in focus groups, I offer you the ideal work situation for Gen Z. You may not be able to create a work environment exactly like this, much less want to, but if you can cultivate even some of these, you will become more attractive to a new generation of workers.

GENERATION Z'S IDEAL WORKPLACE

1. Openness and contact.

As I mentioned above, young professionals prefer an open workplace, where leaders are easily accessible. They like multiple check-ins each day and prefer little to no hierarchy. Organizational charts seem antiquated; they prefer an organic over an organized system.

Question: How could you improve in this area and make yourself more accessible?

2. Fun and play.
In some of my focus groups, Gen Zers described work as a "hobby." Research shows that productivity increases when leaders insert humor and fun into the daily grind. Gen Z wants to feel they're enjoying the pursuit of their goals and that they're working with friends.

Question: How could you turn up the fun and inspire better work through a playful tone?

3. Fluid and adaptive.
Just like their sense of identity may be fluid, their sense of vocation may be fluid as well. Gen Z is likely to adapt to changes in technology quickly and want to update their approach to a task and engage in a variety of tasks each month. It's tough for many to sit still.

Question: How could you introduce change, upgrades, and improvements faster?

4. Meaning and mission.
While Generation Z values a good income (like other generations do), they want to feel like their job contributes to the world and makes it a better place. Gen Zers say they'll take a job that benefits their community over one that doesn't any day. They're cause oriented.

Question: How can you connect the dots for staff between menial tasks and the mission?

5. Growth and learning.

This one is clearer than any other. They want to feel they are growing and learning each year on the job and will leave if they feel stagnant. Employers should offer ongoing personal and professional learning if they want to keep the best Gen Z members.

Question: How can you improve the development opportunities on your team?

> Would your team members describe your workplace with the terms above?

THREE DOABLE IDEAS TO RETAIN GENERATION Z TEAM MEMBERS

When I talk to managers who say they lose young team members almost as quickly as they hire them, I am troubled. Corporate managers are asking a recent graduate to join a workforce that seems impersonal, and they feel like they're a cog in the machine. While we know it's tough for those employees to make the leap from backpack to briefcase, I'm convinced we can take steps right away that are simple and increase our chances of retaining good people when they join.

1. Make their first day unforgettable.

The first day on the job should not be a set of bureaucratic activities on a checklist. It should be a peak moment they want to share later with family and friends. Research from Jason Dorsey shows that a growing number of both millennials and Gen Zers make up their mind whether they'll stay at a company *on their first day*. Did you catch that? On day one. Their generation has short attention spans and, like other generations, makes choices based on a reaction rather than on reflection. A dull first day leads to conclusions that this will be a dull place.

Solution: Create moments on their first day and first week. The folks at John Deere, in Asia, chose to do just that. Their HR staff

THE WELCOME WAGON

collaborated with their customer experience team and created a plan called their "First Day Experience." Shortly after an employee accepts a job offer, they get a note from a "John Deere Friend" welcoming them to the community. It shares the best place to park, what the dress norms are, and that Anita will be in the lobby to welcome them when they arrive at 9:00 a.m. Upon arrival, she points to a flat screen on the wall where the new person's name is headlined and welcomed. When they arrive at their desk, there are balloons and a welcome banner, which also notifies fellow employees there is a new "hire" to be greeted throughout the day. Sitting on the desk is a gift. On their computer screen are the words *Welcome to the most important work you'll ever do.* A letter from CEO Sam Allen is already in their inbox, and it closes by saying, "Enjoy the rest of your first day, and I hope you'll enjoy a long, successful, fulfilling career as part of the John Deere team." Finally, Anita has also arranged to host the new hire for a lunch to answer questions. The result? The new employee feels they belong here.[8]

2. Establish personal connections early.

Whether they'll admit it to you or not, data shows that Gen Z members want meaningful relationships at work. While they're more astute at connecting with others on a screen, they desire connections with a person where they both know more about each other than mere professional information. In the words of Arthur Brooks, they've watched older generations make "deal friends" not "real friends" at work and with clients. It's all transactional. Gen Zers believe "that's for boomers."

Solution: Initiate coffee meetings to get to know each other personally. Too often, we assume a new team member wants their privacy or is an introvert. Perhaps they are. This shouldn't stop your organization, however, from asking to take them to coffee or a meal just to get to know them better. The new hire doesn't have to disclose much, and the message is sent: we want to enjoy a relationship with you that is *more than transactional.* I know several organizations that systematically set up weekly coffee or lunch appointments between new staff and veterans.

In our office, we provide free food for our team, with only one rule: you cannot take the food and eat alone. If people want to enjoy a free lunch, they must do so with others, which fosters community. We even encourage them to converse about topics that are not work related. (Note: if people want to work during lunch, they can certainly go out and get it themselves.) These intentional connections build bridges rather than walls between older and younger teammates. Different generations often embrace a different vocabulary, practice different customs, or embrace different values. Old and young find it harder to connect. It's work. These personal interactive times nudge everyone to do that work. As a result, people find how much they have in common. It's difficult to dislike someone up close.

3. Illustrate how you need them.

This is just good behavioral science. People tend to stay where they feel needed and wanted. Most employers assume they do a good job at this, but most young employees say otherwise. Many leave their current workplaces because they feel they're replaceable or unnecessary. People stay when supervisors and colleagues remind them of the importance of their work and how much they are needed. One in two employees feel only "somewhat valued" and one in ten don't feel "valued at all," according to a January 2023 report by Workhuman.[9] In its monthly Human Workplace Index, 46.4 percent feel a lack of appreciation. Notably, 48.8 percent of females surveyed said they feel undervalued.[10] This is especially true for Generation Z, who has been used to constant feedback from video games or constant affirmation from parents. We can do better.

Solution: Place reminders in your calendar to note how young teammates are doing and affirm any progress and production. Many older managers despise this, feeling staff should not need constant encouragement to do their job. In a perfect world, that's correct. But we don't live in a perfect world. In Generation Z's current state of anxiety and stress, they often wonder if they "fit" in a new workplace. If we want to keep them, we must tell them they matter. Truett Cathy, founder of Chick-fil-A, asked: "Do you know how you can tell someone needs encouragement?" He would pause, then answer his own question: "They're breathing."

I keep a stack of personal stationery on my desk and write thank you notes consistently to partners and teammates. If I am out and about, I'll text people when I notice something. As a young employee myself, I worked for John Maxwell. He would write notes to me, specifically telling me he noticed what I did and how much time it had saved him. I still have several of those notes today, forty years later.

4. Assign a Sherpa guide to train them.

Almost every business believes it provides good training for new team members. Ironically, those new employees frequently say otherwise. Seasoned employees can forget what it felt like to be new and not understand the lingo or insider acronyms. The onboarding process should include someone who builds a personal connection to the rookie and makes sure they are equipped to do what they've been asked to do. Minimally, you want to remove any excuse for poor performance.

Solution: In each department, match your most personable and sharp staff with new hires. The best organizations pair a coach with the new teammate and ensure they understand all the company "lingo" and learn how to do the tasks they've been assigned. If the tasks vary, they may need multiple tutors. Some companies call them "Sherpa guides." A Sherpa guide is part of the Sherpa ethnic group, native to the Himalayas, who acts as a guide and support person for climbers, particularly on expeditions to Mount Everest, using their expertise in high-altitude mountaineering to navigate routes, set up camps, carry supplies, and assist climbers in reaching the summit. They point out how to get your footing, where the dangers are, and how to pace yourself as you move up the mountain. It seems like a fitting term. In essence, it's a personal coach on the job who helps them climb higher, avoid unnecessary pitfalls, and do their work well. Make this match-up an assignment, not a suggestion.

Early in my public speaking career, Shawn Mitchell was my Sherpa guide. He made sure I would stretch to his highest expectations for me. He launched a weekly outreach event for young people, and I was his apprentice some forty-five years ago. At this outreach, kids would see a film that contained a great moral lesson, then Shawn would hop on stage to speak and summarize the big idea. It was inspirational.

At first, my job was to set up the chairs and get him water. So far, so good. One night, however, he met me backstage, and something was different. He looked at me and whispered, "Tim—I don't think I can speak tonight. I may have laryngitis." My eyes grew big as I replied, "What are we gonna do? You're the speaker!" Shawn smiled and said in a raspy voice, "Tim, you're going to speak tonight." I didn't embrace the idea; I saw myself as the guy who sets up chairs and gets him water. But Shawn insisted, gave me his notes, and we traded places that night. It was excruciating for me. After I finished, Shawn approached me and said, "Tim, that was great! From now on, we're going to rotate: I'll be on one week, and you'll be on the next." That was my beginning. And I have been public speaking on a regular basis since that night, thanks to Shawn.

The striking part of the story came decades later. Shawn and I met for dinner one night and reminisced about those weekly events and how I anxiously spoke for the first time. As we chuckled about it, I noticed Shawn was staring at the floor. Something felt wrong. When I asked him about it, he sheepishly smiled and said, "Tim, I have a confession to make. I didn't really have laryngitis that night. I'm sorry—but it was the only way I could think of to get you up in front of a crowd."

At first, I didn't know what to think, but I know what I'm thinking now. I am glad Shawn's goal that night decades ago was not to get the best speaker in the room up on stage. If that were his goal, he would have spoken. His goal, instead, was to be a Sherpa guide for a young man in whom he saw potential. And that should be our goal today.

TALK IT OVER

1. The chapter highlights that Generation Z tends to prioritize work-life balance and values jobs that align with their personal missions. How can organizations structure their onboarding process to make these priorities clear while also aligning with business goals?

2. Chick-fil-A and Toyota have demonstrated effective retention strategies by fostering community, providing growth opportunities, and emphasizing values. What lessons can you take from these examples to create a workplace culture that appeals to Generation Z?

3. This chapter emphasizes the importance of a strong first impression, such as an unforgettable first day. What creative or meaningful onboarding practices could you implement to make new hires feel welcomed and excited to stay with your organization?

AUTHORITY IS EARNED

6

TERMS OF ENGAGEMENT

CONNECT
BEFORE YOU CORRECT

Get ready for a gap.

The issue of engaging Generation Z became the most intriguing piece of data I collected for this book. I will never forget the survey results or the conversations in my focus groups. One twenty-two-year-old, Olivia, described her experience the first year on the job:

> I had preconceived ideas. I thought work would be different. I'm not sure if my leaders know what it feels like to be on the other side of them. It's clear they like being in charge, but it feels like they never got trained to lead.

As you can see, Olivia admits she had some wrong ideas about work. Yet notice her candor when she wonders about her supervisors' self-awareness. She observes her leaders enjoy their power but questions if they know how to lead people. She goes on:

> It's much weirder than I thought it would be. At work, people talk like they're your family, but it's fake. They act like they don't really care. The HR team is powerless. I am young but thought I'd be treated like a full-time staff person. Instead, I'm treated like a "daughter." I'm not taken seriously. I'm like "cheap help." I feel dismissed.

These words reveal Olivia's real challenge. Her leaders and colleagues all use the right language, but in her opinion, they don't live up to those words. And she feels disrespected. She is a full-time team member, but older colleagues treat her in a condescending way.

THE GAP WE MUST BRIDGE

This notion prevails in millions of Generation Z members, and it's not just at work. Today's younger population feels they are not taken seriously in their family—and they resent it. An increasing number of Gen Zers are going "no contact" with their parents once they begin their careers. This growing movement wants to destigmatize severing ties. An article in *The New Yorker* asks: "Is it a much-needed corrective, or a worrisome change in family relations?"[1] In either case, we need some terms of engagement.

There is a divide among young and old, greater than it was when the term *generation gap* was first coined by editor John Poppy at *Look* magazine in 1967. As the screens in our lives moved from public to private, the gap widened. Consider what I've witnessed in my lifetime. As a boy, my family had one screen in our house—it was a television. (In fact, it was a black-and-white TV.) Parents and kids would gather around the TV set and watch a "program" together, such as *I Love Lucy* or *The Dick Van Dyke Show* or *The Andy Griffith Show*. Later it was *The Brady Bunch* or *The Partridge Family* or *All in the Family*. We watched together, laughed together, and talked about it together afterward.

Fast-forward to today—we all have our own personal screens, a smartphone, where we're not digesting the same content at all. In fact, we're in echo chambers with very different people than our kids. Mom and Dad are aware, for instance, that their teenage daughter has an Instagram account, but they have no idea she has three "finsta" accounts (fake Instagram) where she's developed personas for herself and is interacting with absolute strangers. Truth be told, older authorities have less power than they did when I was a kid.

WE'RE IN A WIKI WORLD

Consider what we learn about our world from Wikipedia. It is a self-governed digital site filled with content that's been provided by countless people along the way, and it's fluid. There aren't central scholars or gatekeepers, like Encarta, the digital encyclopedia Bill Gates tried to create. Encarta contained content from the world's top scholars. Yet it was discontinued in 2009 and no longer exists today. We have a wiki culture—and it involves input from everyday people. Let me remind you of Wikipedia's characteristics:

> It is formed by input from anyone and everyone.
> There is not a central authority or gatekeeper.
> It is fluid and always evolving, hopefully improving.

This is the world Gen Z grew up in. So what must leaders do to maximize and capitalize on these Gen Z colleagues? This chapter is all about retaining and leveraging the members of our youngest generation to reach *your goals* and *their potential*. It involves creating a very "wiki" culture that keeps the comment box open, welcoming their naive optimism and allowing them to think and act outside of the box. I will outline tips and tools to engage Gen Z team members well.

Let's begin with our different perspectives on authority.

WHY GEN Z SEES AUTHORITY DIFFERENTLY THAN YOU

My friend Suzanne is a hiring manager for a company in Atlanta. After finishing a series of job interviews with young professionals, she chose to offer one of them a full-time position. When she handed the job offer to her, the candidate smiled, then replied in a serious tone, "Thank you, but my parents are right outside in the car. They said they want to interview you, to make sure you're the right boss for me."

Ah, it's a new day in the workforce. And it's a fluid one.

Throughout my life, I've witnessed society's view of authority evolve. As I've said, job candidates today enter their careers with a high sense of agency and care less about what authorities may think of them. Those of us who serve in positions of authority need to recognize culture's narrative and respond wisely. There are reasons for how we got where we are today.

My mom and dad were part of the Silent generation, often called the Builders. They taught their children to respect authority, regardless of your opinion of them. You respected the police, the mayor, and the president, even if you didn't vote for them. As baby boomers arrived on the job, they brought a more individualistic perspective. At 76.4 million members, they were bigger than previous generations and felt large and in charge since adolescence. Instead of automatically respecting authority, they questioned the establishment and sought to push "reset" on society. A popular bumper sticker during the 1960s was "Question Authority." Jack Weinberg told his listeners to never trust anyone over thirty.

As baby busters arrived at work, they were unimpressed by authority, even when it was the boomers, just ahead of them in age. They were the unplugged generation who often grew up as latchkey kids, problem-solving on their own due to single parent households. As young professionals, many felt they must merely endure authority. Millennials brought with them an even greater sense of audacity, as they grew up in a time of digital customization. They were a "pick-and-choose" population with their music playlists, their college education, and even their faith, mixing and matching what they liked from different religious traditions. Their sense of agency felt like "free agency" to leaders.

Today, Generation Z members are the new kids on the block. They're arriving at adulthood at a very strange time in postmodern history. Their view of authority reflects the times because they've grown up with a smartphone and feel less dependent on authorities to provide solutions for them. Educators are not needed for information or knowledge, thanks to Google, Siri, and Alexa. In a phrase, Gen Z members respectfully explained to me their view of authority: "I'm not sure I even need them."

They've learned how to do things from YouTube, they have notifications popping up on their smartphones that fill them in on everything, and they prefer the collective wisdom of AI on that device over one person's opinion at work, even if that person is in authority. They enter our world with a greater sense of free agency. Further, they've watched the adults in their life, including business leaders, community leaders, and political leaders, setting poor examples of what adult behavior looks like. Can you blame them for not respecting authority today? Civil behavior is rare. Recently, I told a high school senior to set a goal to mature into healthy adulthood. His response? "I haven't seen a healthy adult yet."

Our culture's view of authority is fluid right now. Fewer of us are loyal to leaders or companies, and younger generations (millennials and Generation Z) find it hard, and even unnecessary, to show respect. Consider the protests against police brutality the last several years; consider the January 6, 2021, attack on the nation's capital; or remember 2020, when local school board meetings saw parents showing up divided and ready for a street fight about masks, rules, vaccinations, and quarantines.

Young candidates arrive at a job interview prepared to ask for more money than what the employer offers, to request more PTO, more perks, and more autonomy at the onset. They believe a boss's experience may have made them smarter but also could have made them antiquated. I've mentioned psychologist Adam Grants's term for what's happening. He calls it "the democratization of the workforce." Everyone feels they deserve a voice in decisions, and fewer demonstrate a respect for someone just because they have a title or wear a badge.

SO, HOW DO WE LEAD IN SUCH CIRCUMSTANCES?

Given culture's narrative today, managers must lead with their eyes wide open. The two columns below summarize the shift that seems to be happening in society:

OLDER GENERATIONS ON AUTHORITY	YOUNGER GENERATIONS ON AUTHORITY
1. Position gives you the right to influence.	1. Connection gives you the right to influence.
2. If you're older you have wisdom.	2. If you're older you may be irrelevant.
3. Systems offer order to curb the chaos.	3. Systems must be disrupted to open doors.
4. You should listen to the man at the top.	4. The top person should be listening to us.
5. The top dog wins the debate.	5. The best idea wins.
6. The leader is a gatekeeper.	6. The leader is a guide.

My suggestion? Leaders must lead by permission, not position. We must win our people at the heart level. At Growing Leaders, we've communicated we have their best interests in mind, not just the organization's best interests, by offering team development time and help on personal growth plans. We communicated trust in them by offering unlimited personal time off. We could do this because we hire only highly responsible team members who don't want to let teammates down by failing to get work done. Our leaders are equipped to make emotional connections with their team members. We've created agile teams where teammates of any age and experience can weigh in on ideas. By 2021, we began to allow them to work virtually on Deep Work Wednesdays (where they focus on projects that require uninterrupted time) and Fridays where they can work from anywhere they feel most comfortable and productive. We found if leaders will lean into them, they'll lean back.

> What's your perspective on authority? Is it new or old school? Any change needed?

YOUR APPROACH TO YOUNG PROFESSIONALS

John Mackey was the founder and CEO of Whole Foods from 1980 to 2022. Before he sold it to Amazon for $13.7 billion, he made some remarks revealing his frustration with his young team members across the chain. Despite Whole Foods' "conscious capitalism" policies—environmental sustainability and ethical sourcing of products—young staff were disengaged at work and displayed poor attitudes. Mackey concluded it was just Gen Z's nature. He said, "I don't understand the younger generation. I can't motivate them. They don't seem to want to work."

Looking at the data, however, it appears there were other reasons for Gen Z's disconnect. Other brands were retaining young teammates and not receiving as many poor reviews. Compared to competitors, Whole Foods received twice as many negative reviews from their employees about their experience at the store. Their Gen Zers had different reasons for disengaging. One Whole Foods reviewer described them as having "no respect for employees, literally could not care . . . if you lived or died." Could it be that the issue wasn't a lack of work ethic in Gen Z? Could it be that this retailer had all the right policies but just didn't treat young staff well? David Yeager, research psychologist at the University of Texas, calls this the "generational divide." Older generations feel like they are constantly catering to the needs of young people only to be shamed or blamed for not doing enough.

Here's the key: our perception of them determines our approach to them.

Yeager goes on to reveal three ways leaders perceive young people, which determine how they will treat them.[2] The first two embrace disbelief or doubts about Generation Z. The third perception begins with belief. See if you can find yourself in any of these below. The three mindsets are:

1. **The Enforcer Mindset:** They think Gen Z's immaturity makes them dangerous risks to themselves and to others at work. Leaders must control them.

2. **The Protector Mindset:** They think Gen Z's immaturity makes them fragile and vulnerable if they struggle at work. Leaders must protect them.

3. **The Mentor Mindset:** They think Gen Z is ready to take on tough challenges and achieve great things with proper support. Leaders must challenge them.

The foundation of the first two is disbelief. Leaders with these mindsets doubt Gen Zers are up to the challenge and choose either a punitive posture or a protective posture. The enforcer wants to push them; the protector wants to spare them.

The foundation of the mentor mindset is belief. With this mindset, leaders know each Gen Zer is asking themselves: *Does this person who has power over me think I am competent? Is their hard feedback done out of belief or out of suspicion and doubt?*

The evidence seems to indicate that John Mackey embraced the enforcer mindset, musing what adults have said for years: "Kids these days!" I spoke at a conference for NFL coaches and discussed the best ways to lead Gen Z athletes. As I met each one, I could tell what mindset they had toward young players. While there, I met Roger Goodell, the commissioner of the National Football League, and asked him about his thoughts on Gen Z. He replied, "We'll need to help them develop some grit. Without it, they may not last." While I believe he's right, this "enforcer" approach can make Gen Z want to disengage. It does not inspire them.

In contrast, franchisees at Orange Leaf Frozen Yogurt have taken a different approach. They recognized their young team members would likely stay for a year or two and then move on. It would be easy to not bother to build a relationship with them, much less invest in them. Instead of remaining distant or being agitated at Gen Zers, Orange Leaf Frozen Yogurt decided to embrace this reality by telling potential young team members, "We'll be the best first job you could ever have." When teens go to work there, a manager sits down with them and asks, "What do you most want to learn from a job?" If the young team members say "managing money," hey get to watch the bookkeepers balance revenue and expenses and perhaps even learn to do it themselves. The job becomes rocket fuel for the next step of their career path. While franchisees don't expect most to stay longer than two years, this coaching approach has enabled many stores to keep those young staff and even turn them into leaders who stay around for a long time.

Some leaders call this a "vocation rotation."

What if we built workplaces that made investments in young team members and, maybe, kept them longer because they were getting mentored? In other words, we don't shame them into staying—we win them. Then, knowing they're likely desirous of a "vocation rotation," what if we celebrated change and offered suggestions for their next step with us? What if we equipped them to look for common threads in each of those jobs and find their calling in the process? They are silently asking us:

> Do you care about me as a person, not just a worker?
> Do you offer me developmental and growth opportunities?
> Do you provide help outside of work (such as rideshare, discounts, and so on)?
> Do you provide an app or portal clarifying steps I can take to advance?
> Do you celebrate my growth and future opportunities?

Dayton Moore has served in the front office of three professional baseball clubs: the Atlanta Braves, the Kansas City Royals, and the Texas Rangers. All three have been World Series winners. I watched Dayton meet with a minor league player who was struggling on the field and approach him with the mentor mindset. Dayton spoke words of belief to him. He didn't shelter him by telling him he was awesome when, in fact, he was in a slump. Nor did he scream at him, reminding him how horrible he was doing. He revealed which areas the player needed to improve, calmly suggested some steps, and then told the player

Reflect on your leadership. Which approach do you take with Gen Zers?

he believed he had what it took to make the major leagues. That's a picture of the mentor mindset.

MOVING THEM FROM RENTING THEIR JOB TO OWNING THEIR JOB

A common problem employers must solve today is building a sense of ownership in their young staff. Managers claim Gen Zers don't engage and commit on the job and often don't display a deep sense of responsibility even when the job sounded perfect in the job interview. What happened?

We can answer this question by understanding an assessment psychologist Julian Rotter administered to university graduates in 1954.[3] His hypothesis was that a young adult whose locus of control was internal had a better chance at succeeding in life. And he wanted to measure it. Here's a summary of his terms:

> Internal locus of control. This mindset looks inside for answers. The person believes they must own their success and take responsibility for their life, not blaming others for poor results. They embrace *It's up to me.*
> External locus of control. This mindset looks outside for answers. The person believes that external forces or fate somehow dictate the outcomes of their life. They embrace *I should look externally for solutions.*

Nine years into his research in 1963, Rotter concluded that those with an internal locus of control became measurably more successful in life; they took better care of their health and fitness, their spouse and family, their job and career. It makes sense. We all love seeing young people take ownership of their life.

Fast-forward to today. Over the last six decades, due to the overwhelming amount of information coming at our youth on portable devices and due to the fear narrative so many adults possess about kids' safety, we've taken responsibility for their life. Since we know best, we prescribe every step they take. Consider a kid's life today:

> Parents can be prescriptive in their daily directives, scheduling each day.
> Teachers can be prescriptive in their lesson plans, teaching to the test.
> Coaches can be prescriptive on their instruction for practices and games.
> YouTube and Netflix are prescriptive, suggesting what videos to watch next.
> Amazon is prescriptive, suggesting what other products you might like.
> Employers are prescriptive in their formula to reach the numbers they need.
> Social media apps are prescriptive in their format to keep you scrolling.

Peter Gray from Boston College explains the shift in twenty-first-century kids: "In fact, the shift has been so great that the average young person in 2002 was more External [on Rotter's scale] than were 80 percent of young people in the 1960s."[4] Gen Z is overwhelmed and someone else has owned their life. We've conditioned them to embrace an external locus of control—which frees them to blame someone else for poor results and to disengage. Well-intentioned adults did this to them.

Generation Z will not perform well or "own" their tasks at work with this same kind of leadership. Deep down, I believe they want to own their work, just like we do.

In the 1940s, General Mills released their very first instant cake mix in grocery stores. As society was evolving toward speed and convenience, they were sure their Betty Crocker cake mix would be a hit. After some weeks, they were stunned. Customers were not buying it; they continued baking cakes from scratch. After commissioning psychologist Ernest Dichter to host focus groups to ask why shoppers weren't buying the instant mix, General Mills got their answer: consumers felt like it wasn't real. The original mix included everything but the water. Once Betty Crocker staff took away the two eggs in their powder, sales took off. Customers felt it was their cake once they added more than water. The secret was all about ownership. Who's really making this cake? So it is for Gen Z. They must own it.

A CASE STUDY

Several businesses and nonprofits have adopted our Three Levels of Planning. It's a strategy to enable teammates to gain ownership of a new product or service yet still empower the leaders to run point and make final decisions.

Napkin conversations
These are early conversations when each team member is invited to participate. Like a napkin conversation at a restaurant, this is a volley of ideas where people weigh in on pain points and solutions in small groups. The groups should include varied ages if possible. At this point, nothing is set in stone because people are thinking in "pencil," not "ink." Facilitators record the input. Later, leaders force rank input, prioritizing the best ideas. People tend to support what they help create. Ownership takes root.

Whiteboard conversations
By now, the ideas are further down the road toward completion. At this point, key influencers still offer input, but fundamental

changes are unlikely. Now your team leaders align on the problem to solve and a direction to take. They present to your department influencers on a whiteboard and changes are made. Clarity emerges as people align around steps. The key? If you let them weigh in, they'll likely buy in.

Slide deck conversations
At this point, leaders present a slide deck and request tweaks on improvements, not complete overhauls. Everyone has a voice, but not everyone has a vote. Everyone can attend and offer some input around cosmetic changes or even small changes to the idea you're focusing on. Everyone knows the team isn't brainstorming random ideas at this point but is polishing this best idea, preparing to move forward.

> How do you cultivate ownership in Gen Z team members? Could this idea help you?

So it is with Generation Z. We must help them feel like they own their job.

TEN IDEAS TO KEEP YOUR BEST GENERATION Z TALENT

"Eighteen months," my friend declared over lunch last week. "That's how long my young team members stay on the job. Some only last ninety days. I don't know how to keep them."

As we've noted, my friend's experience is not isolated. Gallup released a report in 2016 called "Millennials: The Job-Hopping Generation." And Generation Z? They feel they know too much to settle for a low-paying job when their talent is worth far more than your wages. They may have eleven jobs in their twenties. They have exchanged that corporate *ladder* for a corporate *lily pad*. They feel in charge of their career path and job experience.

When reviewing the data on today's youngest workers entering the job market, I believe employers will likely need to offer a different kind of opportunity. While Generation Z tends to be a very educated population, many have chosen to "hack" their postsecondary experience. Instead of enrolling in a four-year college, many have gotten creative and learned specific job skills through mentors, MOOCs, master classes, internships, and even YouTube videos. Gen Z witnessed the "great resignation," and millions of them were a part of it in the early stages of their career. The Work Institute, a leading employment consulting agency, estimates that more than forty-two million US workers left their jobs in 2019.[5] By 2021, four million quit their job in a single month. Many employers are desperate to stop the bleeding.

I have found the answer is almost always in the middle. Gen Z will need to learn the ways of the workplace, yet leaders will need to lean in and meet them halfway on how it all works. If we can change our work practices and culture to address these, we stand a great chance at hiring great candidates and keeping them too. What is it we can do to attract and retain the most talented and ambitious Gen Z workers? Let me offer ten ideas based on the data I've read and observed on this new generation.

TEN IDEAS TO ATTRACT AND RETAIN GENERATION Z TEAM MEMBERS

1. Create an internal gig economy.

Since Gen Z loves change and job-hopping, what if you focused on cross-training and welcomed teammates to move around every several months? What if you created an entrepreneurial zone where creatives (including Gen Zers) were invited to join an agile team created to solve a problem with a program, product, or service? What if you set aside funds for the untold fruits of their labor? The team could sunset once the problem is solved and the idea is created—but they'd get to scratch their entrepreneurial itch.

2. Offer flexibility and autonomy.
The pandemic changed most of us. Gen Z has asked for autonomy to work from anywhere and asked for four-day workweeks, working forty hours then having three days free. When leaders offer flexibility and autonomy, it communicates trust to Gen Zers. It relays respect and lets them know they are legitimate team members who add value. Remember, respect and status are sought-after goals for young professionals. Autonomy screams respect.

Train them, then trust that they'll get the job done.

3. Make room for no-collar and new-collar jobs.
Forget blue or white collars. The new workforce may be no-collar pioneers who serve from home. Also new-collar staff have highly specific job skills without a college degree. What if you reconsider traditional requirements for each job opening you have, recognizing Gen Zers are reaching goals through unconventional pathways these days. Let your Gen Z employees know you're open to changing things and pursuing goals in a fresh way. What's important to them is outcomes more than inputs. Hopefully that defines you as well.

4. Provide meaning as well as money.
Gen Z loves knowing how their small task is tied to the larger mission. Also, ensure they see how your mission and products serve the community around them. Although they definitely want money, they want meaningful contributions as well. They want to know the company does more than generate revenue and achieve the income goals for your stakeholders. They're prone to join and stay at companies that are altruistic and philanthropic.

5. Practice the policy: speak as if you're right; listen as if you're wrong.
Management is often viewed as tellers, not listeners. Certainly, leaders must offer direction to their team. Yet in today's world, I'm

committed to a new way of hosting meetings: I speak as if I believe I am right, but I listen as if I believe I am wrong. Young teammates feel heard because seasoned veterans listen to them with as much focus and humility as they would a peer. This enables leaders to practice the paradox of being both confident and humble.

6. Furnish continuous learning and growth opportunities.
Gen Z data reveals they want to work at a place that develops them professionally and personally. Offer training, trips, mentors, Learning Management System (LMS) courses, and experiences that grow them. In fact, my research further shows that Gen Zers will leave an organization if they feel stuck and that they are not growing. Over the years at our team meetings, we offer professional and personal growth opportunities for everyone. In addition, department heads discuss a growth plan with each person on their team. We are all streams, not swamps.

7. Meet to ask them about their "superpowers."
I have found every new teammate who joins our crew brings some obvious and secret strengths or skills. We call them "superpowers," and new employees may not even know how helpful they could be until a manager discovers them. I have a friend who practiced this with her Gen Z staff, and she soon had her company monetizing TikTok and Instagram. She also improved all of her social media marketing and sales processes to young consumers. These simple meetups improved the organization measurably.

8. When possible, embody descriptive, not prescriptive, leadership.
As I mentioned earlier, adults lead youth today by prescribing each step along the way, leaving kids little experience to think on their own. What if you focused on results not steps? What if you described a mutual goal and let them "own" how to reach it? When we are prescriptive, we teach them what to think but not

how to think. Be sure to focus on outcomes, not inputs, and let them determine how they'll reach their goal.

9. Don't gaslight.
When we gaslight, we react to young teammates' comments with impatience, making them feel foolish for making the remark. This is the opposite of a psychologically safe place to work. Labor to cultivate psychological safety for learning and growth. Ensure managers welcome employees to ask what certain terms or acronyms mean without feeling embarrassed for not knowing. This creates the safest space to learn from mistakes.

10. Practice reverse mentoring.
This is when experienced veterans and young rookies meet, swap stories, then offer insights the other doesn't have, based on the generation they're from. This gives dignity to all. Each person in the pair has a chance to mentor the other generation and learn from the other generation. It provides dignity to everyone, levels the playing field, and improves the level of respect, humility, and curiosity among teammates. Everyone checks their ego at the door.

More than anything, practicing these ten ideas connects people who would normally not connect because they are so different. Generations often build walls instead of bridges between them. I love what Abraham Lincoln once said: "I don't like that man . . . I must get to know him better." Perhaps this is the approach we need to take with Generation Z team members. The more I get to know them, the more I like what they bring to the team.

Earlier, I brought up Whole Foods Market as a place that lacked connections with their Gen Z employees. I'd like to close with a question. When *USA Today* polled a panel of food and shopping experts, the study gave a surprising result. Do you know who topped the list as the best grocery store in America? Believe it or not, Hy-Vee earned the title. Why, you ask? There were two big reasons outside of the food they sell. First, the way they treat their team and their customers. The store is known for its catchphrase, "A helpful smile in every aisle," which speaks volumes about the emphasis Hy-Vee places on employee and guest service. The second reason? Hy-Vee's 280 stores are owned by its employees.[6] If Generation Z could describe what would keep them on a job, they'd likely say what any of us would, as young employees: if you want to keep me, show me how much I mean to you.

TALK IT OVER

1. The chapter emphasizes the shift from traditional authority to a more collaborative leadership style. How can leaders balance maintaining authority while fostering a sense of connection and collaboration with Generation Z team members?

2. The "mentor mindset" is highlighted as a key approach to engaging Gen Z. How can leaders effectively implement this mindset in the workplace to challenge and support young professionals while avoiding the pitfalls of the "enforcer" or "protector" mindsets?

3. The concept of moving from a "prescriptive" to a "descriptive" leadership approach encourages ownership and creativity among Gen Z employees. What are some practical steps leaders can take to transition to this leadership style while ensuring team alignment and productivity?

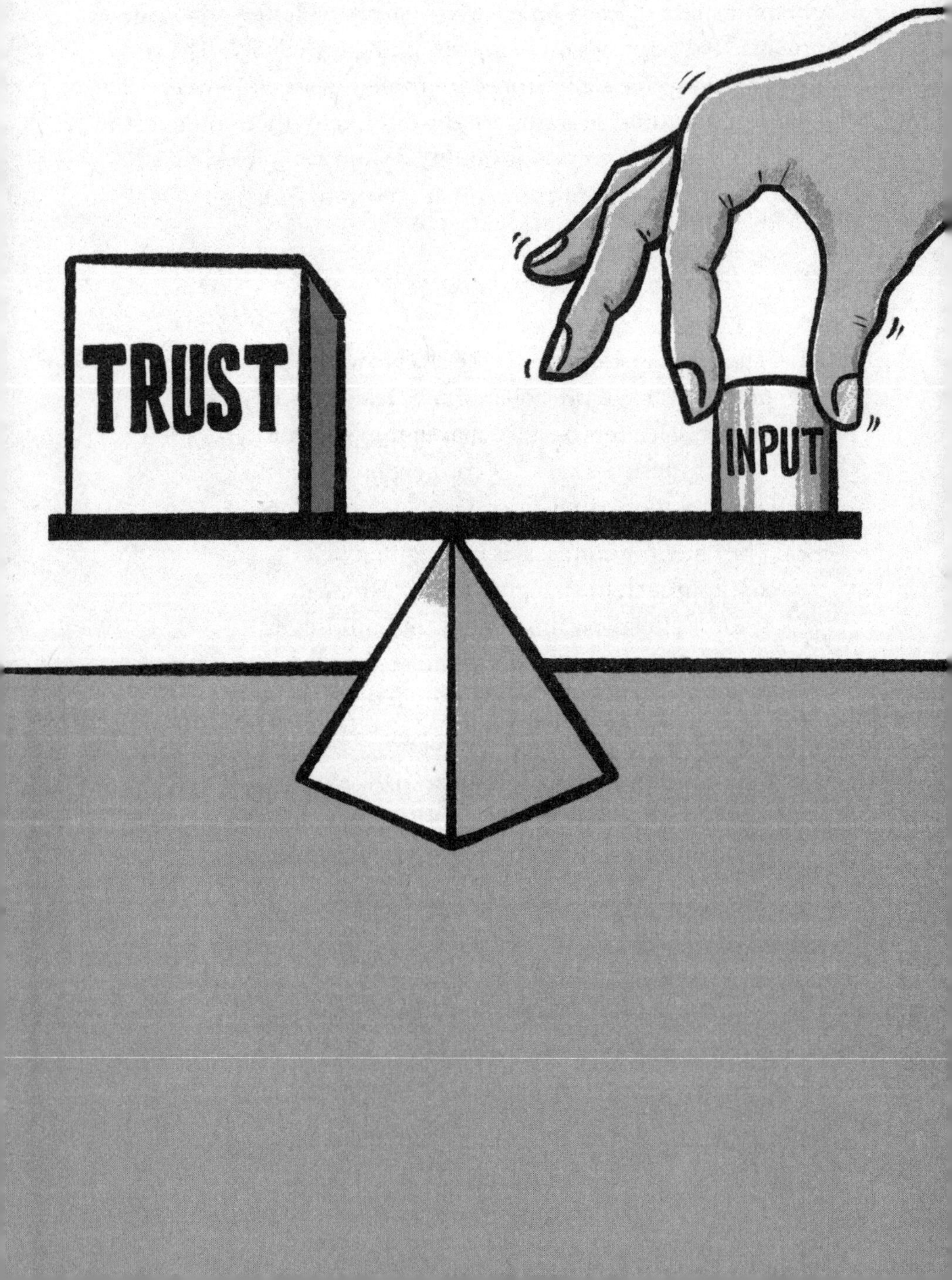
TRUST
INPUT

7

CRITICAL CONVERSATIONS

OFFERING TOUGH FEEDBACK

My friend Branden shared a story with me that illustrates the divide between generations when it comes to handling tough conversations. His colleague Sally recently interviewed a Gen Z member for a job opening she had in her department. We will call him Owen. During their interaction, Sally asked Owen to share a time he faced a challenge but was proud of how he made it through that hardship. He gave his answer, and she was pleased—and decided to hire him. When her HR director called Owen to make the offer, however, the young candidate balked. He retorted, "There is no way I'd work for that woman! She triggered my PTSD when she made me answer that question." He turned down the job.

This scenario underscores a scary reality I've seen emerge over the last fifteen years. When someone says something that's a bit challenging, someone from a younger generation may claim that it's a microaggression, some kind of attack that triggered negative emotions in them. While tough interactions have never been considered fun, something has happened in our day when compared to my generation and certainly my parents' generation. In past times, parents, mentors, teachers, or coaches encouraged you to be strong and face the hardship. Today, the common narrative is to remove hardships when they surface.

This narrative has been evolving since the 1980s, when a fear movement started among parents. In 1981, John Walsh's son, Adam, was abducted and later found dead some miles away. In response, John launched an all-out campaign to prevent this from happening to other families. Soon we saw photos of missing children on milk cartons; Walsh starred in the television show *America's Most Wanted* attempting to help capture perpetrators; and in 1984 he cofounded the National Center for Missing and Exploited Children in Washington, DC. Due to this and other factors, it felt like danger was around every corner. Over the next twenty years, our culture became hyperfocused on kids' safety. Soon playground equipment was removed from schools and parks, based on the belief that certain equipment (like monkey bars) was dangerous. Kids were no longer allowed to venture outside like we used to. Parents did their best to eradicate any unsafe context.

This narrative had benefits and consequences. Unfortunately, risk is a part of a child's maturation. Over the last thirty years, parents have risked too little, rescued too quickly, and raved too easily. These were all well-intentioned decisions, but they reduced the grit and resilience in two generations of young adults. (I will discuss building grit in chapter 13.) You can imagine, however, how closely this is tied to a person struggling to handle feedback that isn't sugarcoated.

I have told parents for years—if we treat our kids as fragile, they will surely become fragile adults. And sure enough, millions of members of Generation Z (and many millennials too) have become fragile to harsh conditions and hard feedback. Two landmark reports on Generation Z—Jean Twenge's *iGen*,[1] published in 2017, and Jonathan Haidt's *The Anxious Generation*,[2] which appeared in 2024—are replete with data documenting that Gen Zers are much more likely than their predecessors to be unhappy, lonely, and mentally fragile.

HARD IS NOW HARSH

In December of 2024, *Fortune* magazine published an article called "Gen Z workers think showing up ten minutes late for work is as good as being on time—but baby boomer bosses have zero tolerance for tardiness, research reveals." Herein lies our problem. Two completely different mindsets about punctuality require a crucial conversation between older and younger generations. One may just feel this conversation is harsh.

I believe this research indicates that those born after 1990 have been the offspring of this narrative from parents and other caring adults. By and large, we worked to prevent them from failing or struggling, we gave them trophies or ribbons just for participating in a competition, we told them they were awesome for putting their fork in the dishwasher, and we asked their teachers to lighten up. By the time our young people reach college, they've been conditioned to think the answer to hardship is to remove it. Think "cancel culture." The university campus was once a place for rigorous debate but now is often a place where students call out detractors. Is it any wonder today that Gen Zers have a reputation for being fragile on the job?

So now, we face a dilemma. How do leaders offer difficult feedback and host tough conversations and not lose their employees? Each day around the world, things people do in the normal course of business have taken on much larger meaning for a junior employee. Managers say one thing, young staff hear another, and a clash happens over interpretations. This chapter examines a strategy for preparing them for truthful and even tough evaluations.

As of right now, anything hard seems harsh for millions in Generation Z.

Before we examine how to manage hard conversations, let's look at an issue that older generations need to master first. To put it bluntly, we've become known for lecturing more than listening. There are times we need to stop talking. Knowing when to be quiet and listen is step one to building a bridge of relationship with them that can bear the weight of truth.

LEARNING TO BE SILENT

Believe it or not, I've discovered the key to constructive feedback sessions has little to do with my position and everything to do with earning permission. Before we talk about how to approach a Gen Z team member and offer tough feedback, I believe it's wise to examine the circumstances where it's best to remain silent and not offer any input. Every now and then, the best way to lead is to be quiet and listen. There have been several times over my career I had to learn to stay quiet. Situations at home, at work, or on the road required me—a teacher at heart—to not share an insight but to remain silent. I recognized silence would achieve more than words. Are you like me?

> "It takes two years to learn to speak, but it takes sixty years to learn to remain silent."

Our family recently decided to see a counselor to deepen our relationships. We all felt we could use a communication tune-up now that our kids are adults and have moved away. In one session, this hit me again. My daughter was speaking up—which I relished—and I wanted to respond. I felt what I had to add was so accurate and helpful. But, alas, I did not. I let her wander verbally and share what she was feeling inside. She needed to feel heard, not informed by her dad.

This is one of the leadership paradoxes we must all face. There is a time to be visible and a time to be invisible as leaders. When we're visible, we set an example. When we're invisible, we empower others to step up and take their place. When we're verbal, people may feel informed and coached. When we are nonverbal, they may just feel heard, understood, and even empowered. While I know this is true, it is so difficult for me. What I've learned at this stage of my career may feel elementary to many, but these are nine reminders about silence I need every week. Many have written about this topic, but these are circumstances when I found silence is golden.

Nine Places to Stay Silent as a Leader

1. In the heat of anger. I'm susceptible to irrationality when I'm mad. My amygdala lights up with more passion than is needed. My description? "I try to kill a roach with a shotgun."
2. If you don't know the whole story. In our world of low impulse control and quick reactions on social media, I am learning to pull back and wait for key details. There's usually more to the story.
3. When you feel too emotional. Emotions are better servants than commanders. When emotions run high, I can say things that I may genuinely feel, but I'll likely regret my words or my tone.
4. If you can't talk without raising your voice. I want to be heard for the reasonable conclusions I've drawn, not because I force my information down their throat. When I raise my voice, I usually shut down my listeners.
5. In times of grief. Too often, we can ruin someone's moment of grief by talking. Silence allows them to

see you feel deeply with them. It's wiser than some cliché or pithy wish you may offer.

6. **If your words can offend a person.** Too often, I assume the truth I share offends others, when it's me who offended them with my tone or choice of words. Our silence may just keep the relational bridge open.

7. **When someone has misspoken.** This one is tough—but when a person misspeaks, a moment of silence often reveals to them their error. The awkward hush can help them rethink their statement.

8. **If the topic is worthless.** Today, people engage in topics that are downright ridiculous and don't deserve our words. It's best to remain silent, and in doing so, we comment on its hollow value.

9. **If your words can destroy a relationship.** A sense of community can be damaged quickly. In a debate, ask what you value more: the person you're speaking with or the words you wish to speak? People matter most.

Sometimes, our silence can save the bonds we enjoy with a young team member. Leaders can often guide them without a word spoken, especially when we're not in a good place to voice what's inside of us. Let your silence serve as guidance.

How well do you discipline yourself to remain silent when necessary?

HOW TO OFFER FEEDBACK IN A FRAGILE WORLD

Grant employs more than two hundred people at his firm and is a friend of mine. He called me recently in a moment of frustration. He said his team was about to go to market on a new product that week when he got a text from one of his employees. The message? "I won't be at work today and tomorrow. I'm just not my best self this week."

Grant was disappointed but also felt he owed his teammate some hard truth. When he saw the young woman later, Grant pulled her aside and explained, "You can't excuse yourself from your tasks because you're not your best self. If you're sick, I certainly understand, but our GTM week is huge for us. I suggest you figure out a way to gather your strength and show up even on tough days." It was at that point his team member gasped as if Grant had assaulted her. She replied that she felt triggered and could not continue the conversation. She left for the restroom and didn't return to her workstation for almost twenty minutes.

This seemed to be the end of the discussion.

Two days later, however, Grant received an email from the young woman's mother explaining that her daughter was "stressed out" and asking him to "lighten up."

FEEDBACK TO FRAGILE TEAM MEMBERS

Offering hard feedback has never been easy, but today it is tougher than ever. Certainly, not every young professional is this fragile, but HR execs say it's a growing problem. We seem to have caved to the idea that young people are fragile and need lots of warning for tough situations. If that's true, it is we who've created this monster. Kids are naturally "antifragile." Toddlers hop back up when they learn to walk; kids forgive wrongs easier than adults do, and they have immune systems that organically combat disease and germs.

These all signal what comes naturally for us. But fragility is up. Consider again what's happening on school campuses:

> They must provide trigger warnings to students.
> They must remove certain books from libraries.
> They must curb free speech and ideas at schools.

This assumption that people are fragile is relatively new. A hundred years ago, we believed kids (and adults) were robust and resilient—and that's a good thing. Life required them to face the Spanish flu, the Great Depression, and World War II. *Life prepared them to become agile, not fragile.* Today, we send the opposite message to our young. It's our fault. Greg Lukianoff, coauthor of *The Coddling of the American Mind*, wrote, "Many university students today are learning to think in distorted ways, and this increases their likelihood of becoming fragile, anxious, and easily hurt."[3] So, let me offer a sequence of action steps to offer feedback.

HOW DO WE OFFER FEEDBACK TO A FRAGILE GENERATION?

1. Gain permission by earning the right to give input. Today, relationships mean far more than positions or titles. We earn the right to offer hard feedback by cultivating a personal and authentic relationship with a young staff person. In short, genuine connection should precede critical input. *We must connect before we correct.* Then, asking permission to have a tough conversation likely earns a receptive ear.
2. Be targeted with your approach. Our feedback has little chance of transforming them if it's a general attack on their work. We must target one

area we'd like to see improved and focus our input on that. Being targeted means we emulate a doctor performing surgery. Surgeons almost always target their operation on one area (a tumor, a bone, an organ) instead of carving up the patient's entire body.

3. **Offer input with belief and expectation.** The key is to offer feedback from a context of belief. You *expect a lot* from them because you *believe a lot* in them. Studies from Ivy League schools prove that effort improves dramatically when leaders communicate this: "I'm giving you this feedback because I have high expectations of you, and I know you can reach them." I'll share more on this at the end of the chapter.

4. **Communicate progress with your words.** I have found I gain a more positive response from someone receiving my feedback if I clarify that I see their current progress. Some time ago, I challenged someone to improve, and she became preoccupied with the fact that I failed to say I noticed she was doing better than before. Once I began acknowledging her progress, she was willing to push further.

5. **Do it in a timely fashion.** Forget the annual review or the yearly evaluations. People need real-time feedback for it to feel authentic. Don't let pent-up frustration build until you vomit emotionally on a teammate. Wait a day until you get over your own emotions, but set a time to meet quickly. I've found it's best to calmly plan to debrief the moment you spot a need but to wait a day or two to meet.

6. Give them the opportunity to practice and implement the feedback. When people receive feedback, they'll be frustrated unless they have a path to improve. In a broader sense, think about where the teammate is going, how they're doing now, and what the next step is to make progress. If you tell them they must do better, furnish a plan for them to do just that. This makes a current suboptimal situation become beatable.

> What have you done to build a bridge to teammates that seem a bit fragile to criticism?

We owe our people this gift of feedback. Don't run from it in the name of comfort or popularity. Winston Churchill said, "Criticism may not be agreeable, but it is necessary. It fulfills the same function as pain in the human body. It calls attention to an unhealthy state of things." To go deeper on this topic, I recommend Jeff Hancher's book, *Firm Feedback in a Fragile World*.[4] The growth and development of our team is our highest calling.

BUILDING TRUST IN A TOUGH CONVERSATION

Nick Saban was the head football coach for Alabama's Crimson Tide from 2007 to 2023, where he won six national championships. Saban was not known for his nurturing style; in fact, he was one of the toughest coaches in the NCAA. Note what he said, however, when he explained how to offer wise leadership to young athletes. "The 2021 Crimson Tide had less veteran experience than past Alabama teams," Saban said in a postgame interview. He then said he had to "nurture" the team to build players' confidence: "We've got a lot of young players that are out there playing. When you've had success the previous season . . . it really takes a long time for us to sort of develop the chemistry on this team from a leadership standpoint. . . . So even though guys have leadership qualities they don't really see that as their role because it didn't have to be their role in the past. But we've had some guys really step up for us and do a really good job. I don't want to call it nurturing, but I felt like we needed to do that with this team, just getting on these guys all the time was not going to help their confidence. It was not going to help the young players develop."[5]

Even Coach Saban recognized when to be tough minded and when to be nurturing with young team members, based on the context and on who they were. I, too, began to encounter Gen Zers who needed nurturing in 2019. By 2020, when we were told to shelter in place, I could see who was struggling with the disruption and uncertainty. Anxiety set in for several of them. It was then I learned a sequence of steps that enabled me to build trust with even the most anxious staff members. I suggest you manage issues in this order:

1. Personal issues before work issues

Knowing I was interacting with struggling teammates, I found that covering personal issues before getting to work items always improved the tone and outcomes of the meeting. When the staff knows their leader is thinking first about them and their well-being, they're able to reciprocate and focus more on productivity. If I didn't, it fostered a "look out for number one" mindset in employees, which distracted them from their work. During the pandemic I continually asked how people were doing and what they needed from me. Our leaders focused first on safety and even discussed ensuring their compensation would stay intact. When we did this, we found productivity went up.

2. Hard topics before easy ones

During difficult times, people's antennae are up; their amygdala is alerted for danger and for anything that feels fake or wrong. So once I ensure they feel cared for personally, my agenda for business begins with the hard news first, before the good news. During the pandemic, for example, our leaders ripped the Band-Aid off and dealt with the tough stuff right away. This communicated we were not afraid to deal with the challenging issues and could be trusted. Then we could close the meeting with easier, happier news. We'd bring up where we were financially and what we'd need to sacrifice going forward. Then we'd offer good news. This kind of candor both deepens trust and breeds transparency on the team.

3. Big picture before details

Finally, during times of disruption, those who are more fragile can be anxious and even illogical. Again, their amygdala kicks in and puts their mind on high alert. They can miss details because their minds can become flooded. I found when you call your team back to the big picture—here's what our mission is this week—they gain clarity on what their role is in view of it. Think about it this way: each person represents a puzzle piece that completes the picture. They need you to show them the lid of the puzzle box to remind them where their piece fits. They're empowered to act in the best interest of the vision. Then you can dive into details, given the context and perspective.

What is an action step you can take as a leader to practice the suggestions above?

WHEN YOU REACH AN IMPASSE WITH A YOUNG TEAMMATE

In 2024, I appeared on the Fox Business channel, where Stuart Varney interviewed me about why Generation Z employees are so difficult to manage. He launched the interview with survey results from a nationwide poll on the topic that I've cited earlier: one in five employers fired a Gen Z member within a week of their start date, according to ResumeBuilder.com.[6] Although I had just a few minutes, I instantly thought about the ideas I'll share next in this chapter.

Because the mindset of a young employee has been shaped by such different social media platforms and cultural norms, they often hold a very different perspective than yours and mine. Workplace norms vary greatly from the college classroom, and millions from the Gen Z cohort have never had a full-time job as they launch their career.

By 2019, I had turned over the hiring and firing of all staff members to our department heads. Some of the hires were wrong ones. They weren't bad people—just not a fit for our culture. I saw conduct I'd never seen before. These young teammates didn't understand professionalism, nor did they see the big picture. After several displays of disrespect and even contempt toward one of our leaders, I was frustrated. As the founder, I worked alongside the department heads to realize that while our principles were worth standing for, we would need to adapt our approach to these young professionals.

A LEG TO STAND ON

Let me paint a picture. Imagine a young staff member has been given some autonomy on a project, and they made what you consider to be a poor decision. It was so illogical and cost the company so much money that you felt angry and frustrated. You know full well if you confronted that teammate right away, you might do or say something you'd regret later. I've learned I must stop getting furious and start getting curious. I must turn my frustration into fascination. Let me provide you with a leg to stand on. Over the past five years, I have used an acronym when I am in such situations. It spells A LEG. I encourage you to note the sequence of steps I now use that result in growth for both of us.

THIS IS A LEG WE HAVE TO STAND ON

A—Ask questions.

Too often, we jump to conclusions, and young team members feel we've accused them of ignorance. Too often, I hear Gen Zers accuse older supervisors of gaslighting. When we begin by asking questions (instead of offering answers), team members feel valued. I found that I fare better when I begin with softer, easier questions before moving toward heavier questions. These deeper questions should be carefully crafted to get to the root of an issue. We may want to begin the conversation with questions like: What were your thought processes that led to that decision? Did you envision the outcomes differently from how they turned out? How are you feeling about the project? What would you do differently next time? Would you be open to some ideas or suggestions? This may lead to another question: On a scale of 1 to 10, how would you rate your satisfaction with your job? It's wise to move from general to specific issues.

L—Listen well.

Once you've posed questions, you've not succeeded yet. It does us little good to ask questions if we're not willing to genuinely listen to their responses. My focus groups with Gen Z reveal they can tell when an older person asks questions "because they know they should, but they don't really care about the response." Members of Gen Z can sense when we're disingenuous from a mile away. In this context, the question is only a way to take our turn next and "preach." We're more successful if we genuinely listen first. When we listen, team members feel heard. Once they feel heard, we have a better chance at collaborating on a game plan for them to respond to the challenge. David Augsburger said, "Being heard is so close to being loved that for the average person they are almost indistinguishable." Listening is loving appropriately.

E—Empathize deeply.

This part of the sequence is vital. Older generations (baby boomers and Gen Xers) are often perceived by younger generations as people who lack empathy. When we don't agree with a Gen Zer, empathizing often feels like we agree with our young staff since we didn't debate the point. It's not true. Empathy is meant to build a bridge rather than a wall between us. When we empathize, they feel understood. Only when a person feels totally understood are they willing to listen and heed advice. Some Native American tribes once used a "talking stick" when in conflict with another tribe. Only the person holding the stick had the opportunity to speak, and they would continue until they felt heard and understood. It was only then they handed to stick to their opponent to allow them to air their perspective. Give your young team member the stick. Then work to understand what they are saying. Simon Sinek put it this way: "Hearing is listening to what's said. Listening is hearing what isn't said." This is all about empathy and understanding.

G—Guide wisely.

Once we've asked questions, listened well, and empathized deeply, we've earned our right to speak from *personal power* rather than *positional power.* Our influence now comes from a relationship, not a title. It's a little like a doctor, who spends several minutes doing a diagnosis, looking at your ears, eyes, mouth, and listening to your heart. That doctor may already know what your condition is and that you'll need penicillin, but they take the time to do the diagnosis before providing the prescription. Ultimately, our response will likely be given with a greater sense of love and compassion if we offer it after listening and empathizing. Our words are well informed, well timed, and wisely given. And they're more likely to be received well.

WHAT I AM PRONE TO DO

Unless I practice these steps, I default to my human instincts, which are usually unhelpful. In fact, let me confess my normal mode of operation. Do you see anything familiar?

I TEND TO	INSTEAD OF
Correct	Ask questions
Lecture	Listen well
Reason	Empathize deeply
Reach an impasse	Earn my right to guide

Evaluate yourself. Do you struggle overcoming your tendency to follow the left-hand column instead of the right?

HOW TO OFFER GUIDANCE: SURGEONS AND VELVET-COVERED BRICKS

I noticed a pattern in myself years ago. As a leader, I would notice a team member who needed correction. Instead of confronting it, I would let frustration build up inside me. Finally, it festered inside me so long that when I offered feedback I would erupt like a volcano, with too much emotion. It was my fault, not theirs. Inspired by my friend Brett Trapp, I created a new Habitude image called Surgeons and Vampires. This unlikely pair illustrate the right and wrong approach to feedback.

Consider a vampire. They sneak up on their victim in a dark room, bite them, and that poor victim never recovers. The poor person doesn't even know what hit them. The vampire benefits, but it only means pain for the victim.

Surgeons are the opposite. They prepare extensively for a surgery; they carefully select where the incision will go—depending on the patient's need. The operation is done carefully and meticulously. That doctor doesn't recklessly slice up the person's entire body—just the area in trouble. The tumor is removed. Everyone wins. Bingo.

Poor leaders offer feedback a little like a vampire. Life-giving leaders do so like a surgeon, even when the feedback is critical and corrective. They operate so that life and health can be restored to their team members. Both vampires and surgeons draw blood, but one takes life. The other gives life.

Here's what I noticed inside of me, as a leader. If I give feedback out of my own need, rather than the benefit of the other person, it doesn't go well. Notice the symptoms in each:

> Vampire leaders offer feedback out of *relief*. They want to relieve their own anger.
> Surgeon leaders offer feedback out of *belief*. They want to benefit the receiver.

Both leaders—vampires and surgeons—induce a little pain. Unfortunately, the vampire results only in pain. The surgeon's pain leads to gain. In fact, the relationship between the surgeon and the patient may even be better after the operation.

Once you know the feedback you need to offer to your team member, be sure to provide it and include two crucial ingredients:

> High expectations (This is the high standard I need you to reach.)
> High belief (I believe you are capable of reaching it.)

Both expectations and belief can positively affect their outcomes, but one without the other is incomplete and can lead to an unhealthy mental state and poor performance. Expectations without belief feels harsh. Belief without expectations feels hollow.

Ideally, high expectations and belief play a positive role in an employee's performance when:

1. The expectations are matched with their potential.
2. The expectations are birthed from healthy motivation.
3. The expectations are combined with belief in the person.
4. The expectations and belief are delivered through a relationship.

Naturally, there are times when we must raise their expectations of themselves, through our high expectations, even when it's not a task they are passionate about. We must adjust our expectations and inspire them to do their best, but don't expect them to become Albert Einstein or Marie Curie. In short, our expectations must correspond to their capacity.

To lead them well, we must become velvet-covered bricks.

Velvet Bricks

The velvet-covered brick is one of our leadership images. The metaphor captures what effective leaders do when leading Generation Z. Picture a brick covered in velvet. Both elements represent an ingredient in great leaders. One is about expectations, the other, belief.

Velvet communicates I accept you, I'm attentive to you, I understand you, I empathize with you, I care for you, and I support you. *In short, I believe in you.*

Brick communicates that because I believe in you, I hold a high standard for you to reach. I won't lower it because it feels difficult. *In short, I expect much from you.*

Consider for a moment what it feels like when a parent or teacher lowers the expectation of a student or, even worse, does the work for the students. At first it feels great. Who doesn't love a day made easier? Over time, however, it begins to backfire. The student feels the adult really doesn't think they have it in them to pull off the goal by themselves. They begin lowering their own expectations and start thinking less of themselves. They believe they need someone to help them perform well. When we lower expectations, it automatically signals low belief. High expectations are an indirect way to affirm them. The bottom line? They need a velvet-covered brick to lead them:

> Velvet = Belief.
> Brick = Expectation.

Consider this: Gen Zers are asking, Does this person who has power over me think I am competent? Is the feedback done out of belief or out of suspicion or doubt?

A group of psychologists from Stanford, Yale, Columbia, and other higher education institutions set out to explore how teachers could offer feedback that would elicit the best effort from students in their middle school classrooms. Researchers had teachers give a writing assignment to their students, after which students were given various types of feedback. To their surprise, researchers found one type of feedback improved student effort so significantly that they called it "magical." Students who received this feedback chose to revise their essay far more often than students who got different feedback. Effort rose a minimum of 40 percent among white students and 320 percent among Black students. The study solves our expectations dilemma.[7] The feedback was simply: "I am giving these comments because I have high expectations of you, and I know you can reach them."

This feedback includes both velvet and brick. It embodies leadership that is both *responsive* and *demanding*. According to well-known research from Diana Baumrind at UC Berkeley, young people need both from leaders, not one or the other.[8] When we are responsive to *them and their needs*, we earn the right to be demanding of *them and their potential.* Ideally, velvet should precede brick. When we lead this way, it naturally cultivates a "growth mindset" in teammates.

Stanford psychologist Carol Dweck coined the terms *fixed mindset* and *growth mindset*. A fixed mindset believes that I am either good at math or I'm not. It's stuck. A growth mindset believes the brain is like a muscle and can get stronger. This person commonly uses the word *yet*. I am not good at math, yet.[9] I have seen belief and expectation cultivate a growth mindset in thousands of people over the last forty years.

The one that hits closest to home was with my own son. Jonathan is now in his thirties and doing well in his career and marriage. I am proud of him and honored to be his dad. There was a time in his younger years, however, that he struggled with some poor choices. (Most of us do.) His sense of identity declined. He began to see himself differently from who I knew he was. I recall meeting with him alone and speaking to him, man to young man, and practiced this kind of feedback. It was easy because it was genuine. I do believe in him, and I expected more of him. That's exactly the fuel he needed. While I don't claim to be his chief influencer, I love who he's become with some added belief and expectation.

Let's embody this with our young team members.

TALK IT OVER

1. The chapter highlights the concept of "velvet-covered brick" leadership, combining belief and high expectations. How can leaders effectively balance these two components when offering

feedback to ensure it is both motivating and constructive for Generation Z staff?

2. With the growing emphasis on fragility in younger generations, how can organizations create a culture where tough feedback is viewed as an opportunity for growth rather than a personal attack? What specific strategies could leaders implement to foster resilience?

3. The chapter mentions the importance of earning the right to give feedback through genuine connections. How can leaders build authentic relationships with their Gen Z team members to create a foundation for open and productive critical conversations?

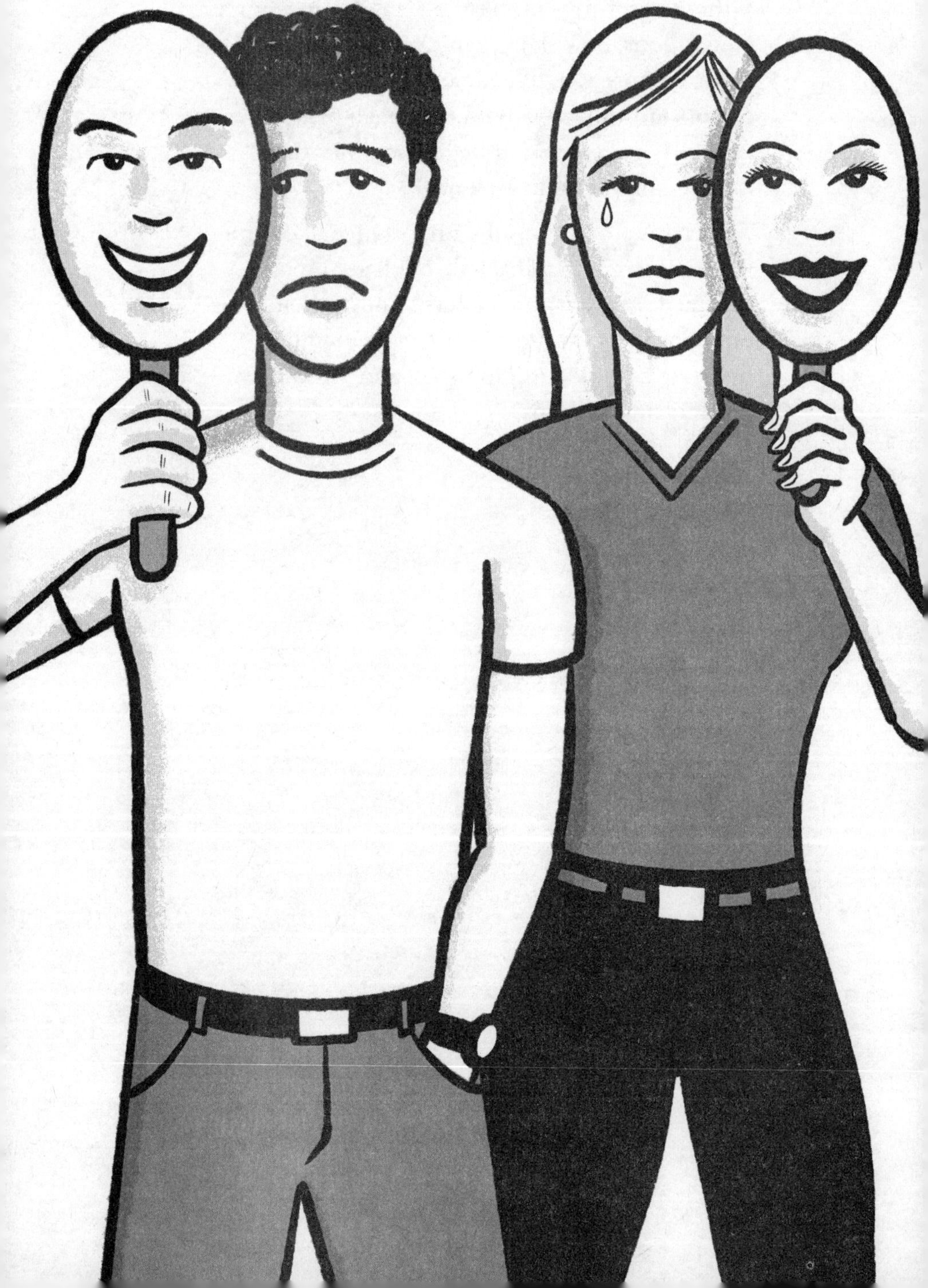

8

CREATING A SAFE PLACE

HELPING THEM MANAGE THEIR MENTAL HEALTH

I met Jasmine last year when she was twenty-one years old. When she asked to meet to talk about her career options, our conversation turned into something far more important. She expressed to me her doubts about life in general and her anxieties about so many issues from climate change to mass shootings. To her, the future looked bleak. Jasmine was melancholy and cynical about the world, when she was barely into adulthood.

The tragic outcome came a month later. Jasmine's body was discovered in her apartment. She had taken her life and left a note that her parents kept hidden for weeks. It read:

> When I look around me, I don't see anything I can trust; I have no passions because I can't see anything I can believe in. I don't see a reason to go on. Sorry.

Jasmine's pessimism may sound extreme, but she's a product of a common worldview.

Mental health is one of the most significant problems that still has a stigma for Gen Z in the workplace. Generation Z struggles with mental illness at higher rates than any other population working. According to McKinsey, more than half (55 percent) of Gen Zers report having either been diagnosed or receiving treatment for a mental health condition, compared to 31 percent of people aged fifty-five to sixty-four, who have had decades longer to seek and get treatment.[1]

One of the greatest challenges for employers is the need Generation Z expresses to guard their mental health. Many see older generations as workaholics, and they don't want to repeat that habit. They also see unethical leadership and want to distance themselves from it. Gen Z will draw boundaries, leave work early, or not show up if they don't feel their best. This chapter offers an empathetic way to meet in the middle and cultivate grit at the same time. Let's begin with a reality check.

THE STRUGGLE IS REAL

Like other generations, Gen Z has had its share of challenges as they were growing up, from mass shootings to the pandemic. Their cynicism reminds me of Gen X, those who were born into the Vietnam War, the Watergate scandal, protests, the OPEC gas crisis, a failed Iranian hostage rescue attempt, and more. It's helpful for me to review the realities that shaped Gen Z before I hire them:

1. They wrestle with mental health issues more than ever.
2. They are aware of national and global tragedies younger than ever.

CREATING A SAFE PLACE

3. They witness more mass shootings each year than we have days in the year.
4. They feel relentless academic and social pressure to perform/compete.
5. They feel they're constantly captured (on video) and critiqued (when posted).
6. They've observed polarized adult generations who often behave badly.
7. They are part of the "pandemic population" living in an uncertain economy.[2]

Add to this list the challenge of social media, which many Gen Zers have used since age twelve, and you have a ticking time bomb. Platforms like Instagram, TikTok, Snapchat, YouTube, and Facebook only exacerbate the issues—no other generation has had such immediate and unfiltered access to the information all their lives, which can lead to stress, anxiety, and other mental health issues. In addition, social media introduced Gen Z to FOMO and FOMU: the fear of missing out and the fear of messing up. When they see others post about that perfect vacation, engaging party, or amazing meal, they feel they missed out on something spectacular. FOMU is fostered because they fear if they make a mistake, painful retribution awaits, or someone will capture it (on their phone) and post it (on a social media site), and they will forever be known for the "fail."

According to McKinsey, Gen Zers are more likely than other generations to admit social media affects their mental health; 27 percent of Gen Zers say social media has a negative effect.[3] This effect is particularly relevant for members of Gen Z who spend more than two hours a day on social media (which is more than a third of them). Studies released by Jean Twenge, author and research psychologist at San Diego State University, illustrate how young adults' vulnerability to anxiety skyrockets once they spend more than two hours a day on such platforms.[4] Sadly, millions of Gen Zers spend the equivalent of a full-time job on social media daily. This is a recipe for disaster as they enter adulthood and their careers.

Obviously, mental health challenges can affect how Gen Z performs on the job. About one in four Gen Zers say their mental health affects their ability to work effectively. However, that doesn't mean we should not hire them. Instead, it means we may want to consider shifting workplace policies to help your team adjust for these mental health challenges, a shift that would benefit everyone, regardless of age.

According to Zippia, more than half of employees (56 percent) who participate in company wellness programs say they have fewer sick days because of them, and 60 percent say they're more productive at work. These programs also positively affect the bottom line: 84 percent of employers reported higher employee productivity and performance and, on average, saw a six-to-one return on investment when they invested in wellness programs.[5]

A PANDEMIC + A SMARTPHONE = MENTAL ILLNESS

What happens when you combine a smartphone with a pandemic? Mark McDonald, a child and adolescent psychiatrist and author of *United States of Fear: How America Fell Victim to a Mass Delusional Psychosis,* said: "The mental health problems are ones I have never seen in my career; not to this degree. Anxiety is up 300 percent. Depression up 400 percent . . . every single mental illness, every behavioral problem, including substance abuse in older kids, is going through the roof."[6]

Now, granted, McDonald noted this a few years ago when the pandemic was in full swing. The aftershock, however, is still occurring. As we all know, aftershocks are reverberations that follow earthquakes, letting us know the shake-up is not over. We are now hiring young professionals who are enduring the aftershock of a very strange four-year period when people were quarantined, avoided each other, wore masks, lived in fear, got sick, and died in the millions due to the virus. Strange but true. The aftershock?

> Young adults' interpersonal skills declined.
> Young adults' anxiety and depression rose.
> Young adults' comfort interacting in person declined.
> Young adults' dependence on technology rose.
> Young adults' confidence in leaders declined.
> Young adults' desire for government intervention rose.
> Young adults' happiness declined.

In fact, the Center for Generational Kinetics released a report suggesting the pandemic was a "Generation Defining Moment" much like World War II was for the Senior generation, and the Vietnam War was for the boomers, and September 11, 2001, was for millennials. Those defining moments occurred as they were forming and making big decisions.[7] The pandemic forced Gen Z to pivot and adapt.

MANAGING THE TENSION

The greatest vulnerability we have when hiring a Gen Zer who suffers from mental health issues is that they can hide it so well. A young professional can post fun Instagram photos or hilarious TikTok videos, and you'd never know they were struggling. Their posts can be a defense mechanism, and they don't even know it. How many times do we hear of a suicide attempt by a teen or a twenty-something and later hear parents and friends say: "We had no idea they felt hopeless." This isn't limited to the US either. I just visited some countries in Latin America, a continent known for joyful expression and hugs and kisses among family and friends. I discovered their Gen Zers struggle as well. The same is true in Asia, Europe, and parts of Africa. Our young have learned how to "appear" a certain way on the outside (social media) and are unaware of how depression has changed their personality. My simple advice? Be on the lookout for telltale signals from them:

> A decline in performance or delaying deadlines
> A withdraw from normal interactions
> Noticeable changes in mood or behavior
> Frequent complaints of physical discomfort
> Difficulty concentrating
> Changes in appearance
> Feeling overwhelmed by normal activity

A second vulnerability you'll face is the tension between stewarding the mental health of the employee and stewarding the performance of the business. Very often a manager is afraid of mishandling this issue due to concerns about litigation. Additionally, members of Generation Z often don't understand what it means to run a business and to generate the revenue to pay the bills. They can come to expect special treatment when it comes to their mental health. This is a slippery slope. Every move you make sends a message.

Some years ago, Ethan, one of our young team members, needed some extended personal time off for his well-being, and any conversation he had with his supervisor about productivity felt like we were insensitive and utilitarian. Nothing short of focusing on his mental health felt satisfying. Our best move was to meet with him and include both his manager and a C-suite level leader. We invited him into the process of managing both his health and the outcomes we needed. The two leaders brilliantly relayed how much they cared for him, personally and professionally. Then, they all looked at the numbers and brainstormed how they could keep him on and still reach the essential revenue and product goals we had. The key was for our leaders to focus on his mental health, then invite Ethan to help us navigate his situation. It was eye-opening for him and eventually led to a mutual decision to part ways.

Another team member wanted to work remotely due to her need to "be away from people and pressure." Carla was a full-time team member everyone loved and appreciated, but her mental health became her preoccupation. She moved away and attempted to work long distance. We soon witnessed a slow drift in her participation on the team. Often in virtual meetings, Carla wouldn't turn her camera on, didn't say anything, and never contributed to the chat column. While everyone tried to understand, this did not reflect the culture we'd built on our team. Further, the very teammates who appreciated her began to resent her. It felt like we lost her, but everyone knew she was still being paid. As our leaders perceived the negative impact, they made a move.

Our HR department was helpful to communicate the legal guidelines, but this situation rarely feels good to the young employee. *Again, anything short of our total focus on Carla's well-being felt harsh.* The relationship became adversarial instead of collaborative; she began to feel she must "look out for number one" since no one else was. She got her mom and an attorney involved, and we soon reached an impasse. At this point, our key leaders stepped in beside Carla's department head and suggested we create a mutually beneficial plan going forward. Each of them (including Carla) got to weigh in. Agenda one was to ensure there was alignment. We all agreed the first priority was Carla's mental health and treatment.

> How do you manage these tensions in your organization? Do you see a need for change?

Agenda two, a performance plan, was put in place where everyone agreed on benchmarks that needed to be reached by a set deadline. We gained agreement between everyone and then signed a win-win agreement. Such scenarios are increasing.

LET'S START WITH THE BASICS

As I spotted mental health issues in my young team members, I first had to acknowledge that I'm not their doctor, therapist, or chaplain. I am, however, a caring leader who wants the best for them, as well as for our organization. I remind them: *everyone is more important than their job, but no one is more important than the mission.* When it comes to creating a mentally healthy workplace, I suggest you talk annually about the fundamentals. Be sure the four practices below are part of your culture and that your managers encourage all your employees to practice them. To go deeper, see my ebook *Stressed Out*.[8]

1. Margin

I mention this element first because it represents the quickest step people can take. Those who maintain a happy, emotionally healthy life are those who create margin in their calendar. They schedule portions of their day where little to nothing is happening. They remove noise and clutter during those portions of time. They experience solitude, quiet, and simplicity. They take control of their day instead of remaining at the mercy of all the busyness going on. They intentionally unplug. They create space for boredom.

2. Movement

Could there be a connection between the increasing hours we sit in a typical day and the climb in our anxiety rates? What if part of our solution was to return to an active lifestyle people experienced more than a century ago? Even technology wizards—perhaps especially tech wizards—know the secret of living well is to get off a screen for part of our day. And for at least thirty minutes walk, run, play, go outside, shoot hoops. Happy chemicals, like endorphins and serotonin, are released when we're active. We were made to move.

3. Mindfulness

If you ask people to define mindfulness, you'll likely get a variety of responses. To define it simply, mindfulness is the basic human ability to be fully present, aware of where we are and what we're doing and not overly reactive or overwhelmed by what's going on around us. It means exchanging our multitasking for "monotasking." One task or thought at a time. It includes putting down all the juggling balls for a bit. It's about embracing the beauty of one thing. The American Psychological Association cites it as a hopeful strategy for alleviating stress, boosting memory, and increasing focus.

4. Management

Probably the most important solution is one people talk the least about. Today, everyone must learn to manage their stress and anxiety levels. We all have them, but stress does not need to turn into distress. Anxiety is a common part of living in a fast-paced twenty-first-century culture, but it doesn't have to be our boss. Talk to the team about steps to manage anxiety, which might include reducing hours on social media, seeing a counselor, or even taking medication. The key is for each one to take control of their life and own their mental health.

> How are you implementing these fundamentals in your workplace?

Neurologists claim that every time you resist acting on your anger, you're actually rewiring your brain to be calmer and more patient. Do you suppose that might work for our anxiety too? If we can resist anxiety by being mindful, practicing quietness, or acting on what is in our control, is it possible to combat our anxiety effectively? I believe this is one important step we can take. *We must listen to ourselves and talk to ourselves.*

HAVING A TOUGH CONVERSATION

Leaders must first remember that people under their care have different temperaments and will react to anxiety differently. It is common during times of strain or stress for young team members to make demands that seem outlandish to older staff. They can display very low emotional intelligence and low professional experience. Obviously, when people are emotional they rarely make logical statements or take rational steps. I've come to appreciate the counsel of Carolyn Frost in such times.[9] She suggests twelve responses that highly emotionally intelligent leaders offer under pressure in a tough conversation:

1. I need a minute to think this through.
2. Help me understand your perspective.
3. That's interesting. Can you tell me more?
4. I notice I'm feeling reactive right now.
5. Let's pause and come back to this.
6. What would a good outcome look like for you?
7. I appreciate your bringing this to my attention.
8. I see this differently, and I am curious about your view.
9. Can we explore other options together?
10. I'm not ready to decide yet.
11. What am I missing here?

> Have you practiced any of these strategies? How could you improve?

12. Let me reflect on that and get back to you.

Each of these statements allows both parties to calibrate their emotions, especially in a high stakes interaction. They can calm anxious moments and allow you to make wise choices.

MAKING THE MOST OF TRAUMA

The Barna Research Group revealed their survey results on Generation Z in 2021. A staggering 82 percent of Generation Z say they have suffered at least one "trauma." Whether you believe that number or not, this is their perception. For many of them, it was facing the COVID-19 pandemic. For others, it's been various setbacks in childhood. They now live with this trauma narrative. Robert Leahy reported boldly, "Teens today endure the same level of anxiety as a psychiatric patient did in the 1950s."[10]

I assumed for years that if someone endured trauma, it would be followed by some level of posttraumatic stress disorder, even if it's just a small amount. While that may be true of many Gen Zers, PTSD does not get the last word for most who face trauma. I have some good news for you. We've all become acquainted with the term *PTSD*. It became popular following our last four US wars. Beginning in the 1990s, psychologists also noticed something else. At least half the people who endured a traumatic event showed no signs or symptoms of posttraumatic stress. Four out of five trauma victims were not plagued by PTSD afterward. In fact, typically they emerged stronger. Instead of being permanently scarred by the tragedy, they experienced posttraumatic growth, or PTG.[11]

Most trauma sufferers end up with PTG. Let's define the terms.

> **PTSD: POSTTRAUMATIC STRESS DISORDER**
> There are varied levels of PTSD where people emerge damaged, triggered, and unhealthy. The trauma can be physical, mental, or emotional, but their life becomes a reaction to it.
>
> **PTG: POSTTRAUMATIC GROWTH**
> PTG occurs when a person endures trauma yet has a guide help them make sense of it and see the positive outcomes. People emerge stronger, kinder, wiser, and more grateful.

While I didn't grow up in a pandemic with a portable device in my hand, I faced my share of triggering events in my younger years, including seven car accidents, a plane crash, type 1 diabetes, and a fall down a flight of concrete stairs. I felt horrible after each of these, emotionally and physically, but each one became a source of growth. Thanks to positive parents and mentors in my life, I was able to turn disadvantages into advantages.

In *The Power of Bad*, John Tierney explains how PTG works: "The growth doesn't come from the trauma, but from the way the person responds to it. These people suppress their negativity bias with an array of defenses that are available to anyone. They choose to become kinder, stronger and more mindful of their joys in life. While a negative experience triggers a stronger immediate emotional reaction than a positive experience, negative emotions fade faster than positive ones do in most people. Repeated experiments with people who've undergone negative experiences prove this. They come into the lab and describe how they feel about recent events, and later return to recall those same events. By then, their feelings have diminished, especially in those who've repeatedly discussed the bad experience with others. Since the initial threat is over, they're prone to recognize positive recovery has taken place. In short, the more you talk about your problems, the more perspective you can gain to ease your anxieties. This is why we feel it's therapeutic."[12]

Did you catch his big idea? The growth doesn't come from the trauma but from the guidance. It's how we choose to think about it once it's over. Our perception becomes our self-narrative. The research shows that when we reflect and see any advantages to our tragedy we enjoy:

> Increased appreciation of life
> Deeper relationships with others
> New perspectives and priorities
> Greater personal strength

A word of caution. PTG does not equal denial. You're not coaching your Gen Zers to pretend nothing bad ever happened or that they don't have anxiety. My kids (both of whom are young professionals today) have struggled with anxiety and depression. Their key was to face it, treat it, and then spot the advantages it has given them to help others. You can imagine, after my plane crash years ago, I gained new appreciation for being alive and for being able to function—I became grateful to be able to breathe, eat, work, and love my family. Both perspective and gratitude remedied most of the trauma in my life.

> How could you or your managers help your Gen Zers shift to PTG?

UNDERSTANDING HOW TO COMMUNICATE

A lesson leaders must learn is how to communicate in emotional contexts. Too often, we can focus merely on results and be blind to how people are feeling. Charles Duhigg released a book in 2024 called *Supercommunicators: How to Unlock the Secret Language of Connection.*[13] In it, he talks about three kinds of conversations we have each day and how to recognize them when they surface. He argues that people have trouble connecting when they don't know what kind of interaction is taking place. To connect, we need to recognize the type of conversation and match it. The three are:

1. Practical conversations. These interactions are all about transmitting information and contain little emotion. They revolve around the subject matter. No one gets hurt or offended. It's just the facts.
2. Social conversations. These are interactions that focus on people and what happened. There may be passion or levity because they revolve around who we are. Others engage since it's about identity.
3. Emotional conversations. This may appear to be social or practical, but these interactions are about how we feel about ourselves or what's happened. They revolve around how we feel.

In practical conversations, facts and details matter since it's about what we know. In social conversations, details are less important, since it's about our sense of who we are. In emotional conversations, it's all about how we feel. Be sure to recognize when you're having an emotional conversation.

Frequently, conversations surrounding mental health for staff aren't informational but emotional interactions. I recall talking with my daughter about a question regarding counseling for parents. She is a counselor and at the time was not a parent. She asked whether, if I had a choice to see a counselor about a parenting issue, I would prefer to see one who was trained well or one who was trained and was a parent. Thinking we were having a practical conversation, I replied, "All things being equal, I'd see a counselor who was actually a parent." I had no idea how much it hurt her. I misunderstood our interaction. I thought it was practical, but it was an emotional one. This happens at work all the time. When there may be misunderstanding, follow these steps:

> Answer their question with a question to clarify what they really need from you.
> Watch body language and listen to their tone to see if it's about more than facts.
> Be truthful, but always try to leave them feeling hopeful about themselves.

MOVING FROM EMPATHY OR COMPASSION

A high school principal recently told me that the mother of one of his students requested her daughter be taken out of her civics class and moved to a different one. When he asked why, Mom explained that her daughter was distracted and anxious in her current class. When he inquired why a different class would be better, the mother explained her daughter's former boyfriend was in her current class, and it would help to get her out of that environment.

This mom was displaying empathy, and it offers a case study for us.

We celebrate empathy in our day. We'd all agree *empathy* is certainly better than *apathy*. But empathy is only a stepping stone to what Gen Z really needs from us: compassion.

WHAT'S THE DIFFERENCE BETWEEN EMPATHY AND COMPASSION?

Empathy is not feeling sorry for someone in pain. That's sympathy. Rather, empathy is mentally putting yourself in the suffering person's shoes to feel their pain. As Harvard professor Arthur

Brooks reminds us: "It's the difference between 'get well soon' and 'I can imagine how much discomfort you must be feeling right now.' Evidence suggests that empathy really can lessen other people's burdens. In a series of experiments documented in 2017, participants enjoyed significant physical pain relief when someone expressed empathy."[14]

But it's a stepping stone. A means to an end.

When empathy grows into compassion, it becomes more helpful for both you and the person for whom you demonstrate it. Each one leads to a different response:

> Empathy is feeling their pain and wanting to remove the hardship they're enduring.
> Compassion is to feel their pain and to equip them to overcome it from now on.

WHY GENERATION Z NEEDS COMPASSION FROM US

In the example above, the mother felt sympathy for her struggling daughter and was prompted to remove the struggle. That's empathy. Compassion is feeling deeply for your daughter and working with her to become tough enough to face the hardship and continue. Having raised two adult children, I know that's what they needed from me—to leave them in a better spot, able to face similar tough times going forward.

Yet it is rare today.

You move from a shared feeling to a redemptive action. It's the difference between a friend and a nurse if you're a patient in the hospital. Your friend is comforting because they sit beside you, express empathy for you, and perhaps get you some water to drink. The nurse sees your pain and takes action to remedy the disease. Both are nice, but one is better. Empathy feels good to give, but you may feel their pain so deeply you're not even able

CREATING A SAFE PLACE

to act. Compassion allows you to rise above the pain so that you can treat the need. Consider the nurse once again. What if your nurse felt empathy for you but couldn't stand the sight of blood? You need them to be able to act objectively in the presence of pain and blood. Employers must move from empathy to compassion for Gen Z.

Because compassion enables you to rise above the negative emotion and act, it often moves you to lead contrary to empathy so you can benefit the other person.

> Empathy means giving a man a fish. Compassion is teaching a man to fish.
> Empathy *feels* the hurt, but compassion *heals* the hurt.
> Empathy thinks short term. When displayed, we make things feel nicer today.
> Compassion thinks long term. We make things better for them years from now.

So, how do you move from empathy to compassion? First, I urge you to camp out in the land of empathy for a while before you move to compassion. Be sure they know you feel their pain. Step two is to work on your own toughness. To be tough in the presence of another's pain does not mean you feel it less. It means to feel the pain without being impaired to act. Empathetic parents suffer with their kids when they're struggling at college; compassionate parents resist the urge to call the dean or to drive over to the university and treat them like children. Here's how I break it down:

EMPATHY	COMPASSION
A shared feeling	A redemptive action
Feels the hurt	Heals the hurt
Removes the hardship	Equips the person
Focuses on detection	Focuses on development
Means giving them a fish	Means teaching them to fish

Dan is an incredible example of a compassionate employer. A year ago, Samantha, a young staff person, approached him saying she struggled to keep up as she battled anxiety. Dan replied, "I'm so sorry to hear that, but I'm glad you told me. Let's work together to beat this challenge, what do you say?" She smiled and said, "What do you have in mind?" Dan then created something he called his "training wheels" plan. He placed some "training wheels" on her work shift until she felt she could do the work well, without much mental anguish. She "peddled," but someone was with her to make sure she kept moving forward.

Truth be told, Dan said he began to look at his team much like general managers look at their baseball teams. They sign talented players—athletes they know not only have major league potential but could be all-stars. First, however, they let them spend a little time in the minor leagues to get ready. Dayton Moore did this for Alex Gordon, Salvy Perez, Eric Hosmer, and Mike Moustakas when he was general manager of the Kansas City Royals. He knew the talent was inside them but took time to develop them. They not only became major league all-stars but won a World Series.

Dan did this for Samantha as a retailer. He prioritized development before duty, knowing if he developed his sharp young hires, the duties would take care of themselves. That's exactly what happened for Dan and Samantha. She became an all-star teammate for him.

CREATING A SAFE PLACE

TALK IT OVER

1. The chapter highlights the impact of social media and global crises on Generation Z's mental health. How can leaders create workplace policies and practices that mitigate these stressors while fostering resilience and well-being among employees?

2. Empathy and compassion are described as distinct approaches to supporting employees, with compassion focusing on equipping individuals to overcome challenges. How can managers strike the right balance between offering empathetic understanding and fostering long-term growth through compassionate actions?

3. Posttraumatic growth is introduced as a potential outcome of adversity when the person is guided effectively. What specific strategies can leaders adopt to help Gen Z employees transform challenges into opportunities for growth while maintaining a supportive and inclusive work environment?

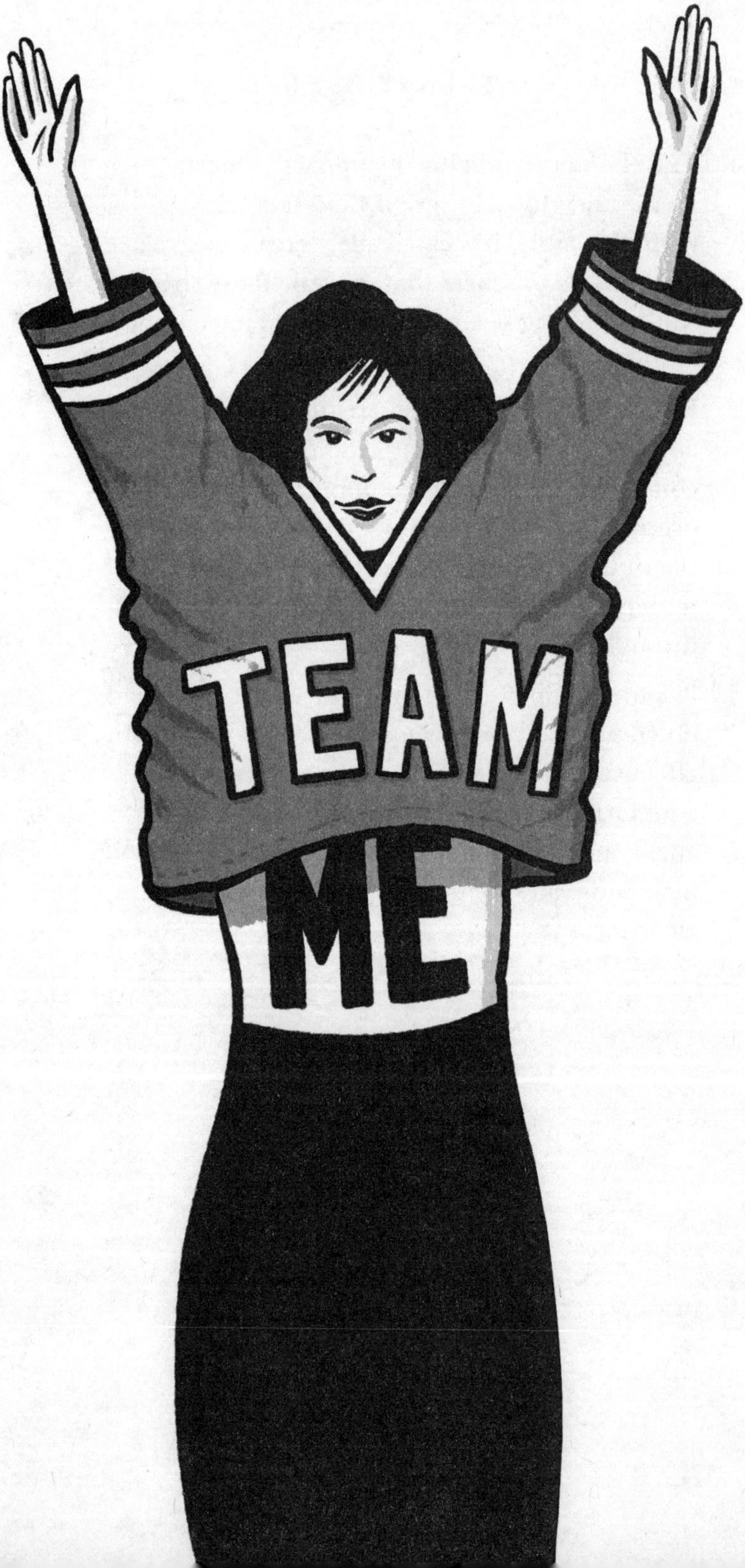
TEAM
ME

9

RIGHTSIZING THEIR MINDSETS

MANAGING UNREALISTIC EXPECTATIONS

My wife has been taking dance lessons for more than a year now, and (in my humble opinion) she's gotten quite good at it. In November 2024, she had the chance to dance with one of her favorite TV personalities, Derek Hough, from *Dancing with the Stars*. It was an unforgettable evening for her. On that night, only a handful of people from the audience got to take a moment or two and dance with this professional who's at the top of his game. My role was to shoot the video of her spin with Derek.

I noticed a few things very quickly. First, some of the dancers weren't ready. Although they could've watched footage before this dance and prepared, they did not know the steps and could not keep up with him. Derek had to slow down. Others were clunky because they thought they knew what the steps were, but they didn't. Once again, Derek had to slow down. My wife, on the other hand, had been taking lessons and stayed in step. She smiled the entire time as they did salsa; he spun her and swung her, and they ended with a dip. I caught it all on video and was so proud of how she kept up. It was beautiful. What made it work is that they stayed in step. Both Derek and my wife played off each other. Each responded to the other as they moved in rhythm.

Life works very much like a dance. In fact, teams on the job work like dancers. When people are in sync, it's beautiful. When they're not, it can be clunky. And when things feel clunky, it's often because team members are on different pages; they bring different expectations to the team. And in my experience, this is most likely to happen among people from differing generations. My focus groups with Gen Z employees were telling:

> "My greatest fear is that I'll get stuck in a job that's miserable, and I can't get out of it because of my relentless bills." —Dillon, age twenty-four

> "I don't want a third of my life to be depressing, where I am shackled with golden handcuffs, and I won't really see it until I'm old." —A. J., age twenty-two

> "I don't think like my boss does; he lives for his work; I don't want to be like that. I want a life; that's why I approach my job differently." —Sam, age twenty-two

> "Most people at my work feel their jobs are dismal. I got scared my first week because I thought: *Is this normal for people here?*" —Amy, age twenty-three

DEFINING THE CHALLENGE

The result of all this is that Gen Z team members can enter their careers with their guard up. It appears to their manager that they're not committed; they may show up late or not at all. They seem distracted from what their supervisor needs them to focus on. While I'm not excusing Gen Z, this gap in expectations has a reason. Gen Z may distance themselves for self-protection, as a defense mechanism. To use the dance analogy, Gen Z may want to do the tango, but their manager wants to waltz or do salsa. The expectation is just not the same. It requires a conversation and maybe, just maybe, meeting in the middle.

Consider this: Gen Z often begins their career without any full-time job experience, leaping into the workplace with only classroom experience. Millions of their parents told them to *not* get a job in high school and college and focus instead on academics. This creates a gap as they enter their careers with unrealistic expectations about their compensation, their autonomy, and their authority. This chapter offers a game plan for leaders to make the jump mentally and rightsize their expectations on career progression and the speed they will likely climb the ladder.

THE PROS AND CONS OF GENERATION Z

So, when Gen Z shows up at work, what can we expect? How does this generation appear to the team? Let's look at the data. Recently graduated students entering their careers bring with them pros and cons that differ from those of, say, a boomer or an Xer. Below are some pros and cons for you to examine and discuss. Have you spotted these?

THE PROS	THE CONS
1. They may feel bewildering agency.	1. They may feel bewildering anxiety.
2. They own the "tech" world.	2. They may expect fast and easy results.
3. They catch onto new ideas quickly.	3. They may struggle with long-term projects.

THE PROS	THE CONS
4. They can multitask naturally.	4. They can find it hard to focus on one task.
5. They're often the focus of parents.	5. They often find it hard to cope with reality.
6. They hunger to change the world.	6. They may expect it to happen quickly.

Let me add a caution. We must be careful to not stereotype or to be guilty of fundamental attribution error, as I suggested earlier.[1] It's easy for bosses to see only the cons in the right-hand column and miss the pros on the left side. Not long ago, I met with Jalen, one of our young team members, who was struggling with a poor attitude and critical nature. I told him I wanted to understand where he was coming from, so we played a little game crafted by Sheryl Sandberg, former COO of Facebook (Meta Platforms) years ago. Here's how it goes: when you meet for an evaluation, each of you asks, What's it like to be on the other side of me? I asked this question of Jalen, and then he asked it of me. I shared the two columns above and told him I saw all the pros in him but wondered if he was aware of the cons he brought with him. It was an epiphany for him.

HOW WORK TENDS TO WORK

Recently, a department head spoke to me about the number of young team members who expected immediate freedom on the terms and times of their labor. She said, "Millennials and Gen Z employees often expect to set their own hours, establish their own boundaries, and even dictate the tasks they'll take on."

A vice president told me he had three employees approach him questioning him about their "career path." It's a term describing the course each person will take to be promoted, receive pay raises, and ultimately arrive at an ideal position in the organization. The VP frowned and said, "I would have never brought that up to a supervisor when I was young. I would have felt selfish, focusing on my own growth rather than the company's."

I had to agree with him. Today, times have changed.

FOUR RULES THAT GOVERN OUR WORKPLACE

There's a natural order of laws that govern the way freedom, influence, and promotions tend to operate at work. While there are exceptions to these rules, the following are four that usually make sense to Gen Zers when you discuss them.

1. Autonomy Increases with Productivity

In 2019, we had a growing number of team members who requested days each week to work from home. It's quite normal in our culture today. Over the last decade, we've allowed several team members to do this. But I've always based my decision on a simple principle: *autonomy increases with productivity*. We all earn our right to work on our own terms. Those who demonstrate they are producers and need little or no supervision to meet and exceed expectations get to enjoy greater levels of freedom. Each director must evaluate the production of employees and make that judgment. Freedom isn't free; it's earned.

2. Promotions Always Follow Testing

When team members inquire about promotions and pay raises, our leaders are not put off by that conversation, but we always try to clarify: *testing always precedes promotion*. By this we mean tenure alone doesn't earn the right to be promoted or given bonuses. Academic degrees alone don't automatically translate into pay raises either. Just like a product in a store is never used until it is tested, so it is with team members. The deeper the testing and the more team members demonstrate that they can pass those tests with flying colors, the more likely they are to be invited into greater levels of responsibility and be rewarded with greater remuneration. Simply doing a job doesn't equal progress. Promotion follows performance at a higher level.

3. Rules Decrease as Results Increase

Sometimes it's hard for a young, inexperienced team member to see a supervisor experiencing high levels of independence and authority. Just like "autonomy increases with productivity," this second cousin explains that the more results a person produces in their work, the fewer rules are needed to legislate their activity on the job. Working under John Maxwell for twenty years, I learned this rule quickly. John was clear about the fact that results were his "love language." My work ethic and my achieving outcomes were all he needed to allow me great independence, even in my twenties. *He never asked me to clock in; he only asked me to put out.* I was happy to do so. This is how work usually works.

4. Influence Rises by Providing the Scarcest Resource

This one occurs naturally, but few people notice it. Our influence (and ultimately our leadership role) rises when we provide a rare resource. Consider a simple example: if you're with a group of people in a car, traveling in an unfamiliar city, and only one person has a GPS, they are the one with the most influence. Similarly, if I bring to my team a skill, a talent, or an ability that is scarce, I tend to gain more influence. It's just how the marketplace works: *supply and demand.* If what you have is in short supply and great demand, you're in good shape. In fact, the scarcer your ability, the more remuneration and the more influence should come your way.

One disclaimer. I don't mean to sound utilitarian. I love each of our team members and enjoy working with them,

REFLECT

Would you modify these four rules? What would you add?

regardless of their role. But freedom and advancement are privileges we all earn through our diligence and results.

REQUESTS COME IN THREE FORMS

In chapter 5, I mentioned five issues we must clarify with our young teammates. They spelled PERKS and offered a way to discover the expectations of Gen Zers during a job interview. Let's look at three levels of "requests" in employees that often get confused in inexperienced staff. Let me clarify what leaders must recognize in discussions:

1. Preferences. Leaders must discover if a desire in a Gen Zer is merely something they prefer but is not a hill they feel is worth dying on. It's an opinion not a conviction; a desire not a demand.

2. Expectations. This one is stronger. Leaders must discover what Gen Zers expect or assume will be true. Conflict expands based on the distance between expectations and reality.

3. Demands. These are nonnegotiables that job candidates feel entitled to receive. They consider them essential to their job satisfaction. Some can confuse wants and needs. When they think they need something, they feel they can demand it. Also, if they think they need something, they can judge a boss's level of care and support based on their willingness to meet that need. This can be dangerous. Be sure to discover demands as soon as possible.

> **REFLECT**
>
> As you consider expectations and entitlements how could you discuss these?

THREE METAPHORS TO TALK ABOUT

A disconnect in expectations between leaders and employees can result in quiet quitting. Management can be on one page, the teammate on a completely different one. Fortunately, I've had to deal with this only a handful of times. When I did, however, I framed the issue with three metaphors, either one-on-one or with entire departments. These metaphors are part of our Habitudes series I mentioned earlier. One of these images is for you, the other two for your team.

1. Dentists and Cavities

I'm sure you've noticed that when your dentist finds a cavity in your mouth, they say, "Could you stay a bit longer and I'll fill it now? If not, when's the soonest you can return for me to do it?" They want to fill it quickly because they know if they don't fill that cavity, bacteria will fill it. Something damaging often fills an unfilled cavity. The same is true with people in times of uncertainty. They have mental cavities that need to be filled. And leaders must be dentists. As teams endure conflict, people can assume the worst. Suspicion occurs. Gossip ensues. Emotions can spiral. Quiet quitting often happens as a result.

Leaders serve as dentists as they convene meetings to relay accurate information, helpful updates, and life-giving hope. They must commit to truth-telling and filling those cognitive and emotional cavities. As the old saying goes, "A lie gets halfway around the world before the truth has a chance to get its pants on." Truth is always better than speculation in anxious people. When truth isn't clear and thorough, people frequently experience cognitive distortions: they personalize, catastrophize, minimize, and overgeneralize.

I've learned that when teams feel uncertain, leaders must overcommunicate with them. Clarify and repeat. Encourage and repeat. T. S. Eliot wrote, "When we do not know, or we do not know enough, we tend to always substitute emotions for thoughts." I have found:

1. The larger the cavity, the greater the possibility of inaccurate narratives in people.
2. The larger the cavity, the more leaders must overcommunicate with their teams.

My conclusion? Quiet quitting diminishes when leaders stay in touch and tell the truth.

2. Crock-Pots and Microwaves

We've all tasted food that was heated in a microwave oven. While the food cooks quickly, it doesn't taste the best, especially a few minutes later. Hot dogs are rubbery; pizza is soggy. You know the drill. We give up taste and quality for speed. A slow cooker, on the other hand, is just the opposite. My mom put a roast in that pot, and it took hours before it was ready. But when she served it, it was delicious. Tender meat, tasty vegetables, soft potatoes. Mmmm—my mouth is watering as I write this. With a slow cooker, you give up speed for flavor and quality. It's a great trade-off.

It is easy for young staff to expect their careers to work like a microwave. They assume folks will spot their talent and move them up the organizational chart quickly. Maybe they'll be vice president by age twenty-five! You and I both know, however, that good careers usually work like a slow cooker, not a microwave. Things take time, more time than we expect. But it's worth the wait.

My good friend David Salyers told me about life after he received his degree from the University of Georgia. He had two job opportunities: one was from a major company that could pay him very well immediately, while the other was a starting position at Chick-fil-A corporate headquarters. The latter role didn't pay quite as much, but they promised they would move him forward as he "added value" to others in his career. He chose this option and, over time, became a key executive for Chick-fil-A. David ignored the "traditional" approach of selling himself to the highest bidder and pursued an "outlier" path, focusing on adding value not extracting it. When we do this, we usually gain both.

My conclusion? Quiet quitting diminishes when leaders right-size expectations.

3. Half-Hearted Mountain Climber

Anyone who is a genuine mountain climber knows—you don't accidentally climb a mountain. It takes intention and commitment to make it to the top. In fact, if your ambition isn't to make it all the way to the top, you're not a true mountain climber. Did you know the word *mediocre* is a mountain- or rock-climbing term? It literally means, "middle of the rock." It describes someone who began climbing and got only halfway up and stopped. Sounds like quiet quitting to me. It describes a halfway effort. There is no such thing as a half-hearted mountain climber. You either are one, or you're not.

I've yet to see anything good come from half-hearted effort. Humans must choose to get in or get out, but quiet quitting only wastes people's time. Commitment, while a fading virtue, is still important. In today's world we find it easy to "sign up" for new, novel, and shiny opportunities, but find it increasingly difficult to stay committed. We start well but we don't finish well. Jobs. Workouts. Marriages. Volunteering. We're like the young brother and sister who practiced piano together. During one rehearsal, the boy hopped off the piano bench before the song was over. When his sister complained to Mom, he explained frankly, "I just got done with the song before she did."

That never feels good to anyone else.

The word *decision* comes from Latin roots: *de* meaning "down" or "away from" and *caedere* meaning "to cut." A decision means cutting other possibilities. A true decision means you commit to pursuing a result and stop with the FOMO. Your level of commitment shows up in three places: your calendar, relationships, and bank account. No matter what you say, those three categories reveal what you're truly committed to in life.

My conclusion? Leaders need to act like dentists. Our careers will usually feel like slow cookers. Team members need to act like mountain climbers.

> **REFLECT**
> How could conversations on these metaphors deepen engagement from Gen Z?

WHEN I DESERVE TO HAVE A VOICE AND A VOTE

During a Q-and-A time with business leaders in Guyana, a woman asked me why so many young employees today expect to have a say in how things are done at work from day one. She was baffled by the sense of entitlement she's witnessed. But before I had the chance to explain my research on the issue, she volunteered her perspective. It was so profound I wanted to grab my tablet and take notes. Her wisdom was simple yet thoughtful. When did she believe someone gets to weigh in?

"When you start caring for something or someone other than yourself."

GENERATION Z WANTS TO HAVE A VOICE

One of the heart cries Generation Z employees bring to the workplace is the desire to be "heard." A growing body of research shows they despise the phrase *pay your dues* and want to weigh in on issues immediately, even with little experience.

I can understand both sides of this issue. Generation Z has grown up in a world of social media platforms where they instantly and constantly get the chance to speak their mind, voice what they like, and comment on posts that please or displease them. Why not continue this as they enter the workplace? After all, they're part of the team now.

On the other hand, supervisors and seasoned staff wonder why anyone should listen to someone who has no job experience and has been around only for a short amount of time. Veteran employees tell me they would not have dreamed of expecting their manager to listen to their opinions early on. After all, you earn the right to have a voice. What young team members often fail to recognize is the principle of leverage. When a new staff member demands rights or perks, it can come across as nonsense to a tenured supervisor because the person has so little to leverage. Negotiations, even friendly ones, operate based on leverage—what value do you bring that would persuade the boss to adapt to your request? Someone with nothing to leverage has little power to get their way.

HOW TO GAIN LEVERAGE ON THE JOB: OWNERSHIP AND RESPONSIBILITY

Young and old frequently represent two paradigms at work. Call it old-school and new-school thinking. The businesswoman's comment in Guyana struck me because of its common sense. There is such a thing as "work maturity." It comes over time as employees gain a sense of ownership. It's not just about age. Sometimes young team members mature quickly as they assume a sense of ownership rapidly. Like perspective, maturity comes with responsibility—when you start caring for something or someone other than yourself.

When our nation was birthed, US citizens couldn't vote until they owned property. Why? Our forefathers believed that once you were a landowner you had some stake in the game, a sense of ownership in the future of America. For years, the voting age was twenty-one since that was when you gained a sense of ownership of your life, moving away from your parents to live on your own. During World War II, the US government needed more soldiers, so they lowered the qualifying age for the military to eighteen. When they did, however, they realized if the government was asking young men and women to fight for their country, they deserved the right to choose who their commander in chief should be. That's when the voting age was lowered to age eighteen. Once again, it's about stake in the game.

I realize we must strike a balance on this issue.

As I've said, there is an unwritten social contract people must adhere to if they want to succeed in life. *To offer rights without responsibilities creates unhealthy people.* In fact, it's a mild form of abuse as it ultimately creates unrealistic expectations in them. Adults (that is, parents) have often done a poor job clarifying to Gen Z how life works. Influence is earned. People listen to us when we demonstrate we deserve to be listened to, which happens when we show we care about things beyond ourselves. What did Uncle Ben teach Peter Parker in the Spiderman story? *With great power comes great responsibility.* We do a disservice to our young staff if we fail to model this. Privilege and responsibility go together. This perspective flies in the face of our cultural narrative. It may be why one in eight managers say they've fired a Gen Z employee in their first week.[2]

TAKING STEPS TO MEET IN THE MIDDLE

Resolving this issue on your team may take longer than you think it should because you are both stewarding your organization and developing a new generation of leaders who will be in charge one day. Let me suggest three best practices:

1. Everyone has a voice, but not everyone has a vote.
I mentioned our team decided to meet in the middle. We established a policy that basically said: "Everyone has a voice, but not everyone gets a vote." This meant we'd hold staff meetings that

presented a concern or an issue and allow people to weigh in. We knew if we let people weigh in, it would foster buy-in. Once the perspectives were voiced, everyone knew that our leadership team ran point and would ultimately make the decision on what direction to take. We distinguished between voice and vote.

2. Voice increases when value does.

I touched on this earlier. We must clarify a reality to young team members that all veteran employees understand—your influence deepens as you execute your job well and produce results. Autonomy and power both expand when a person adds value to the mission. Power increases with productivity. If young employees want people to listen to them, there is one sure way to make that happen, and it has nothing to do with how loud they are. Instead, it has everything to do with how helpful and beneficial they are to the rest of the team.

3. Teach staff to speak as if they believe they're right but listen as if they're wrong.

I adopted this mantra five years ago with no regrets. Both young and old should practice this habit in meetings: speak to others with confidence (as if you are right), but listen to others with humility (as if you might be wrong). This was a game changer for me, both with my team and my own adult children. When I listen to others in a teachable manner, it communicates value and helps them feel heard. David Augsburger said, "Being heard is so close to being loved that for the average person, it is indistinguishable."

> How could you relay these steps with your Gen Z staff?

McKinsey and Company reports, "Gen Zers who are 'taking a long-term approach to planning their careers' are now referred to as the 'road map generation,' according to a recent *Business Insider* article.[3] These ambitious budding professionals are weighing whether job offers—and the benefits and development opportunities that come with them—set them up for success in life. Our own research on what Gen Zers want from work supports that notion: when evaluating a new job, salary comes second to career development and advancement potential." This is news that gives me hope.[4]

HELPING GEN Z EMPLOYEES LEARN TO BE TEAM PLAYERS

Years ago, one of our department heads hired someone right out of college. He learned quickly that there's a trade-off when fresh graduates join the team. On the one hand, they often bring new ideas, energy, and creativity. On the other, these grads have often never worked a full-time job and may not know how to be a team player. That was the case with Tracy (not her real name).

Tracy fit the mold for the Generation Z demographic. She'd grown up with smart technology, she struggled with anxiety, she felt strongly about social justice, she wanted to have a voice instantly, and she distrusted the "establishment," all of which made her prone to "speak truth to power." If she felt something or someone was wrong, she wasn't afraid to say so. Within her first few months, we watched Tracy sabotage herself:

> She publicly disagreed with our president on a Zoom call, implying he didn't know what he was talking about. It felt disrespectful to the team.
> She didn't seem to recognize professional behavior and frequently acted like she was still in a college residence hall. It felt immature to the team.
> She'd submit projects along with colleagues and defend why hers was superior, even when teammates disagreed with her. It felt selfish to the team.

While none of these missteps are horrific, her very presence brought discord to her team. Disagreeing with an executive or defending your work is acceptable on our team, but how she did it vividly displayed she didn't know how to "play well with others." Like millions from Gen Z, she needed to learn to be a team player.

LEARNING TO SACRIFICE WHAT I WANT FOR WHAT I NEED

A look at the data on Generation Z members reveals they are strongly individualistic (note the variety of terms for gender preference), they desire self-expression (check out their tattoos), and they've been conditioned to learn alone on a screen (think COVID-19 quarantines). They're different from millennials and often require supervisors to teach them teamwork. They long to be part of a community, but many don't know how to experience it. Consider this fact. Inside of every human being, there are two desires:

1. I want to be me.
2. I want to belong.

Maturation is the process of balancing these two desires so that we can maximize our joy and meaning in life while also succeeding on a team. Like all youth, Gen Z felt the strong tug inside called "I want to be me." They may wear unorthodox clothing; they pierce parts of their bodies and tattoo other parts seeking to make a statement about the unique person they are. As people age, however, we recognize how much we need others to be complete. We need others' support, advice, talent, listening ears, food, products, money, help, and so on. Eventually, we acknowledge we want to belong to someone or to some community. The tug-of-war occurs until we find a place of contentment. We learn that we must sacrifice some of our self-centered desires to gain something greater. This does not mean we demand that Gen Z surrender their sense of identity. Quite the opposite, it requires them to be who they are but on behalf of a greater community or team. Research psychologist Brené Brown explains there is a difference between fitting in and belonging. I mentioned this idea in chapter 4:

> Fitting in requires a person to compromise who they are to blend in with others.
> Belonging requires a person to embody who they are but for the benefit of others.

So being a team player doesn't mean that your *identity* changes but that your *perspective* changes. You play the cards you have in your hand (your gifts, your personality, your unique role), yet do so to benefit the team's progress. I recently spoke to a Gen Zer who asked me if I felt he needed to compromise on an opinion he had regarding a department project. I told him: "I know you feel strongly about expressing your opinions. If you can do so in a collaborative manner, go for it. It's likely, however, you'll need to sacrifice what you want [call it individualism] for what you need [which is community]."

Psychologists teach the "social identity theory," which reminds us we're meant to belong to a group.[5] We are social creatures who flourish only when living and serving within a community. Globally today, however, more people than ever travel alone, dine alone, and live alone. Trends now show we are drifting away from an essential community. I believe work teams can play a role in defeating this trend.

STRATEGIES THAT ENABLE GEN ZERS TO BE TEAM PLAYERS

1. Discuss this truth about humanity's social contract.
If it's helpful, use this information to launch a conversation about the perks and price of participating in the social contract. You might use a whiteboard and list two columns, one containing the benefits of collaboration and community, and the other the benefits of going alone. Believe it or not, our world is experiencing a "loneliness pandemic." We know we need other people, but we're determined to avoid the hassle other people bring when they enter our world. We've all heard the saying, "If you want to go faster, travel alone. If you want to go further, travel together." Discuss what they value most and what you value most.

2. Assign a task that requires them to ask for help.
One of the best remedies for both loneliness and individualism is to give the person a task that they cannot do alone, one that requires them to approach teammates for help. Each of us are designed to be part of something bigger than ourselves, and I believe many young adults have not experienced that yet. To be honest, I'm convinced most people want to be part of something that's very important and almost impossible. Why not force the issue and give them an assignment that's too big for them and watch them collaborate?

3. Teach them there is such a thing as "duty."
For all that we "want to do," there will be some "ought to do" activities we must embrace. If this is their first full-time job, you may need to host this conversation. I've met members of Gen Z who feel they shouldn't have to do something that compromises what they want to do. This sentiment is nothing short of immature. Remind them of the "duties" other team members perform that

the entire team (including them) benefit from. Help them see the larger benefits of belonging. When we're selfish, we usually lose more than we gain.

4. Explain Pyrrhic victories.

A Pyrrhic victory occurs when someone wins an argument but loses more than they gain. This centuries-old term comes from King Pyrrhus. His army defeated an enemy at a devastating cost. When he was congratulated on his victory, he replied, "One more such victory and I shall be lost." These victories happen daily at work and at home when we win a battle but lose a war. We debate customers, spouses, and colleagues due to our egos and fail to see we may lose a relationship. Teach Gen Z to ask: Is this issue worth debating? Why do I want to win? What will it cost me to insist on my own way? Avoiding Pyrrhic victories can save a team.

5. Ask them: If everyone lived the way you do, what kind of world would we have?

When selfish moods arise, imagine the world if all of us lived this way all the time. Have them describe the way they truly want to live, then visualize what the team would look like if every person lived that way. Discuss it. Show them that the best life is one of support and accountability. Retaining these communities of support and accountability deepens our happiness, diminishes our loneliness, and increases our sense of purpose.

THE VALUE OF SEEING THE BIG PICTURE

As I write this, I'm on a flight from Manila to Tokyo. It's about 10:00 a.m., we've just enjoyed our breakfasts, and a flight attendant is now making her rounds asking each person to close their window shades so that others can sleep. It wasn't bedtime, but I watched each passenger kindly lower their shade on behalf of others. Not one person refused, demanding their individual right to look out the window. Call it a collective sense of community we each felt. "*I want to belong*" trumped "*I want to be me.*"

Years ago, I heard the story of four young men who chose to climb a snowy mountain in the Alps. As they ascended the mountain, they faced a strong wind that turned into a blizzard. It was too much for one of them. The freezing temperatures got the best of him, and he fell into the snow, unconscious. The other three debated what to do, and two of them concluded they had to go on. They would all freeze to death if they didn't continue to the other side of the mountain. The fourth climber would not leave his friend to die in the snow. So while the other two marched ahead, he placed his buddy on his shoulders and climbed more slowly. Hours later, he found the two who insisted on moving faster lying in the snow. They had frozen to death. The fourth climber had actually saved his own life by carrying his friend and benefiting from his body heat. Both were spared.

These kinds of sacrifices and compromises mark the power of belonging.

I opened this chapter by talking about my wife, Pam, a baby boomer, getting to dance with a professional, Derek Hough, a millennial. It was beautiful because they were on the same page; their expectations were aligned. Let's see if we can do this with Gen Z.

TALK IT OVER

1. The chapter reveals the need to align expectations between Gen Z employees and their supervisors, likening it to staying in step during a dance. How can leaders foster open conversations to bridge the gap between Gen Z's expectations and workplace realities?

2. Generation Z often values autonomy, quick results, and significant impact, yet the workplace operates

on principles like earning freedom through productivity and promotions through testing. How can organizations effectively communicate these principles while maintaining Gen Z's enthusiasm and engagement?

3. The chapter discusses the concept of quiet quitting and its impact on workplace culture. What proactive steps can leaders take to address and prevent quiet quitting while ensuring that team members feel valued and motivated to contribute fully?

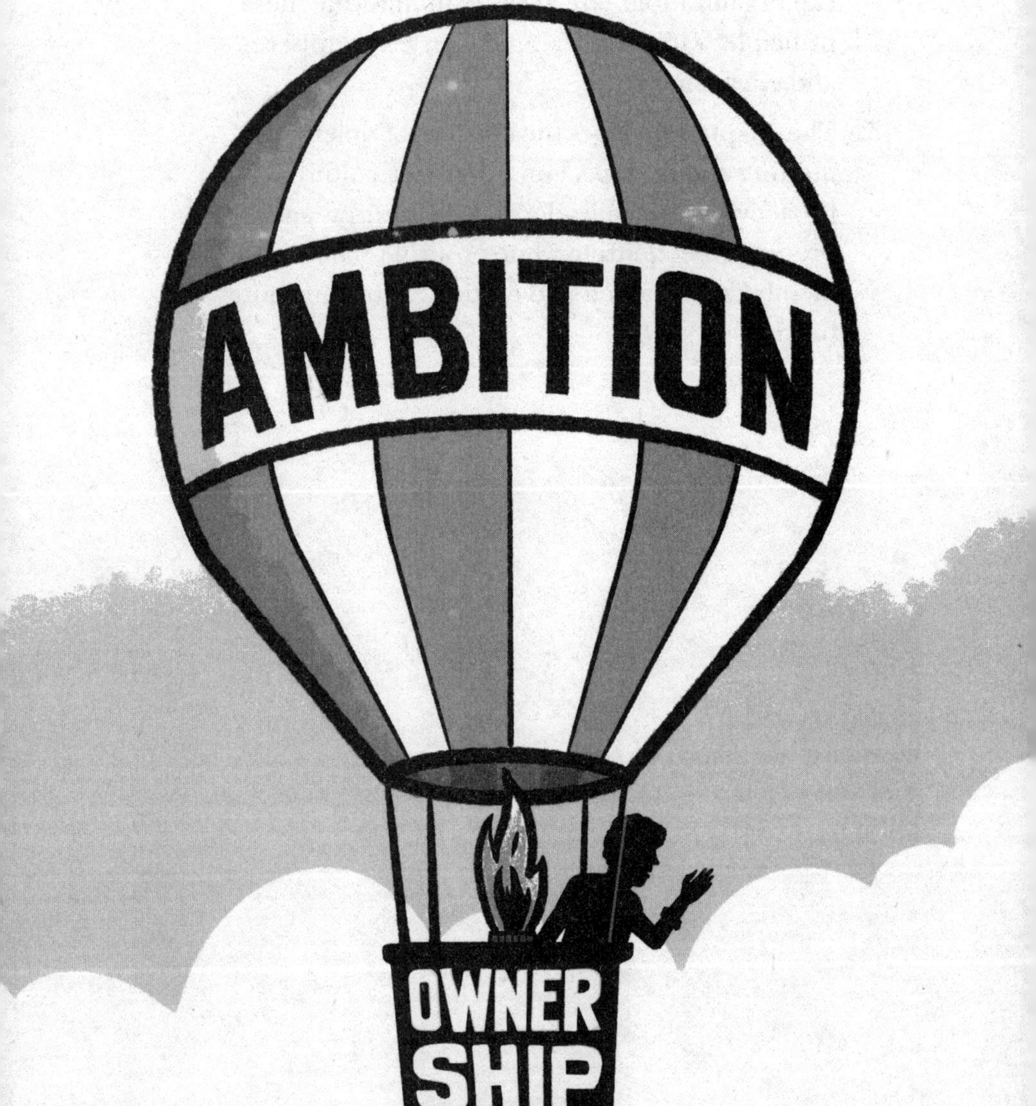
AMBITION
OWNER
SHIP

10

AWAKENING AMBITION

MOTIVATING AND INCENTIVIZING THEM

I have known Josiah Moore since he was born. He's a twenty-something who's ventured into a fascinating career as a commercial artist. His story represents the path so many young professionals are taking these days.

Josiah was attending Sheridan College, a prestigious art school in Ontario, Canada. As a student, he faced loans he began to feel uncomfortable carrying. So to reduce his debt, he decided to get a job and pay for his tuition along the way. This left him with a decision.

He wondered: What kind of job will cover my cost of living and let me stay in school?

He decided to freelance as a digital game designer during his second year of school. He admired the work others posted on Kickstarter and decided to post some of his work on it too. It paid off. Even without a degree from Sheridan, Josiah was asked to work on a small project for three months. The company was so pleased, they kept him on for a year and a half. Soon the workload was so demanding he faced another decision.

He wondered: Do I keep pursuing my degree or continue to make money?

He decided his opportunity to work was promising, and while Sheridan was a great school, it offered no guarantee of employment after graduation, only tuition debt. So he continued to enjoy working. The jobs proved to be both lucrative and satisfying. He loved seeing the results, the fruit of his labor. It beats a school assignment any day. And it provided him an incredible sense of ownership, a need we discussed earlier in this book.

Today, Josiah is a freelance artist and is flourishing. He told me, "These days, so many companies care more about your portfolio than a degree." On top of that, he explained, "When I saw the school curriculum for the third and fourth year, it was not nearly as valuable as what I was doing. I loved what I was learning both at school and at work, but the choice was a no-brainer. I had to pay for school, and I was getting paid for work."

Josiah has become a small-business entrepreneur. He told me, "It's all about providing a service to meet a need. The internet is the marketplace; and it's about finding places where people like and want my work." He's a member of community who creates content for digital games and has found a subculture who loves those games.

To be clear, Josiah does not claim to be some shrewd businessman. He simply makes use of the world in which he lives. Upon posting his work, momentum happened. He's now using his talent as much as he wants and making full-time income. I'm proud of him.

WHAT'S MOTIVATING ABOUT THIS SCENARIO?

When I pause and reflect on Josiah's story, the pattern is clear to me, a pattern that is true for many young professionals today:

> He gets to be the boss of his own calendar.
> He gets to choose how he'll use his gifts.
> He posts his work so he can get noticed.
> He works hard because he owns the work.
> He gets to figure it all out on his own terms.

My question for you is this: Is there a way your workplace could provide anything close to this scenario? It would motivate Gen Z. While every member of Generation Z has a unique personality, the cultural narrative for them is: we want to pioneer something fresh, updating and upgrading anything that feels obsolete; we want to harness AI; and we want to own what we do. Josiah's career reflects the research shared by Daniel Pink in his book *Drive*. He found that people no longer respond well to carrots and sticks (rewards and punishments) but flourish in work environments where they experience:

1. **Autonomy**—The team member gets to operate without micromanaging.
2. **Mastery**—The team member believes they are mastering their tasks.
3. **Purpose**—The team member believes they contribute to a larger mission.[1]

Does your staff experience these? Incidentally, Josiah's older sister, Alaina, has her own story, illustrating how motivation works. She and her husband, Patrick, began posting music they'd written and performed. People saw it, then subscribed and followed. Soon thousands were following. They formed a band called Tennis, did concert tours, and the crowds got bigger and bigger. Eventually an executive from Sony Music asked to take them to dinner. While his big offer was flattering, Alaina and Patrick had heard horror stories of record labels who bought music and controlled it, sometimes never releasing it to the public.

They turned the offer down and chose to grow organically, maintaining their intellectual property. They signed with smaller labels who were committed to developing talent rather than going for the fast money and maintained more of their rights and autonomy. By 2016, the two launched their own record label, called Mutually Detrimental, a tongue-in-cheek commentary on what happens to musicians and labels today. Tennis's first self-produced album, *Yours Conditionally*, was released in 2017 on Mutually Detrimental. The album was a commercial success, debuting at number three on Billboard's Alternative Albums chart and number two on the Vinyl Albums chart. What does Tennis love besides creating and playing music? The fact that nobody owns them.

Younger generations often prefer to start something than join something.

HOW DO WE FOSTER AMBITION?

This chapter illustrates how Generation Z might just make you a better leader because of who they are and how they approach work. We'll look at ideas to inspire and motivate them. As I've hinted at already—it's not just about traditional factors like money or titles. It's often about building a sense of ownership in them.

A report from Johns Hopkins University summarized our challenge well: "Every few years, a new generation joins the workforce, bringing with it its own set of qualities, traits, and values. For example, when searching for employment, baby boomers sought job security, Generation X sought work-life balance and professional progress, and now, millennials and Generation Z seek everything from a company's ethics to a decent work-life balance. These distinctions have an influence on how employees interact and are managed."[2]

This should encourage us to consider—how does motivating a twenty-something differ from motivating a fifty-something? For example, a boomer or Gen Xer might be highly motivated by a corner office, a bonus, and a C-suite position. A Gen Zer might say they prefer more flexibility, autonomy, and some help paying off college debt. It works like buying a gift for someone on a birthday or holiday. You consider the person before purchasing a present for them, right? Getting a generic pair of socks for Uncle Bob and for your teenage niece won't thrill either of them. Why? You didn't put any thought into who they are or what they value. Gratitude increases as the receiver recognizes how thoughtful you were. The same is true with motivation. Did your leadership match your receiver?

> **PAUSE AND REFLECT**
>
> What do you imagine motivates your Gen Zers on the job?

FROM STAPLES TO HOBBIES

On the chart in chapter 2, I provided the results of my research on how various generations view work and career. Views have evolved over the last century, and we can avoid an unnecessarily strange conversation by understanding this issue. Let's do a quick review of each generation's viewpoint on jobs based on the culture that shaped them. A century ago, the Builder generation entered the workforce, on the heels of the Great Depression and World War II. Few were talking about "finding their passion and purpose." The goal was to find a job that provided for a family. It was an exchange of money for talent. At the end of your career, you got a gold watch. Today—the times have changed.

The boomers: jobs are a central focus.
Baby boomers, born between 1946 and 1964, grew up in a time of idealism, optimism, and lots of change. Their parents had

memories of V-E Day in World War II, as America surfaced as the major world power. Hope filled the air as shopping malls popped up everywhere and quick-service restaurants were franchising. Families with lots of kids were everywhere (hence the name baby boomer), which led to heavy job competition for the 76.4 million young professionals in this demographic. Outside of those protesting the Vietnam War, millions placed their career front and center and still focus on it to this day. Often, when a Gen Zer looks at a boomer, they see a "workaholic," and they don't want to repeat that mistake. They saw how it added stress, consumed time, and ruined families. If they were honest, Gen Z would say to a boomer: "You live to work. We work to live."

Generation X: jobs are a necessity to endure.
Gen Xers entered their careers in the shadow of the 1970s and '80s, when times had evolved into a season of turmoil and distrust for leaders. The Vietnam War drew mixed reviews at best as news footage looked very different from the story President Johnson was spinning. As the war ended, the Watergate scandal took center stage, which deepened the mistrust in our country. In the subsequent years, we endured the OPEC gas crisis, huge inflation, and a failed rescue attempt for American hostages in Iran. As a result, Gen X entered their careers a bit jaded; corporate America felt greedy and corrupt. They longed for authenticity as they began their careers in workplaces that seemed pretentious. They viewed work as a necessity to put up with; the phrase TGIF surfaced: Thank God It's Friday. Gen X, by and large, looked elsewhere for fulfillment—likely not their jobs or careers.

The millennials: jobs are a place to serve.
These were the kids of the 1980s and 1990s. Both of my children are part of this generation. They are called millennials because they'll spend their entire adult life in a new millennium, the twenty-first century. Times had shifted again. Kids grew up in a

more hopeful time, where the economy expanded again, where innovation and technology played a huge role in how people felt and thought. Start-ups were everywhere, and Bill Gates and Steve Jobs became household names. Millennials are the largest generation in US history (even bigger than the baby boomers), and by and large, they grew up hearing about changing the world and making it a better place. Jobs were connected to this big goal, and young adults entered a job not merely to make money but to make a difference. We soon learned they would even take a job or leave a job based on how the company benefited the community.

Generation Z: it's my hobby.
This cohort joining the workforce today was shaped not only by the media but by social media. (They spend more hours on their phone screens than their TV screens.) Those smartphones have been a source of both entertainment and anxiety. As I met younger Gen Zers, they described work as a duty, something their parents made them do. Yet joining the workforce over the last several years, they've seen employers lay off or fire people abruptly. During the pandemic, which is indelibly etched in their memories, they saw huge layoffs as they began their careers. As new hires, they were often the first ones to be let go. Workplaces came to be seen as machines, and employees were only tools. Natalie, a Gen Z professional, said to me: "I love staying busy, so I don't mind work, but I won't give any more than forty hours a week and not a minute more unless I'm paid. This organization isn't giving me any more than the bare minimum, so that's what I'm doing. I am part of a machine. I feel replaceable so I will look at this company the same way."

So how have jobs come to be viewed as a hobby?

To survive the current job climate, Gen Z has chosen to be picky. We all know retailers or restaurants who are always looking to hire more workers or wait staff but Generation Z, unlike past generations, is not as quick to take many of these entry-level jobs.

They're looking for work that feels like it fits them, something that is fun and that they enjoy. One of their big fears is ending up in a career that they hate or that is unsatisfying. So, in one sense, they look at work like a hobby. In several focus groups with people, ages sixteen to twenty-six, this idea came up repeatedly: a hobby. At first, this feels wrong to employers. Bosses who have heard this said to me, "That's problematic. In fact, it's foolishness. A job isn't a hobby; I am paying them to produce results. I pay them to work hard and get a job done." Another employer added, "That's why we call it 'work.'"

But what if we reimagined work?

Reflect for a moment on a hobby in your past. Perhaps growing up you had a hobby like stamp collecting or baseball cards or even a train set in your basement. (I had all three of these when I was a kid.) If you really enjoy that hobby, the times goes fast. You might even lose track of the time. Your best work may take place at midnight, not noon. Why not enable Gen Zers to do this on their job? What if we profiled their tasks as a hobby, where they can get to the goal their way, not just our way? What if we shared the outcome we desired (as a supervisor) and let them choose the steps they'd take to reach it?

Obviously, once they attempted the task, they'd be much more likely to receive input from you. Your history on the job will help them reach their goal faster. But you let them own the job, like a hobby. You value outcomes more than inputs, meaning the steps toward the goal are not nearly as important as reaching the goal. They get to choose the inputs, like a hobby they're passionate about. Consider Josiah and Alaina's stories above. He creates digital games and she creates music. We use the term *playing* video games and *playing* music, don't we? And yet they are working.

> As each year begins, what if you met and discussed how to approach work like a hobby?

TURNING WORK INTO PLAY

Evelyn Glennie was a teenager when she applied to one of the most elite conservatories in the UK. For four years she'd practiced as a musician—a percussionist to be exact—and at this point, Evelyn felt ready. Sadly, the Royal Academy of Music didn't accept her. Multiple experts expressed concerns for her lack of ability and concluded she had no hope as a professional musician. Surprisingly, less than ten years later, Evelyn became the world's first full-time percussion soloist. Normally drummers are part of a larger orchestra or band who play in the background. But not Evelyn. She's won three Grammy Awards as well as awards for Best Chamber Music Performance and Best Classical Crossover Album. Not long ago, she was the first percussionist to win the Polar Music Prize, the music equivalent of a Nobel Peace Prize. Glennie was even knighted by the queen of England.

So, what happened? What took Evelyn Glennie from a person who lacked ability and didn't have an ear for music to a prize-winning performer? You should know that when the Royal Music Academy concluded she lacked ability they weren't wrong. Technically, she didn't have an ear for music; in fact, she could not really hear at all. The world's first solo percussionist is legally deaf. Evelyn lost her hearing in elementary school. Over time, a percussion teacher named Ron Forbes taught her to play without good ears, and his strategy was genius. Instead of convincing her to grind through tedious drills in music, he gave her a framework to see music like a fun hobby. She adopted a different learning style, learning to sense the vibrations in her arms, her stomach, her cheeks, and her scalp. She saw her whole body as a giant ear. She started practicing barefoot to feel the vibrations more intensely. It was interesting and even energizing for her.

When organizational psychologist Adam Grant spoke to her about her music, Evelyn said she loved the challenge that Forbes had given her, raising the bar, as she mastered various levels.

Evelyn said, "I was like a sponge!" Yet her greatest explanation for her achievement surfaced when she said, "There was never a distinction between fun and hard work."

Grant went on to explain, "We're often told that if we want to develop our skills, we need to push ourselves through long hours of monotonous practice. But the best way to unlock hidden potential isn't to suffer through the daily grind. It's to transform the daily grind into a source of daily joy. It's not a coincidence that in music, the term for practice is 'play.'"[3]

If we could help Gen Z profile what they do at work as a source of passion and even fun, it will make a radical difference. What did Mary Poppins say to Jane and Michael Banks? "In every job that must be done, there is an element of fun. You find the fun and snap! The job's a game." We must help young teammates develop a passion for the play of a task.

Passion is a descriptive word for what we feel when we are active in a hobby. We move from "I have to do this" to "I want to do this" and eventually to "I get to do this!" The value of passion isn't limited to music, either. In 127 studies involving more than forty-five thousand people, persistence was more likely to translate into performance when passion was present.[4]

I'll never tire of telling the story of Burberry Coats in London. In 2006, the luxury coat brand was in decline, and Angela Ahrendts was invited to become the CEO. Their customer base needed to grow beyond "rich, older ladies" and include a new generation. So what did Angela do? She met with her youngest employees (including interns) and brainstormed with them: *What should we do to reach your generation?* They came up with ideas for the website and creative steps in their stores.

Between 2006 and 2014 (when Angela left), the brand more than doubled in revenue. Angela would say it was because she turned conventional wisdom on its ear. Instead of asking her executive team for ideas and telling the young staff to implement them, she enlisted her younger staff to come up with ideas. She said, "In a way, we're right back to our roots. I always remind employees that we didn't found the company. Thomas Burberry did—at the age of twenty-one. He was young. He was innovative. We say that his spirit lives on, and that it's this generation's job to keep his legacy going." Angela tapped into the passion of her young team. I bet it felt like a hobby.

> **PAUSE AND REFLECT**
> How can profiling "work" differently be a game changer for your Gen Zers?

VIEW OF WORK: IT'S MY HOBBY

Let's talk about profiling work as a hobby, as my Gen Z focus groups have described it. This may feel like mere semantics, but the way people view situations makes a lot of difference in how they approach them. Below are clear and simple terms to profile work as a hobby.

H—It can be a source of *happiness*, not drudgery.

Like a good hobby, their job can be the source of satisfaction and fulfillment. Something they see as challenging yet worthwhile as they develop their gifts. It is an extension of themselves. And like with a good hobby, people engage for a different reason; they may do their best work at midnight, not midday. Work can actually offer meaning to life.

O—It can be approached as an *opportunity*, not an obligation.

What if we profiled their job as an occasion to contribute? What if they saw it as an opportunity, not an obligation? Something they get to do instead of have to do. This can turn a negative emotion into a positive one, using the same energy. It's the difference between saying you are nervous and you are excited. The approach can be a difference maker.

B—It can be seen with a *broad* perspective, not as a boring task.
When a young team member feels they've been given a job that's beneath them, it doesn't feel good. It feels mundane. What if you could help them see how their tasks are connected to the broader scope of the organization's mission? Would it feel different if they saw how their effort directly tied into the big picture? We must show them the lid of the puzzle box.

Which of these ideas could you improve upon as you lead Gen Z?

B—It can *build* them into a more knowledgeable person.
Above all, it can be a source of development and growth, professionally and personally. Since Gen Z values learning and improvement, remind them how they will become more valuable with each year they serve. It can prepare them for that ideal job in the future. What they'll learn at work will grow them into better teammates and maybe even quality leaders.

Y—It can *yield* many positive benefits.
As opposed to working a hobby from home, work furnishes social connections. It engages your talents, it can boost your brain activity, and it helps to pay your bills. It's easy to focus on the faults and flaws of colleagues, but we do well to remember that a steady job offers all kinds of social capital. Depending on the workplace, jobs can yield amazing advantages.

CHANGING YOUR APPROACH

Like those in every young population, Generation Z includes all kinds of personalities, both extroverts and introverts; optimists and pessimists; initiators and responders. Certainly, there is not one right way to engage young professionals. But—as a sociological cohort—Gen Z demonstrates they view work differently than my generation does and will need us to adapt and lead them differently. My question for you? Are you willing to adapt to connect and engage them at the heart level? Here are three shifts I made.

1. Don't appeal to their sense of duty; appeal to the significance of the task.

As a rule, boomers and Xers are old school. They value duty, punctuality, work ethic, and so on. While these are noble and some jobs require punctuality, expecting Gen Z to share these values from the beginning may be a stretch. What if you appealed to the importance of the task you've given them or built a sense of passion for its significance to the mission? Early on, my wife and I appealed to our daughter's sense of obligation (that is, you should attend this event), but it never motivated her. Once we shifted to reminding her of how the event aligned with her passion or to its significance, we got buy-in. At work, a leader may explain to seasoned veterans why launching a new product is a responsible decision. To younger employees, however, that leader might use a different tactic, clarifying that a new product will bring all kinds of value to people, increase customer leads, and result in bonuses that quarter.

2. Don't appeal to "majority rules"; appeal to equity for everyone.

In my early career, many of our team decisions were based on the majority benefiting from those decisions. In short, it was a democratic choice. It reflected our American rationale. Since Gen Z values the marginalized and the outlier, the democratic process isn't always motivating for them. They wonder how decisions affect the outsider, the minority. This is noble, but it may require you to change how you clarify actions you take and choices you make. For example, it makes sense to employees over forty-five years old that a choice is best for the majority, but those under thirty need to know it provides equity for the minority. Explain how the marginalized also gain from the decision and how it improves their condition. Gen Z must see that the lowest-paid staff people, not just the leaders, gain from the choice.

3. Don't appeal to morals; appeal to the benefit they'll receive.

I am a man of values; living by my moral standards is important to me. They drive my major decisions in life and at work. It's all about doing the right thing. I soon learned that it's different for many Gen Z team members. It's not that they don't have values; it's just that black-and-white morality is not the norm for them. As a generation, they value inclusivity and tolerance. Personal convictions feel intolerant. So leaders may get more mileage out of appealing to the benefits of a decision, not that it's right or wrong. Describe the personal plusses or bonuses it represents for the team members. Years ago, our team discussed a decision our leaders had made, and I explained our board felt it was the right thing to do. I noticed that those over forty-five years old nodded in agreement, but those under thirty stared at me with a blank face. It was then I appealed to the practical advantages of this decision. Their countenance changed. Soon, everyone got on board.

TWO METAPHORS TO FRAME YOUR CONVERSATIONS

For this chapter, I have two Habitudes that will inform you as you motivate Generation Z. Here are my Habitudes for leaders:

Chess and Checkers

Think about these two games. While they're both played on the same game board, they are very different. In checkers, all your pieces look alike and move alike. In chess, all your pieces are different and move differently. I believe wise leaders play "chess" with their people, not checkers. They recognize people are motivated differently and possess different strengths. These leaders connect with people based on their strengths, personality, and generation, and those people flourish. As a leader, I discover:

1. Their strengths and weaknesses
2. Their personality
3. Their triggers that motivate them
4. Their learning style

The Waldorf Principle

George Boldt ran a motel in a Pennsylvania town a century ago. When an elderly couple ventured into his motel from a storm, he couldn't turn them away, even though he had no vacancies. George gave this couple his personal room. The next day, the elderly man asked George for his name, saying that one day, he planned to build the finest hotel in the world—and because Boldt served him so sacrificially and extravagantly, he wanted him to run it. Years later he did. The man was William Waldorf Astor. He put Boldt in charge of the Waldorf Astoria Hotel in New York. But it wasn't because of George's keen intellect. It was how he honored his guests as he led. Below are seven paths to power with others (from lowest to highest), and George chose the highest path:

> **REFLECT**
> How could you inspire your Gen Zers by practicing these two metaphors?

1. Force (people feel threatened as you induce pain; people act unwillingly)
2. Manipulation (people feel coerced, as if they're backed into a corner)

3. Intimidation (people feel emotionally bullied and fear they may be fired)
4. Exchange (people see a transaction—you both give something to each other)
5. Persuasion (people are moved to cooperate through incentives you provide)
6. Motivation (people are inspired by your passion and sacrifice for the result)
7. Honor (people follow as you respect, value, and honor them through service)

TWO LEADERSHIP ACTS THAT DRIVE TEAMMATES TO GIVE MORE

I spoke to two NCAA athletes about their effort in a recent competition: one, a football player, and the other, a swimmer. The football player was a defensive lineman who admitted to me he gave a less than stellar effort in the last weekend's game. The swimmer, a sprinter on a relay team, overcame her opponent in the last leg of a race to win. When I asked about why they'd given the effort they had, their answers were telling. The lineman felt he'd done a fair job but knew he had two All-Americans on the line with him who were more capable of doing the "heavy lifting." The swimmer said she gave extra effort knowing her teammates were "counting on me."

So, why do some teams enjoy motivation and others don't?

Why does one person let his team down, while another sacrifices even more? Believe it or not, teamwork is motivating for some but demotivating for others. How come? The answer lies both in how we are hardwired and the environment in which we work.

In America, we've all heard the acronym for *team*: Together everyone accomplishes more. In German, one acronym for *team* is: "Great. Someone else will do it."

Psychologists have a term for people who reduce their effort when they team up with others: "social loafing." The idea that working on a team can lead people to give less effort is the target of much psychological study. Researchers from Ohio State University suggested that "social loafing can be regarded as a kind of social disease."[5] It lets teammates down and reduces their chance to win. We might assume working together would raise a team member's effort due to accountability. While it does for many, it doesn't for some. Research from the University of Florida argues that teamwork represents a social dilemma, in which people must choose between two options:

1. What is best for the team (sacrificing to achieve great team performance)
2. What is best for themselves (withholding personal effort to save resources)[6]

What teammates choose to do depends on how coaches lead their teams.

TWO KEY FACTORS TO COACH FOR TEAMWORK

Leading well involves understanding behavioral science. To get the most out of staff, we must understand two important factors: perception of dispensability and pulling triggers.

The Perception of Dispensability
When people who serve on a team perceive their work as dispensable—it doesn't make a meaningful contribution to the outcome of a team—they tend to show less effort than they would when working alone. It's a psychological perception. Subconsciously, these people feel their effort is not needed as much as others' efforts and that it makes sense to save their energy. On the other hand, when a

person is convinced that what they do is tied to the big picture goal and that it makes a huge difference on the overall outcome, they'll give mammoth effort. They feel their work is indispensable. In the first, their work feels redundant. In the other, it feels meaningful. The four most motivating words in the world are: "You make a difference." The six most depressing words are: "You really don't make a difference."

In the story above, the football lineman knew he had a job but felt his effort was not nearly as important as the two All-American athletes he stood next to on the line of scrimmage. In contrast, the swimmer gave "extra mile" effort for her teammates. Think of Kobe Bryant, who continued playing after he dislocated and then relocated his finger. Think of Curt Schilling, who continued pitching with a bleeding ankle in the World Series. Think of the times a key player got injured in the playoffs but teammates stepped up and gave superhuman effort to win. This effort doesn't make sense unless you understand motivation. Effective leaders clearly demonstrate to each of their team members how their personal work is tied to the overall mission and is absolutely essential to reaching the goal. They even take time to clarify what happens if that team member *fails* to fulfill their duty and its impact on the whole team. Our brains need this clarification and illustration to make sacrifices and endure pain. This is especially true for a young employee.

The Pulling of Triggers

The second component to motivating team members is recognizing the different emotional triggers people possess. Not everyone is driven by the same motivators. This is why leaders can make a difference when they tap into the triggers of each player, a little like playing with pieces in a game of chess as opposed to checkers. You treat them differently since they're different. For one, comparing their abilities to a teammate can be motivating, challenging them to step up their efforts; for others who perceive their abilities are so different from a teammate's, it can have the opposite effect. They will never catch up so what's the use? Great leaders remove the comparison trap and leverage triggers in each team member.

Three Triggers for Teamwork

> - Affiliation. This *social motivation* demonstrates I care for my teammates.
> - Results. This *outcome motivation* demonstrates I care deeply for the goal.
> - Influence. This *persuasion motivation* demonstrates I care to make an impact on the team.

In short, when we recognize some are motivated by not wanting to let their teammates down, we should tap into this trigger as we communicate. For another whose motivation is primarily to reach a goal, we should focus on outcomes. And for a third with "influence motivation," which is all about having an impact on the team to reach a goal, we should talk about their influence on others. It's important for coaches to not assume everyone can be motivated the same way. We must tailor our words to the listener. The bottom line for us?

1. Leaders must clarify the indispensability of teammates' assignments. The result: they feel they really matter.
2. Leaders must understand and leverage their teammates' triggers clearly. The result: they feel their leader knows them.

In the end, it's essential to move their motivation from *external* to *internal*. Outside accountability from you is fine, but ownership of their assignment is better. When leaders and teams perceive their individual effort is absolutely indispensable, it moves the needle. When we tap into what drives people internally, we turn average performance into amazing. How much talent a person has is not in our control, but how much effort they give is.

I opened this chapter by telling the story of Josiah and his sister Alaina. The fact is, another sister in the family, Ashley Rae, has a story of her own. Rae worked service jobs early in her career, but none were jobs she felt passionately about. She remembered her mother had taught her how to sew when she was seven, but it had been only a hobby. Rae enjoyed sewing clothes more than anything and wondered if this hobby could be a vocation. So she went for it. She met Kate, a professional seamstress, and took a bold step. Rae said, "If you'd be willing to coach me, I'll work on projects for you for free, just to learn."

Kate was a harsh leader and demanded hard work, but after six months of daily work without pay, Rae was offered a job where she got very good and made money doing her hobby. A decade later she moved to Los Angeles and worked on small projects until she got noticed. The rest is history. Rae began working for Seventh Bone Agency, a high-end tailoring company. Both the agency and Rae took a risk—but it has paid off big time. As of today Rae has designed garments for the Kardashians, Cher, the Jonas Brothers, Julia Louis-Dreyfus, and others. Not bad for a hobby. It's amazing what we'll do when we love our work.

TALK IT OVER

1. The chapter emphasizes Gen Z's preference for autonomy, mastery, and purpose over traditional motivators like money or titles. How can organizations design roles and environments that align with these motivational drivers to inspire greater ambition and productivity?

2. The idea of treating work like a hobby suggests allowing employees more freedom in how they approach tasks. What strategies could leaders use to balance this freedom with the need for accountability and measurable outcomes?

3. The chapter introduces the importance of understanding individual motivators, such as affiliation, results, and influence. How can managers effectively identify and leverage these triggers to inspire their Gen Z team members to reach their full potential?

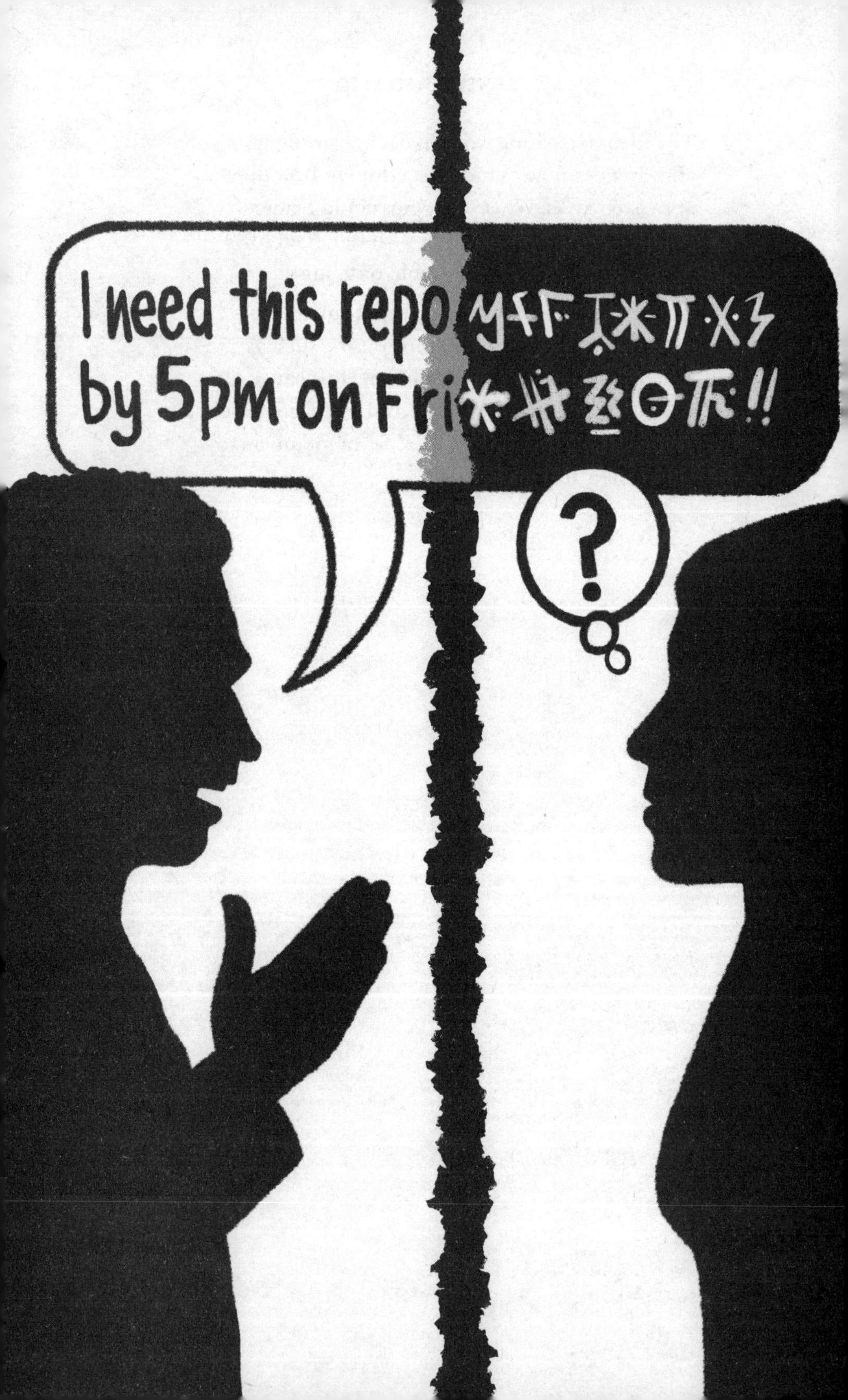
I need this repo
by 5pm on Fri
?

11

TAPPERS AND LISTENERS

HOW TO GET THROUGH TO THEM

In 1990, Elizabeth Newton performed her PhD project at Stanford, called "Tappers and Listeners." Chip and Dan Heath mention it in their book *Made to Stick*. It was a simple exercise where a group of individuals was divided into two teams. The first team was called "tappers," and their job was to choose a song from a list of twenty-five well-known songs (such as "Happy Birthday" or "The Star-Spangled Banner") and tap out the song on a table with their fingers. The second team was the listeners. Their job was to simply guess the song by the rhythm being tapped. Sound simple?

In reality, the listener's job was quite difficult. Of the 120 songs that were tapped out in Newton's experiment, only three were guessed correctly. That's 2.5 percent. Not a very good score. Now here's what made the experiment newsworthy. Before they began, each tapper was asked to predict the odds of their listeners getting the song right. The tappers predicted their odds were 50 percent.

They thought they would get their message across one time out of two. Interestingly, the tappers got their message across only one time in forty. Why? It's simple. When tappers tap a song out, they're hearing the song in their head. Most listeners didn't hear the song at all, even though they heard the beat. These tappers were stunned at how hard the listeners were working to guess the song.[1] Isn't it obvious?

Unfortunately, this little exercise is repeated daily in workplaces across our country, especially when it comes to communicating with Gen Z. You have a clear message in your head, but somewhere between your lips and their ears, the message gets lost in translation. You assume they'll "get it." It's simple. The fact is, their minds are in so many different places before hearing you speak—their biases may cause them to misunderstand the message you're sending. One supervisor said her young employees were "good with portable devices but not with people; they're social but not relational."

"The single biggest problem in communication is the illusion that it has taken place," wrote George Bernard Shaw. I think he's right. Time and time again, managers say one thing, young employees hear another, and there's a clash over the interpretations.

UNDERSTANDING THE PROBLEM

On top of this challenge, young job candidates may arrive with little to no work experience. In fact, most of the communication problems with Gen Z on the job surround:

> Professionalism. The young employee doesn't understand proper conduct or communication.
> Engagement. The young employee isn't engaged on the job or doesn't care to meet standards.

For example, numerous office managers have told me when they've called a meeting to discuss an important issue, a Gen Z team member will reply that the time doesn't fit their schedule, then add a digital link for the manager to choose a spot on their calendar when the Gen Zer is available. They are unaware of authority structures and assume their boss will work around their schedule.

I had a difficult time believing two human resource executives in a focus group. I asked each of them about their experiences with communicating to Generation Z. Were they different or the same as past younger generations entering their teams?

Two of them shared that in the middle of a job interview, the Gen Z job candidates got a call on their mobile device, and they both took it. Yep, during the interview. The hiring managers sat for an awkward moment listening in and waiting to resume the interview. One of Gen Zers asked the caller to wait a moment, then covered his phone and asked the hiring manager to step out of her office so he could take the call.

You can't make this stuff up.

Obviously, those young job seekers were not trying to be rude. They were there to get a job. It was simply normal to take a call if the person on their smartphone looked interesting; no one taught them that an interview is an inappropriate place to take one. Job interviews were new for them. Phones were not.

The truth is, each new generation for over a century has created language and habits that they understand but for which other generations need translations. Over the last few years, phrases such as "left no crumbs" or "say less" or "what's poppin', slime?" have raised a few eyebrows on the faces of those over forty-five years old. And ghosting became normal.

And now, those Gen Zers serve on our teams. Some are already leading.

DEFINING OUR CHALLENGE

Generation Z brings differences not only in their communication but also in their preferences for communication. What's more, they often need more explanation from you on your directions than older generations do. Getting through to them may require offering a "why" before your "what." Getting through clearly and convincingly is a must for leaders today. This chapter offers ideas on how to get Gen Zers to engage and "own" your request.

Sadly, we live in the "information age" but not the "communication age." It seems we are becoming poorer at good communication as time marches on. According to Sydney Harris, "The two words *information* and *communication* are often used interchangeably, but they signify quite different things. Information is giving out; communication is getting through."[2]

Melanie got her first job the summer following graduation and was excited to show her supervisor her skill set. Unfortunately, she got in her own way. She brought her cell phone to orientation and kept checking incoming texts during the training. This irritated her manager. In addition, when she was late getting a project done and was criticized, she got defensive in an email. (She broke rule number one by sending emotionally charged messages electronically.) When team members began growing distant, her supervisor asked her if she had any idea why. She did not. That's when Melanie got a crash course in communication from her boss:

> Screens are for information, not for emotion.
> Leave your phone at your desk when attending meetings.
> With two ears and one mouth, we should listen twice as much as talk.
> If possible, begin discussions face-to-face before using phones or email.

Albert Mehrabian, author of *Silent Messages,* conducted several studies on communication. He found that 7 percent of any message is conveyed through words, 38 percent through tone and attitude, and 55 percent through nonverbal elements (such as facial expression, gestures, and posture).[3] This means 93 percent of communication has nothing to do with words and can't be done well from a screen. So how do we do it well?

Authentic communication usually requires me to step into the shoes of the Gen Zer I'm speaking with and imagine what they will need to understand my message. What words will best be comprehended? What voice tone should I use? Do I need to give an example of my point? Should I ask a question? How can I listen well and earn my right to speak? What methods for communicating should I use: email, text, phone call, Slack, social media, or face-to-face conversation? These are all legitimate questions if you care about getting your message across. According to psychologist Rollo May, "Communication leads to community, that is, to understanding, intimacy, and mutual valuing."[4] Even though it is work, good communication is always worth the benefits it yields.

THREE HOOKS TO HELP YOU CONNECT WITH GEN Z

Sometimes, a good "hook" helps me follow through on what I intend to do as I lead. Let me offer you three hooks or metaphors to cling to as you attempt to connect with Gen Z. When I struggle to get through to a young teammate, these hooks (which I briefly mention in other parts of the book) help me establish the right mindset.

HOOK ONE: Think Foreign

The same effort required to interact with someone in a foreign country may be required interacting with someone from a different generation. If you flew to Thailand, for example, as you landed you'd mentally prepare to work hard to communicate with a local person there. Why? They speak a different language, embrace different values, and practice different customs. Bingo. This is true about Gen Z members. If we're willing to do the work to connect in Thailand, why not here at home? What if we committed to work that hard at communicating with Generation Z?

HOOK TWO: Think Gifts

You can always tell the people who understand how to give good gifts at either birthdays or at holidays. They're the ones who spend time observing what Uncle Charlie or your niece Ashley really wants for a gift. A simple pair of socks doesn't thrill anyone. Generic gifts are not nearly as appreciated as gifts chosen specifically for the person receiving them. Good leaders communicate personally with the receiver in mind. Their style, tone, and language match the receiver, like a good gift, and that person can tell you're invested in them. This includes feedback, rewards, motivation, you name it.

HOOK THREE: Think Highlighters

When I read a good book, I use four differently colored highlighters to mark up the text. One is for good quotes, another for stories, another for research, and another one for key content. Each serves a role in helping me benefit from the book. Just like my colored highlighters represent different facets, different generations highlight various perspectives that organizations can gain from. Each sees issues slightly differently, including Gen Z. You must value each one. Be sure to let Gen Z highlight your work from their perspective. They may have visibility on cultural realities that you don't.

> Consider some situations you could practice these "hooks" to help you connect.

COMMUNICATION COMFORT ZONES AND PREFERRED ZONES

The research is interesting on Generation Z and communication. The data show that Gen Z is most comfortable working from home and communicating on a screen, but they prefer to be in person with the team and to build relationships. Here are the comfort zones of each generation in the office today:

- Boomers: email, phone, or in-person conversation
- Gen Xers: email, text, or phone
- Millennials: text and Slack messages
- Gen Zers: digital

While this is accurate data gathered from all four generations, note that Generation Z's communication *preferences* differ from their *comfort zone*. They feel most at home on a screen, but they distinctly want in-person contact at work. In fact, they requested it more clearly than any other generation. My theory is—while they like the comfort of hiding behind a screen (don't we all?), they recognize they need to build social capital, and the quickest way to do that is to interact face-to-face, getting to know colleagues, discovering what makes them tick, and letting them know what makes you tick.

According to a report from Johns Hopkins University, Gen Z wants improved in-person interaction. Fifty-one percent of Gen Zers prefer speaking to friends, family, and coworkers face-to-face rather than by text.[5] I suggest businesses can nurture this mentality by:

- Suggesting video calls over phone calls
- Choosing frequent gatherings to offer Gen Z a personal connection they need

- Having managers check in frequently, provide insightful input, and schedule weekly feedback and performance evaluations
- Organizing social activities that promote team bonding

COMMUNICATION GEN Z NEEDS FROM US IN TIMES OF DISRUPTION

The toughest time to send a message is during times of disruption, anxiety, and confusion.

People need leaders who offer clear boundaries, tangible targets to hit, and the confidence that they can reach those goals. This is even more true in ambiguous times.

Leaders must remember first that people under their care have different temperaments and will react to anxiety differently. People need three items most from their leader in tough times. After collecting data on communicating with Gen Z since the pandemic, I saw a pattern. Wise leaders seemed to understand their people and offered them three gifts.

1. Context—*This offers perspective.*

Max De Pree wisely taught us *the first job of the leader is to define reality.* We must clarify where things stand in a realistic manner when life feels confusing or unfamiliar. I discovered that during uncertain and disruptive times, people need context to minimize anxiety and panic. I reminded our team that COVID-19 was the fourth pandemic we faced in the last century, and we not only made it through each one, we made progress. It busted the myth that we've never seen anything like this before and gave context. People need perspective from their leader.

2. Applications—*This offers clarity.*

Especially in times of disruption or confusion, people need clear objectives and action steps to take. People need boundaries, clear targets, and a path to pursue the vision. Clarity is the greatest gift a leader can offer their people. My friend Andy Stanley reminds us: "We can all live without certainty; we do it all the time. But we cannot live well without clarity. It gives us energy." During the ambiguous 2020 year, I told our team we don't know what next year holds, but we do know this week: we have two priorities to work on; please work from home and limit your daily news watching to an hour.

3. Belief—*This offers hope.*

More than ever, people need inspiration from their leaders to stay steady and to continue. When leaders express that they not only believe the organization will make it through this difficult time but will be better for it, it instills belief in followers. After one difficult time, I shared with our team how we improved and found new systems to use. It sparked new energy in teammates to see how a disadvantage can become an advantage. Confidence begets confidence. Gen Z must be led from both the head and the heart—and belief is from the heart of the leader to the heart of the team. Napoleon Bonaparte said: "Leaders are dealers of hope."

> **REFLECT**
>
> Have you been successful communicating with Gen Zers in tough times?

Those three words above spell CAB. While it sounds cheesy, when I meet with young staff who are feeling anxious about a situation, I tell myself: *I gotta hop in a CAB to reach my goal.* Communicating these three fundamentals can meet their need for assurance.

BECOMING AN EPIC COMMUNICATOR

The best leaders have changed the way they communicate ideas and initiatives to Gen Z team members. Leonard Sweet, a long-distance mentor, taught me something years ago that I have attempted to practice ever since, especially with young staff. To explain it in a memorable way, I'll use an acronym: EPIC. I strive to be an EPIC communicator:

E—Experiential

Too often, leaders remain bland and forgettable because they use only words to say something. Gen Z is an experiential generation; they are not looking for a "sage on the stage" with a lecture but a "guide on the side" with an experience. The best leaders create an environment or an experience for team members that sets up their message. In fact, listeners stay engaged because it's not just a talking head up front.

For example, I took a group of young staff out to a graveyard before hosting a discussion on thinking long term and making long-range plans. I had them pair up, walk around the gravestones, and read the epitaphs. They did this for ten minutes. Afterward, we made a circle, and I asked them: "What did you read?" One replied, "Well, I noticed that some people lived a long time and others did not. Some died really young." Another said, "I saw that some people had really nice things said about them, while others . . . not so much." This continued for another few minutes before I asked the big question: "What will people say on your gravestone? Will it just be about how much money you made, or how funny you were, or your car?" Each began to think about the one sentence they'd want others to remember them by. It was emotional for some and set up a great opportunity for me to communicate the power of focus, priorities, and long-range planning.

On another occasion, I spoke to my first-year staff while at a bakery. We sat outside, and as we enjoyed our bagels and cinnamon rolls, our waiter came by to remove some plates. I asked him, "What's your favorite menu item at this bakery?" He smiled and replied, "Oh, I don't eat anything here. I just serve it to customers." The waiter was a friend of mine who discussed with me his personal growth plan each year. I had planned this experience to spark a discussion on a Habitude called "The Starving Baker." The metaphor is the baker who spends all his time baking bread for others and never eats it himself. We discussed the practice of planning our personal growth and ensuring we feed ourselves intellectually, emotionally, and even spiritually to avoid burnout.

P—Participatory

This one is key for Generation Z. They want to participate in deciding where a project or an initiative is going; in fact, they want to have a say in where your message is taking them. If it's a typical message you give each year, they wonder: Is it any different this year because they're involved? Will it feel like it's theirs and they own it? I learned a principle a long time ago: "People support what they help create." They want to upload their thoughts not just listen to you download yours. Kara Powell, from the Fuller Youth Institute, put it this way: "What young people are telling us is that they want to actively cocreate, not passively watch."[6] It's messier and riskier—but the impact is well worth it.

I've stood in front of our first-year staff and placed a set of images on the screen. The slide looked like a Bingo card of pictures. Each represented a topic I wanted them to embrace, but it felt like they had a "say" in the message because I let them choose which images to focus on in our hour together. Again, it was not merely me delivering my thoughts but the listeners directing the conversation. When I let people weigh in, I usually get buy-in.

A friend of mine teaches college biology and chose to put this principle into practice. She began her class each semester by passing out the syllabus. Inevitably, students would ask questions that she had already addressed in the syllabus. (They obviously weren't reading it.) So she scrapped that strategy and began her class by letting the students create the syllabus and determine how the class would go. She started by asking, "This is biology. What do you want to talk about regarding the subject?" Interestingly, she told me they listed the very topics she wanted to teach. Then she asked, "How many tests should I give you?" When one student yelled out, "Just one!" classmates protested they didn't want their grade to rise or fall on one exam. They ended up choosing four, the very number of tests she'd planned to give them. Finally, she put them in pods of five students, assigning different parts of the textbook for each pod to explain to the others in the class. She found that young adults never learn so well as when they must teach it themselves. The class resulted in a messier but far more effective time. The outcomes were amazing.

I—Image Rich

This ingredient may be most important of all. Generation Z grew up with screens full of images on Instagram, TikTok, Snapchat, and other platforms. When they were in high school, some called them "screenagers." Because so much of their schooling engaged the left hemisphere of their brain more than the right, they love pictures over lectures. Images are effective because they activate the right brain, which governs imagination, emotion, and creativity. This has always been true. Centuries ago, Aristotle stated, "The soul does not think without a picture." More recently, Leonard Sweet declared, "Images are the language of the twenty-first century."

So, how could you harness the power of a picture, a video, a metaphor, or an image to invite Gen Zers into the learning process? I'm not merely talking about using an image in your talk; what if you let the image anchor the big idea and invite conversation around it? I mentioned earlier, I created an entire curriculum around images, Habitudes, and it has been our bestselling product by far. You've learned a few of them in this book. Why are they engaging? Because the axiom is true: a picture is worth a thousand words.

As I mentioned earlier, there are several companies, nonprofits, health care organizations, schools, and sports teams that use these images to teach and learn. I have found if I let the picture do the work, listeners will discover and learn without me talking all the time. For example, the first time I taught our Habitude Thermostats and Thermometers, my young audience instantly recognized the difference between these two instruments. One sets the temperature, the other only reflects it. It launched a great conversation about how people set the climate on a team. We soon recognized there are layers of meaning to each image. One young man raised his hand after an epiphany. "Dr. Tim, I just remembered that inside of every thermostat is a thermometer, informing it whether to raise or lower the temperature when someone sets it. In the same way, leaders must read the room to determine whether to turn the heat up or cool the room down." It was brilliant.

I get to meet NCAA and professional athletes—baseball, football, hockey, and basketball players—who've learned life skills and leadership through these images. They are as simple or deep as you allow them to get. A child can understand the iceberg picture at their maturity level, and brilliant PhDs can grasp the same image at another level. Leaders at the White House and the Department of Justice have used them, on the one hand, as have inmates at prisons and juvenile detention centers. The images get through barriers.

C—Connected

Finally, Gen Z wants to connect with both the person presenting as well as others in the community. Our communication should be interactive, inclusive, and feel organic, not just organized. Allowing true connection makes things feel genuine. Unlike former times, these young team members wish we would learn what

Charles Duhigg, Ted Gioia, and others have discovered as they communicate:

> You gain more trust when seated, not standing.
> Don't speak *at* people—speak *with* them.
> An informal tone is more persuasive now.
> Conversations have more influence than speeches.
> Tips and sound bites are less influential than storytelling and spontaneous remarks.

Psychologist Adam Grant understands this as he influences Gen Z students each day at the University of Pennsylvania. In one class, he gets students to share a personal problem they don't have an answer to, nor the means or the connections to resolve it. Once the problem is clearly summarized, the entire class takes turns combing through their connections to people or creative ideas until they collectively solve each of the problems in the class. He insists it gets a group connected with one another by solving problems and serving people as they grow. What's more, everyone learns how much their own personal well-being is improved when they help others. The bonds this creates are tremendous.

Socrates used a method for communicating that now bears his name: the Socratic method. It's not about delivering a message or a speech but about interaction and connection. He claimed he wasn't especially clever, but great things came from him because his students learned through processing concepts out loud. Socrates's entire reputation was built on conversation. He never wrote a book, or anything else, as far as we can tell. He knew that other teachers might give "speeches finely tricked out with words and phrases." He, on the other hand, would seal ownership of his wisdom by connecting people and concepts.

I realize you might be saying, "Are you serious? Turn my communication into an image-rich, experiential conversation, just to keep my Gen Zers engaged?" Yes, that's what I'm saying.

My nonprofit, Growing Leaders, enjoys partnerships all over the world, which means I get to travel and meet some of the best international leaders. In late 2024, I got to visit our partners in Brazil, at Universidade da Familia (University of the Family). The founder uses the Habitudes (in Portuguese) at both their nonprofit (UDF) and his company, Instituto de Desenvolvimento (Development Institute). This company employs forty-five hundred team members who are invited to "grow" as they "work" in the business. On my last trip there, President Jorge Nishimura sat down with me to share the results of their multiyear EPIC learning communities that used Habitudes. He commissioned a report in response to some of his managers who questioned if it was worth it to spend money on these learning initiatives. Jorge told me, "For every R$1.00 they invested . . . they got a return of R$8.16." In short, the employees become more valuable. That's an eight to one ROI. You bet he believes it was worth it.

> **REFLECT**
>
> What are some steps you can take to become EPIC?

WORKSHOP:
SEVEN PRINCIPLES FOR GETTING THROUGH

Let me close this chapter with some quick, practical principles I use when I communicate with young staff. They're seven principles from my book *Habitudes for Communicators*. These images (metaphors) remind us of how to get through to Gen Z:

1. Windows and Mirrors Principle—The transparent message gets through.
When leaders offer listeners a window into their own souls, they provide a mirror for listeners to see themselves. Being real and transparent doesn't reduce their respect for you; it raises it. Vulnerability is the key to believability. They identify with your humanity.

How could you share a personal story and reveal your struggle with the topic?

2. House on Fire Principle—The urgent message gets through.
Before you talk about the importance of water, light a house on fire. Gen Z learns on a "need to know" basis, so give them a need to know. If you give your listeners a why they're incentivized to learn almost any what. Show why your message is urgent.

What dilemma can help you launch your topic? What will persuade them to engage?

3. Facebook or TV—The interactive message gets through.
Young generations spend more time on social media sites than they do watching TV. Why? They prefer raw and interactive experiences. Your message should allow time for people to interact about your topic. The best learning happens in a social context.

What questions could you ask listeners to enlist them to participate in the topic?

4. Number Three Pencil Principle—The simple message gets through.
Why do people use number two pencils more than number three pencils? Because number three pencils are too hard. Good communicators keep their message simple, not hard, knowing they'll lose people if it becomes too complicated. It increases your chances that they'll respond.

How could you simplify your message, offering a simple takeaway for them to grasp?

5. The Faded Flag Principle—The clear message gets through.

Years ago, a tragic train accident occurred because the flagman waived a faded red flag that sent no signal about the bridge being out. The engineer didn't get the message. It was deadly. Too often, leaders wave their "flag" passionately and don't understand why people don't act. It's often not that their challenge is off but their lack of clarity.

How could you clarify the clear action step you want listeners to take?

6. The Thomas Nast Principle—The visual message gets through.

Thomas Nast drew editorial cartoons that helped oust corrupt politicians. Folks didn't read the articles, but they understood his images. Great leaders use imagery to ensure their message is memorable. Pictures beat lectures every day. Visual is stickier than verbal.

How could you identify an image or metaphor to anchor the big idea you're sharing?

7. School Yearbook Principle—The relevant message gets through.

When you got your school yearbook, what's the first picture you searched for? It was your own. So it is with audiences. As they listen to communicators, they're looking for themselves. Listeners must see how your talk applies to them, or you'll lose them.

REFLECT

This week, how can you leverage these principles?

How can you ensure you illustrate how listeners will find your message relevant?

A POINT, A PICTURE, AND A PRACTICE

Here's the bottom line. To effectively communicate with Gen Z team members, I utilize a simple strategy to get my ideas across. These three steps engage their minds and hearts and usually convince them to join me on the journey:

1. Give them a *point* for their head. Identify the one, clear big idea you want them to embrace. What do you want them to know? What should they understand?
2. Give them a *picture* for their heart. Offer an illustration or example that shows them what your big idea looks like in real life. What do you want them to feel?
3. Give them a *practice* for their hands. Offer an understandable and doable application to your message. What action step do you want them to take? What should they do?

Tom Peters said it best: "The best leaders . . . almost without exception and at every level, are master users of stories and symbols." This means we commit to good communication.

Doug Conant was hired as the new CEO of Campbell Soup Company in 2001. The organization was in serious trouble at the time because the food industry was consolidating. Doug was brought in to turn the company around, and that's exactly what he did. The challenges he faced, however, were gigantic. At the time, the culture at Campbell Soup Company was toxic. Most of the employees were disengaged, with no passion for their work.

What's more, leaders had been hired from various companies like Pepsi, Procter and Gamble, and General Mills, each bringing with them their own preferences and ideas. Compounding all these issues, there were four generations working there and many rookies on the team. People weren't connecting. Communication was just plain bad.

So Doug started to rebuild.

He began to create a culture of communication. First, they established communication norms. Next, he set an example of noticing the good work people did and thanking them; then he affirmed them in front of others. He wrote ten to twenty handwritten notes each day to people on staff, just to let them know he'd seen their good work. (Doug wrote thirty thousand notes in ten years.) He taught his executive leaders to view all the buzz, phone calls, emails, and people stopping by not as interruptions but as opportunities to make the company better. In short, Doug got people to connect both online and offline. What's more, he launched a cohort of promising leaders to meet with and mentor, knowing they were the future of Campbell's. He got them communicating well . . . which created an energized culture. Soon, he had people on the same page and focused their efforts on the mission. This was the secret to Campbell's huge turnaround—a leader who got people connected.

TALK IT OVER

1. The "Tappers and Listeners" experiment highlights how communication can often be misunderstood. What specific strategies can leaders use to bridge the communication gap with Generation Z and ensure their messages are not lost in translation?

2. Generation Z is described as comfortable with digital communication but preferring in-person

interaction for building relationships. How can organizations balance these preferences to foster effective communication and stronger team dynamics?

3. The chapter emphasizes the importance of becoming an EPIC communicator—experiential, participatory, image rich, and connected. Which of these elements do you think is most critical for engaging Gen Z in the workplace, and how might you apply it in your leadership approach?

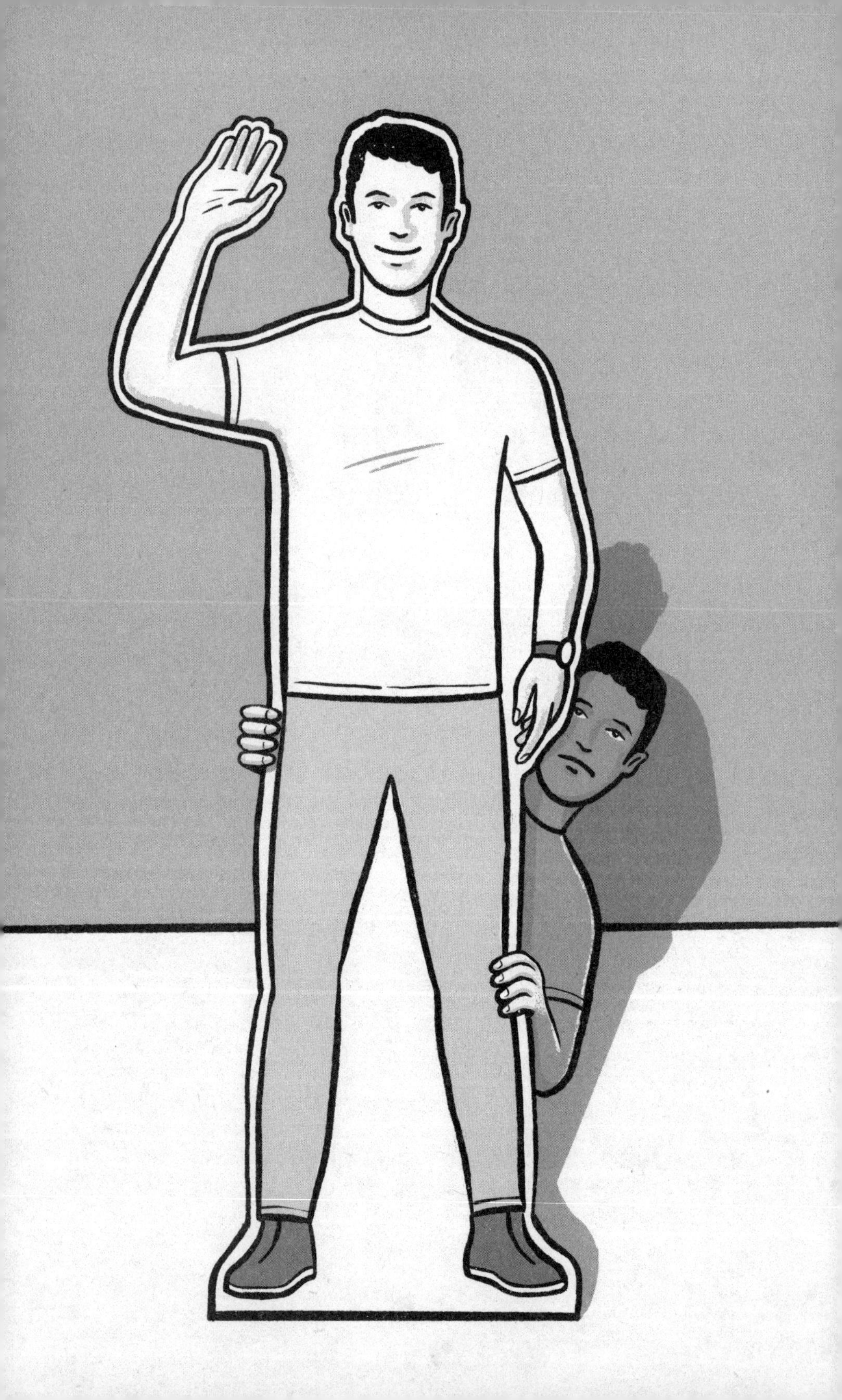

12

CULTIVATING SOFT SKILLS

BUILDING THEM INTO LEADERS

Gavin just joined the staff of a software company not far from where I live. I happen to know the human resources officer who hired him. It's been interesting to hear Gavin's opinion of his job compared to his manager's perception.

Gavin feels his leaders don't really know what they're doing. They're not up to speed on new technology, they seem stuck in past strategies, and they come across to him as a bit antiquated. His manager sees things differently. When I inquired of her, she told me he's a nice enough young man but has a condition she's not seen before. He comes across self-assured, like he's got the world by the tail, but when his skills are tested, he crumbles. There is a veneer of confidence, but he's not confident at all. When responding to direction, he gives no eye contact and is vague in his language. She calls it a "word salad."

Gavin is cocky but not confident.

This scenario is happening more and more frequently. It feels like an oxymoron. How could a Gen Zer come across so self-assured and a minute later lack self-assurance? We must remember they were conditioned by twenty-first-century realities that frustrate older leaders:

> They can look anything up in seconds and feel like experts the same day.
> Most have not taken service jobs because waiting on customers is challenging.
> Many perceive current leaders as selfish and greedy, so their respect levels are low.
> They've spent so much time on phones that they can be socially awkward at work.

Not all members of Generation Z reflect these traits, but a growing number of employers are reporting them. Earlier I mentioned the survey by ResumeBuilder.com saying that 74 percent of employers find Gen Z more difficult to work with than other generations.

Supervisors have noticed a scenario among members of both Gen Z and millennials. Two therapists I know use a term to diagnose them: "high arrogance, low self-esteem." It may be the result of input by caring adults who told them they're remarkable, but the words were hollow. Adults consciously worked to cultivate kids' self-esteem but took shortcuts, merely voicing how amazing our children were without getting out of the way to let them demonstrate it. Hence, they can be cocky but not confident. Their identity is artificial.

ARTIFICIAL SELF-ESTEEM

Over the last forty-plus years, the self-esteem movement took root. We began to lead our young differently. Truth be told, people under forty need to fumble, fall, and fail en route to success. Unfortunately, millions of us over forty didn't let them. We felt that failure would negatively affect their identity. We wanted to build their self-esteem by telling them they're awesome, but we kept the stakes low, not wanting them to risk failure. Robust self-esteem comes from trial and error and then success. Artificial self-esteem comes from verbal input, no trial, and then trying to convince them they're successful. The symptoms?

> They'll quickly quit a job without having another one lined up.
> They'll insist on keeping their boundaries but often not respect others' boundaries.
> They find it troubling to endure hardship or uncomfortable situations.

WHAT'S OUR TAKEAWAY?

Please don't get me wrong. I'm not insulting Gen Z. They are products of our making. We failed to prepare them for the challenges ahead. Now we must help them catch up.

Allow me to be blunt. Teachers and leaders should not try to build their self-esteem. For that matter, parents should not try to build their child's self-esteem. Instead, we must work to build their capabilities. When we do this well, their self-esteem will be authentic and take care of itself. They will know where their strengths lie and have a realistic perception of themselves. This is the path of all accurate self-perception.

Do you remember the story of the Golden Buddha?

It's one of our Habitudes. More than sixty years ago, the largest chunk of gold known to humankind was discovered in Bangkok, Thailand. At the time, there was a concrete statue of Buddha set in the city square. It had been there so long that it was stained and dirty. So a crew was hired to move it inside to clean it. When the crew picked up the statue, however, they dropped it, and it cracked. They were mortified. That is, until one of the crew noticed the concrete was only a shell. Inside that shell was an eight-foot-tall solid chunk of gold. Needless to say, their bad day turned into a very good day.

This is an analogy for each of us, especially for Generation Z. The shell on the outside is just that—a shell. Inside there is gold, but we must get past that outer veneer and discover the gold inside. The exteriors we see may be a cocky attitude or impulsive media posts. Those are only shells. Finding the gold will affect how both you and they perceive reality. It will also positively affect their performance on a team.

This chapter is about how you can build the interpersonal skills in Gen Z so that everyone can discover the gold inside of them. But it will be a challenge. Generation Z can make us better leaders because of *who* they are, *how* they respond to both authority and to peers, and *what* skills they may still need. En route, your leadership will improve as you develop them as leaders. This all begins with their greatest need: soft skills. Once they cultivate their interpersonal (social) skills, they'll be less prone to sabotage themselves and can use those hard skills they bring to the team.

THE SOFT SKILL PROBLEM

The term *soft skills* was coined by the US Army in the late 1960s.[1] It refers to any skill that does not employ the use of machinery. (Those are called "hard skills.") The military realized that many important activities represented a new category; they were the social skills necessary to lead groups, motivate soldiers, and win wars. These were skills they had not yet cataloged or fully studied. Today they are more important than ever. In fact, I believe hard skills depreciate over time because machinery and technology are constantly updated and upgraded. Soft skills appreciate over time. Sadly, we don't act like it. In this age of artificial intelligence, leadership will change in two ways. Our hard skills will increasingly be replaced by AI, and our soft skills will become increasingly more important.

Now, here's my point. Many employers recognize that Gen Z arrives on the job comfortable with smart technology but lacking in interpersonal skills. Some call them power skills, not soft skills, because they differentiate great employees from average ones, much as superpowers do. Psychologist Nicholas Humphrey famously stated that social intelligence, rather than qualitative intelligence, defines humans.[2]

The Nobel Prize–winning economist James Heckman claims that "soft skills predict success in life, that they causally produce that success, and programs that enhance soft skills have an important place in an effective portfolio of public policies."[3] Employers now say these skills are more important than GPA (once considered the most important factor in making decisions) in hiring a new worker.[4] To be honest with you, I don't know an employer who's asking young job candidates about their GPA. I do know many who ask candidates about their ability to work on a team, communicate well, listen well, and about other social skills. Because college graduates are often not learning these in a classroom, employers need to cultivate them in their young professionals.

The good news is, many are doing just that. Some industries now focus on these power skills and offer professional training in such skills to their teams. Deloitte offers intentional mentorship and leadership development programs for young professionals. New hires are informed about them and encouraged to participate. They've created Deloitte University to cultivate interpersonal skills and to coach Gen Z in networking. En route, they become more and more valuable to the company.

PricewaterhouseCoopers does much the same. PwC, a large accounting and auditing firm, provides extensive coaching and feedback for new hires. They inform Gen Z candidates that this norm is in place to accelerate their growth. Their "career coach" model pairs young professionals with mentors to guide their career development. This meets two goals: to instruct Gen Zers in the fundamentals of their culture and work and to establish relationships with them.

McKinsey and Company is known for investing heavily in the personal and professional growth of its consultants, particularly young ones. They offer extensive mentorship and training programs for young (Gen Z) professionals. They establish relational connections with Gen Zers, which is the bridge to all progress. Believe it or not, one division does primary research on Generation Z and publishes it in a newsletter that I enjoy regularly.

Google is known for its internal mentorship programs, where they focus on employee development, particularly for those who are new to their careers. They're so famous that in 2013 Vince Vaughn and Owen Wilson starred in a comedy film called *The Internship*, playing trainees at Google who were less tech savvy than their younger counterparts. Each year, Google focuses on continual learning and offers Google Career certificates.

REFLECT

What are you intentionally doing to develop Gen Z's soft skills?

It's time all of us give attention to building these skills in young professionals.

THE BUILDING BLOCKS FOR BUILDING SOFT SKILLS

Before we jump into some of the most valuable soft or power skills your Gen Zers need, let's identify a system for building them. Too many have counted on mere instruction on these topics to instill people skills and have been disappointed at the results. Do you remember our discussion on EPIC communication in an earlier chapter? Let me offer a recipe of four ingredients that I've found are transformational with Gen Z team members.

Conversation—They need to talk about it.
Step one is to introduce a soft skill competency to your Gen Zers in a conversation. Keep in mind, some of these skills could be new to a young professional, so this step may just introduce a concept they've never considered. As I mentioned, our team conversations are usually launched with an image that represents the soft skill. Because pictures are worth a thousand words, we immediately get engagement from them. In our hour together we ensure they understand the big idea before moving on to the next step in the process.

Demonstration—They need to see it in action.
We recognize for most Gen Zers a mere conversation is insufficient. We all learn better when we get to see a skill set in real life, right? I like to say, "Show and tell beats tell and tell any day." People do what people see. Bosses can give great speeches, but if they model a lifestyle opposite of what they just spoke about, it's hollow. People follow the example not the speech. In this step, mentors model the skill, or they point to an example of someone who is embodying the skill. Now the words and actions bolster each other.

Application—They need to practice it themselves.
I believe that we never really learn something until we've practiced it. Discussions and examples are powerful, but the skills leave the realm of theory and become more powerful when Gen Zers put it into practice and apply it. Practice doesn't always make *perfect*, but I've found practice does make *permanent*. We must find safe places for our Gen Zers to try out the concepts we've discussed and see how they work in real life. It can be role-playing in a workshop setting or even experimenting with their teammates later that day.

> **REFLECT**
> Do you have a setting where you could implement these fundamentals?

Evaluation—They need you to assess what happened.
I bet you've heard the phrase "Experience is the best teacher." I don't believe that, because I've seen young staff have a bad experience and come to the wrong conclusions. I believe experience with evaluation is the best teacher. When you take time to assess the experience they had trying to practice a soft skill, it equips them to take even a bad experience and learn from it. Later, having this appraisal under their belt, they can improve and become quite good at embodying it. But remember—this feedback time can be hard. Ask them for permission to offer it and remind them your goal is to make them even better.

FIVE BIG CONVERSATIONS

As I met with hundreds of Gen Z employees, I asked them, How would you coach your former self as a rookie on the job? In what areas do you wish someone would've prepared you for the job? Their answers were: swallow your pride, be patient, take initiative, use the systems that are in place, and "own" your job. On our team, we frame these conversations with metaphors we call Habitudes.

These word pictures spark conversations with young staff about the varied qualities and skills I just mentioned. They may be helpful for you too.

1. Coffee Step (Swallow your pride)

Years ago, Kerry felt insulted that she was asked to get the coffee for the executive-level meetings each week. She wondered if the company knew she had a college degree or that she had some real work experience. And did they ask her because she was a female? Fortunately, she swallowed her pride and served the coffee. She told me later she's so glad she did. Serving coffee to the executives got her in the room interacting with key influential people. The next thing she knew they were asking her questions and getting acquainted; eventually she was asked to sit down at the table for a session. Kerry learned a valuable lesson. Early tasks are more about earning trust than showing talent. Young staff must be willing to execute small jobs with excellence and earn the right to take on bigger ones. Getting the coffee (or doing the small task) is a step in the right direction.

2. Crock-Pots and Microwaves (Be patient)

We've all tasted food from a microwave oven. A moment after that hot dog was zapped, it's cold again and a little rubbery. The preparation was fast, but it didn't taste good. A slow cooker is the opposite: that pot roast takes hours to cook, but once it's ready, it's delicious. Our jobs usually work the same way. We wish our careers were prepared in a microwave and that we'd shoot to the top in a short time. But the best careers take time. We must be willing to wait to be great. Our path usually takes longer than we assumed necessary. Slow and steady wins the race, and for that matter, it's not really a race. Think pace, not race. Too often we watch highlight reels of star athletes performing, but we never see the years of practice they put in privately. We see posts of our friend's vacation but not their preparation. We must learn to delay gratification to enjoy a future celebration.

3. Early Birds and Mockingbirds (Take initiative)

Every workplace has two birds: mockingbirds merely imitate others, while early birds take initiative and set the pace for others. Most young staff are preoccupied with avoiding any mistakes, so they watch others and imitate them. They blend in; they don't stand out. Rare staff decide they'll set the pace for others, getting a jump on what needs to be done. I had an intern ask for the office key two weeks into his internship. It felt a little presumptuous to me until he revealed why. He told me he loved his projects and often arrived early and stayed late to work on them. Frequently, he arrived and left when no one else was there. I smiled and quickly gave him an office key. He is an example of an early bird. Mockingbirds are not bad people; they just do the minimum tasks expected of them. And sometimes, that's sufficient. In the long run, though, early birds look ahead and get ahead.

4. Trains and Tracks (Work with the systems in place)

It would be easy to assume that a train track prevents a train from moving freely, but it's just the opposite. It would be ridiculous for a locomotive engineer to get frustrated and decide to jump the track and attempt to take the train up a mountain. He wouldn't get very far because the tracks help the train move swiftly and make progress. Often a young staff person can feel the systems in a workplace hinder their flow or productivity. All teams actually need systems and processes to accelerate the workflow. Like a train track. Systems are simply an organization's approach to get things done. They improve results, deepen collaboration, accelerate speed, and expand your ability to scale. Gen Z staff, especially those who are creative, must learn to appreciate them and capitalize on them. Systems, like train tracks, help you keep your promise to reach a destination.

5. Apartments or Homes (Own your job)

People usually take better care of their home than they do an apartment. Why? Often it's because the home belongs to them. We rent an apartment and realize it doesn't genuinely belong to us. Renters might not pay close attention to damage that occurs because they know a landlord will take care of it. When we buy a home, we tend to spend time caring for it and cleaning it because now it is ours. This mental shift must take place on the job. Leaders need young team members to own their work, not rent it. It should feel like it belongs to them, not to someone else. Once someone feels a sense of ownership, it shows up in their work ethic, their initiative, their creativity, and their problem-solving. The change has nothing to do with talent or IQ. It's all about a shift in attitude. You look inward not outward for answers.

> **REFLECT**
> How could these images spark change in your Gen Z staff?

Years ago, I noticed our need to continue reviewing the same soft skills with our new hires, especially our interns. Even though our young staff claimed they understood what habits and attitudes we desired in our office, their conduct revealed they really didn't. Concepts like the ones above required annual review and discussion to ensure they were practiced, not just understood. So I created resources to spark these discussions such as:

> *Habitudes for New Professionals*
> *Habitudes for Career-Ready Students*
> *Habitudes: The Art of Connecting with Others*

These books became the foundation for the skills we want on our team. Each book is filled with thirteen images resulting in thirteen conversations on interpersonal skills. You can find these Habitudes books at GrowingLeaders.com.

THE ROOT OF THE PROBLEM, THE HEART OF THE SOLUTION

Amber looked down at her phone and noticed Rob was calling. Although Rob was her boss, she wondered why he'd be calling her at 8:00 p.m. She was not in a good place emotionally that night. Did Rob need something? Did she miss something? She answered to discover Rob had heard Amber's mother just passed away, and he wanted to express his condolences. It was a sympathy call. Amber, touched by his empathic words, thanked him and shared some poignant details about her mother's long illness and how it felt to lose her. Amber and her mom were very close, and she now felt quite alone.

As she continued, however, she heard the clicking of computer keys at the other end of the line. She slowly realized Rob was typing, answering his email while on the call. His remarks became increasingly empty of feeling and perfunctory. When they hung up, Amber felt so disheartened she wished he had never called at all.

She was on the other side of what philosopher Martin Buber called an "I-it" interaction. It's when two colleagues interact but at least one feels no attunement with the other. They go through the motions, but they're not really connecting. Amber's conversation with her boss, Rob, felt hollow to her. He made the call, checked it off his list, and likely gave himself a pat on the back. But Rob represents our problem: he knew what to do and he performed. Like Rob, we have our checklist of behaviors to execute, but Generation Z can spot a fake a mile away. Did we get the cart before the horse? Let's put the heart before the course.

Our soft skills must develop from the inside out, not the outside in.

CULTIVATING SOFT SKILLS

To accomplish this, I have assumed four postures with my young employees. As I've said, I use metaphors to help me frame what I must do to connect with Gen Z. I must model soft skills before attempting to teach those skills to them. Here are my metaphors:

A Host. You know what a good host does, don't you? They initiate connection, they provide for the needs of their guests, and they offer direction at a party. I challenge you to engage in each interaction with your Gen Zers as a host, not a guest. Don't be passive; be active. Come to meetings ready to initiate, make them feel welcome, and launch the discussion.

Think of specific steps you can take to embody these metaphors.

A Doctor. A good doctor doesn't engage with patients by instantly offering a prescription. They are taught in medical school to take several minutes and to probe where it hurts. They examine your mouth, your ears, your eyes, your heart rate . . . you get the idea. Come to meetings ready with some questions, ready to discover where their pain point is.

A Counselor. Effective counselors are brilliant listeners. In fact, they lead with listening. I believe great leaders today must be skillful, active listeners. Your people do not have an innate need to get their own way, but they do have a need to feel heard. Come to meetings ready to listen and empathize with Gen Zers so you can understand them.

A Tour Guide. Tour guides differ from travel agents. Travel agents tell you where to go to enjoy a great vacation. Tour guides take you on the journey. Similarly, leaders must coach and mentor Gen Zers, remaining by their side as they learn and develop. Come to meetings ready to "show the way" and "go the way," especially if they have little experience.

LEADERSHIP QUALITIES THAT ARE STILL RELEVANT IN THE AI AGE

I consulted with a focus group of employees from Generation Z, all between sixteen and twenty-four years old. While their comments were energizing, one of them voiced a future concern that the others agreed with quickly. Can you guess what it was?

Will the job I'm dreaming about even be around in ten years?

Artificial intelligence is replacing jobs at a stunning pace. Goldman Sachs reported on the BBC that AI may replace three hundred million jobs by 2030. Since 2000, automation systems have already eliminated 1.7 million jobs, and this number is only going to increase. Some have predicted that AI is going to take away eighty-five million more jobs in 2025.[5] Not surprisingly, workers ages eighteen to twenty-four are 129 percent more likely than older workers to worry that AI will make their job obsolete. Here are skills I believe are "AI proof," at least in the foreseeable future. *Forbes* created an expert panel, the Forbes Business Development Council, to identify the skills they see as relevant in an AI world.[6] (Special thanks to Forbes for this helpful research.) Inspired by them, I expanded their list and recommend you find ways to cultivate these in Gen Z staff.

SIX QUALITIES THAT WILL INCREASE IN VALUE IN THE AI AGE

1. Authenticity and transparency

Today's employee values leaders who come across as genuine and real. It's a human quality that not everyone possesses, and certainly not robots. At least yet. Think about what AI is today. Generative AI tools are not objective. They're subject to the biases of the humans who make them, and any biases in the training data may show up when they are used. They're not reliably factual. AI tools might feel authoritative and credible, but the responses they generate are routinely riddled with inaccuracies. This will deepen our craving for authentic and transparent interactions. There is a human element people will miss in the day when half of our interactions are with robots by the mid-2030s, according to the Pew Research Center.[7] Even now, people say they enjoy purchasing a hamburger from a screen at a quick-service restaurant but miss human interaction at the restaurant simultaneously.

2. Emotional intelligence

This so-called soft skill may be the umbrella under which the others stand. Emotional intelligence is a crucial leadership skill because it requires an understanding of the nuance that AI lacks. EQ is all about self-awareness, social awareness, and how to manage emotions as we interact with others. It's reading the room. It's about knowing how to read a person before you lead that person. I believe the higher someone rises in an organization, the more important emotional intelligence will be. Consider this. Success in school is about 75 percent IQ and 25 percent EQ. In our careers, it's just the opposite. Emotional intelligence plays an even greater role in our success with people. If I had to choose between hiring an intelligent person versus an emotionally intelligent one, I'd take the latter. We love the convenience of AI, but it is not human.

I believe teams that practice genuine, emotional connections will build deeper trust and prevail in the future.

3. Identifying needs for growth

With AI, leaders are now able to create tailored coaching for any skill they want to improve. Mike Villalobos from Seedtag put it this way: "Want to become a better listener? ChatGPT will quickly generate a plan with tactics and exercises to help you develop that skill. Wonder how to deal with a difficult situation? It's likely that AI can summarize the world's knowledge on the subject. It's a brave new world." Consequently, building the human skill to identify where the greatest growth needs are on a team will become extremely valuable. In short, like all new technology, people need to repurpose their abilities to complement their new reality, just like horsemen had to do when automobiles were invented. Nearly everyone knows their team can improve, but not everyone recognizes what areas are most vital. The ability to identify those needs will differentiate you.

4. Adaptability and agility

Since AI is about the sum of what we've learned from the past, adapting to tomorrow's unforeseen changes is vital. The future will be different from what we've accumulated from history. We're moving into uncharted territory, like "marching off our maps." The ability to rapidly shift to new realities with positive, curious attitudes will be valuable. Tony Ambroza, of RealTruck, says, "Adaptability is the most relevant leadership skill, which can be developed by continuously learning about AI advancements, embracing the power of these changes, and fostering an innovative culture. Since technology evolves rapidly, ongoing and frequent training is a must. This allows teams to fully embrace how AI can scale your work." I believe the two metacompetencies that are most important in this century are resilience and resourcefulness. Both require adaptability and agility. When plan A doesn't work, teams must adapt and leverage the resources they have, not the ones they wish for. Thus far, AI cannot do this as well as an agile team member.

5. Humility and team awareness

A subset of emotional intelligence is being aware of the big picture when interacting with teammates. This means we need to check our egos and logos at the door and see others' internal needs. Jacob Dearstyne, from Optizmo.com, believes we all must accept that certain longtime aspects of our jobs will vanish in the face of AI. Embracing this, rather than fighting it, will help you to take advantage of the flip side of the coin: we will need to stay teachable and humble. The ability to communicate clearly and with humility is a timeless skill. This will separate us from others who understand AI but are poor at interactions. Because content is easier than ever to create and to fake, teams will need people who are aware of what's right and true and then humble enough to go with the best ideas. Humility and perspective will always be in style and in need.

6. Timing on decision-making

This skill is intuitive and nuanced, and those who have it will be extremely valuable. Jonathan Nikols, from Verizon Business, states, "The ability to interpret the data and make action-oriented decisions will be the most important skill for leaders in the age of artificial intelligence. Decisions like real-time pricing adjustments, real-time promotions, and real-time placement will all be enhanced and executed with AI. Those who use AI to make faster, more informed, and timely decisions will give their company a competitive advantage." This talent, in fact, is one that complements what AI can do. John Maxwell taught me, "The wrong decision at the wrong time can be a disaster. A wrong decision at the right time is a mistake. A right decision at the wrong time leads to rejection. And a right decision at the right time results in success."

A HUMAN TOUCH

A few years ago, I spoke to Tim Tassopoulos, who then served as the president and COO of Chick-fil-A restaurants. When I asked him why Chick-fil-A wasn't emulating other quick-service restaurants, utilizing touch screens instead of people for consumers to order food, he replied that they were "betting on" their people. He reminded me that Chick-fil-A aims to make an emotional connection when they can with their guests. Whether it's by helping a single mom out to her car with the food she's just purchased for her three children or refreshing people's drinks in the dining room, they believe maintaining a human touch will differentiate them, at least in the foreseeable future. So far, he's right.

Smart technology cannot offer that human touch. In fact, those who've used any version of artificial intelligence will tell you it is loaded with inaccuracies and errors at this point. It is far from perfect, but it is getting better and will be an essential part of the future. This means we must cultivate complementary and unique skills for this new world. I believe human elements will always be in demand. This chapter is a great place to start.

TALK IT OVER

1. The chapter highlights the prevalence of "cockiness without confidence" among Generation Z, stemming from artificial self-esteem. How can leaders create opportunities for young professionals to build authentic confidence through trial, error, and growth?
2. Given the increasing importance of soft skills in the AI-driven workplace, how can organizations effectively integrate the development of these "power skills" into their onboarding, training, and mentorship programs?

3. The chapter outlines four steps to building soft skills: conversation, demonstration, application, and evaluation. Which of these steps do you believe is most critical for developing interpersonal skills in Gen Z employees, and why?

CHAOS

ISSUES

BUDGET

DOUBT

GRIT

13

BUILDING GRIT AND FOSTERING GROWTH

I'd like to introduce you to the most extraordinary person you've likely never heard of or met. His name is Cliff Young, and he became famous in 1983, for a very strange feat.

Cliff was a potato farmer living in Australia. His family was so poor they couldn't afford a four-wheel drive truck or any horses, so he harvested potatoes and herded sheep across a two-thousand-acre plot of land on foot. He had no teeth and wore pitiful looking but functional clothes and rubber boots to do his job.

In 1983, Australia hosted their first ultramarathon, from Sydney to Melbourne. It would be the world's most grueling footrace, 544 miles in length, a contest that would take days to finish, if anyone did finish. (To put this race in perspective, it was the equivalent of 21.6 marathons.) Experienced runners entered the race knowing their regimen would be to run for eighteen hours, then sleep for six hours, then get up the next morning and do it all over again. And then again. Only serious athletes even applied.

THE FUTURE BEGINS WITH Z

Except for one guy, Cliff Young.

Cliff decided it might be fun to test his grit. After all, he'd herded sheep on foot for three or four days straight. He'd run around a huge plot of land in rubber boots. Maybe he could see its effect on his sixty-one-year-old body. So, he registered for the ultramarathon. When the race started, the other runners took off at a fast yet sustainable pace. Onlookers began to chuckle at Cliff, this toothless potato farmer, as he began to shuffle along, far behind his opponents. He was like a real-life Forrest Gump.

Days later, the crowd assembled at the finish line to see who would win. Imagine their shock when they spotted Cliff, shuffling to the finish line, far ahead of anyone else. Cameras began flashing and the crowd roared as Cliff, a senior citizen, was the only runner in sight, for quite a while. The race was not even close.

HOW DID HE DO IT? HOW COULD HE?

Cliff's secret is what this chapter is all about. You see, Cliff's life had been a preparation for this ultramarathon. All day and all night, this old man had shuffled across fields, taking care of his sheep and potatoes. His focus was "pace" not "race," which enabled him to win, not unlike the story of the "Tortoise and the Hare." Here are my takeaways:

> - Cliff's daily regimen was tougher than the race itself. He herded sheep on foot for three to four days straight without stopping. So while other runners ran for eighteen hours then slept for six, Cliff just rested for two hours and kept on running. As they slept, he passed them all up. *Key: Make your daily disciplines harder than your job.*
> - Cliff had learned to maximize his resources. He shuffled his feet, without picking them up off the ground, which helped him use less energy and

> continue longer. In fact, afterward other runners began imitating Cliff's shuffle, preserving energy and enabling them to endure. *Key: Steward your resources with great discretion.*
>
> > Cliff utilized only what he needed. Not only did he survive on minimal sleep, but he consumed only water (for hydration) and hot chocolate (for energy). That's it. This enabled him to keep his pace while others required stopping to eat. *Key: This is a lesson in choosing your essentials and avoiding needless extras. Be a minimalist.*

At the race's end, Cliff had no idea there was a trophy and a big check awaiting him. He just wanted to test his endurance. When he was given the prize money, he replied that every runner had worked hard and deserved something too. So Cliff shared the money with them all. At this point, he had established himself and taught everyone a valuable lesson. He is the embodiment of resilience and resourcefulness. Before he passed away in 2003, Cliff had set six world records, offering a new model for long distance running in Australia. And this potato farmer became a bit of a national hero.

GRIT AND GROWTH

I think you'd agree with me that Cliff's story is the antithesis of our lives today. We're not bad people; we just live in a world filled with smart technology where many of our wants require only a quick click. As I've stated, life is on demand and instant access. And this is especially true for those who've grown up in the twenty-first century. Our culture has not helped them delay gratification.

Psychologist Angela Duckworth has created a Grit Scale that measures a person's level of perseverance and ability to recover from failure.[1] Her studies frequently showed a lower average grit score for Gen Zers compared to older generations. My research demonstrates that employers (by and large) don't see high levels of grit or resilience in Gen Z employees. In fact, the managers I've studied say that young staff will more likely choose to "quit" over show some "grit." Older generations can feel as if they're constantly catering to the needs of young people, only to be shamed or blamed for not doing enough. Sadly, I believe Generation Z has lots of grit, but millions of them are so afraid of landing a miserable job that they'll leave before they learn to press through hardship and find satisfaction on the other side. An African proverb reminds us that we all prefer our tasks to be:

> Fast
> Easy
> Excellent

It makes sense. Who wouldn't want these words to describe their daily job? The problem is, we can't have all three. At best, we can have only two of the three. We must choose. If it's fast and easy, it likely won't be excellent. If it's fast and excellent, it likely won't be easy. And if it's easy and excellent, it most likely won't be fast. We can't have it all.

Sadly, older adults have not taught this lesson well to younger generations. Kids got ambushed by technology and crippled by anxiety, which has nudged parents to remove stressors in their lives. After all, if our kids are already stressed out, we certainly don't want to add more stress to their life, right?

So, how do leaders equip Generation Z to not only stick around but to grow from difficult challenges? This chapter reviews the data on Gen Z and reveals the steps

---

REFLECT

Considering Cliff Young's story compared to ours, what do you conclude?

---

leaders can take to deepen resourcefulness and resilience in them. Further, we'll look at how they can turn a disadvantage into an advantage if we can learn to lead them differently.

HOW DID WE GET HERE?

Let's talk about how Gen Z is in the shape they are in. While I believe they'll be amazing and will disrupt the workforce one day, the journey toward that goal may be bumpy. There are several obstacles they face that have diminished their grit today. Let's look at two of them.

1. Cancel Culture
Believe it or not, cancel culture didn't begin on social media or on a university campus. It surfaced in our middle-class homes as Gen Z was growing up. As I've said, parents see their anxious kids and don't want to add more stress to them. We want to remove it. So millions seek to relieve their kid's hardship instead of coaching them on how to face it. I shared the story of a parent who called the school principal and asked to take their child out of a class because a former boyfriend was present; I know parents who've marched down to the school to negotiate a better grade on their child's project; and I know parents who've actually done their child's homework for them at Starbucks. Parents can now "rent a mom" to visit their kid in college. Daisy Bug Delivery is a concierge organization offering a "second mom" service that freshmen may need. Students can have their bed made, their laundry done, their room tidied up, and even be picked up in a car. This service is well intended, but it illustrates our tendency to reduce experiences that are hard or unfamiliar. Decisions like this can reduce Gen Z's grit and problem-solving skills.

On the college campus, cancel culture has reached a peak. Over the last decade we have seen an assault on hardships through cancel culture. Students who once championed "free speech" and "open debate" in the academy now wanted schools to cancel controversial speakers, demanded speech codes, called for trigger warnings, and requested schools to police microaggressions. While I understand the desire for safe spaces, the consequences of this shift are sinister—and we didn't see them coming. I believe there's a correlation between *cancel culture* and *diminished grit* in Gen Z. While I believe cancel culture has produced some positive results, I believe the solution to overcoming hardship is rarely to remove it. Grit doesn't grow without adversity. So while you feel compassion for your struggling Gen Zer on staff, find solutions that help them face their hardship instead of taking it away.

2. Binge Culture

Our culture has also played a role in reducing grit levels, especially in younger generations.

Let's face it—society today compels us to pursue comfort and pleasure, and we can find sources for both faster than at any point in history. With those sources at our disposal, we don't excel at practicing moderation. We naturally fail to develop grit, resilience, and resourcefulness. Why? Because we choose pleasure over pain. Stanford research psychologist Anna Lembke explains our brains naturally send chemicals into our systems to balance pleasure and pain. Chemicals like endorphins, dopamine, serotonin, and oxytocin make us happy when we feel pain or discomfort. When you run for several miles, your brain recognizes the strain you feel and sends endorphins into your body, giving you a "runner's high."

When we consume pleasureful inputs the opposite happens. Our brain seeks balance. The problem is, we live in a day where we can binge on about anything, from TikTok, to opioids, to alcohol, to nicotine, to porn, to romance novels, to Netflix, you name it. Bingeing on these pleasures can cause an overdose on dopamine. At this point, the science gets ugly. The more people become addicted to a stimulus, the less pleasure they receive. Eventually, this cycle creates "anhedonia"—the complete absence of enjoyment in an experience originally pursued for pleasure. It's the law of diminishing returns. They feel depressed and lack the tenacity or resilience to push through without pleasure.

Over the last century, our leisure time has evolved, but not in a good way. Ted Gioia describes this in his Substack "The Honest Broker," where he brilliantly summarizes what's happened to us.[2] Over a century ago, we spent free time in the *arts*, including theater, symphonies, opera, concerts, and the like. Decades ago, the arts began to be displaced by *entertainment*, including movies and television, stand-up comedy, and later home videos. Eventually, we got smartphones, and *distraction* replaced professional entertainment in our leisure time. It's ordinary people doing silly things on platforms. Today, we've devolved. Distraction is being replaced by *addiction* because we can continue to consume the pleasure we want almost whenever we want it. For millions of people (especially Gen Z) doomscrolling is the norm thanks to Silicon Valley. We've become drunk on dopamine.

> **REFLECT**
>
> Have you noticed lower grit in today's culture? What have you done?

How has this affected us practically speaking?
- It has lowered our levels of happiness.
- It has raised our levels of addiction.
- It has decreased our levels of discipline.
- It has increased our levels of depression.
- It has expanded our levels of narcissism.
- It has reduced our levels of grit.

Each day, our work teams combat a force that pulls them toward shortcuts and easy fixes. Call it a "pleasure addiction." As I've mentioned, we want projects to be fast, easy, and excellent at the same time. Consider how this binge culture, flowing with dopamine, affects our daily lives. Even in my lifetime, I have witnessed this evolution that Ted Gioia describes in the table below:

THE RISE OF DOPAMINE CULTURE

	SLOW TRADITIONAL CULTURE	FAST MODERN CULTURE	DOPAMINE CULTURE
ATHLETICS	PLAY A SPORT	WATCH A SPORT	GAMBLE ON A SPORT
JOURNALISM	NEWSPAPERS	MULTIMEDIA	CLICKBAIT
VIDEO	FILM & TV	VIDEO	REELS OF SHORT VIDEOS
MUSIC	ALBUMS	TRACKS	TIKTOKS
IMAGES	VIEW ON A GALLERY WALL	VIEW ON A PHONE	SCROLL ON A PHONE
COMMUNICATION	HANDWRITTEN LETTERS	EMAIL	SHORT TEXTS
RELATIONSHIPS	COURTSHIP/MARRIAGE	SEXUAL FREEDOM	SWIPE ON AN APP

HELPING THEM CHOOSE RESILIENCE OVER AMBIVALENCE

As an employer, I've noticed a pattern with young teammates who are not resilient. Resilience and ambivalence are opposites. When one is present, the other is absent. When a young team member attempts a task that's hard and they see measurable progress, they become more engaged. It's difficult to remain ambivalent. They gain hope and commit to seeing it through. On the other hand, a young staff person may try a hard task, fail, and give up. Afterward they usually become ambivalent. When they're convinced that they cannot conquer something, they stop caring or trying. They don't bounce back after failing. It's easier to be apathetic than to try harder until you conquer an obstacle. Feeling that "it's not worth it" can cause them to quit or be guilty of quiet quitting (giving you bare minimum effort). Both ambivalence and resilience are learned behaviors.

During my years working with John Maxwell, I recall him sharing a story with me from his boyhood. He remembers wrestling his older brother, Larry, in the living room. Larry was bigger and more experienced, which meant he beat John every single time, pinning him on his back. Over time, the defeats came quicker and quicker, as John became conditioned to lose. One day, his dad was watching and challenged his son John to a match. As they wrestled, Dad put up a fight, but as John exerted effort, his father allowed John to pin him down and win. Young John smiled from ear to ear. As an adult, he remembers this key moment. He also recalls his brother Larry never pinned him again.

John's dad knew that once he tasted victory from his effort, he could associate that effort with winning and keep on trying. He also knew that if his youngest son never won, eventually he would experience something called "learned helplessness."

Let's look at the science behind this strategy to increase resilience in Gen Z.

WHAT ARE THE EFFECTS OF LEARNED HELPLESSNESS?

"Learned helplessness" is a term coined by psychologist Martin Seligman in his 1967 research at the University of Pennsylvania as an extension of his interest in depression.[3] In experiments, Seligman and his team discovered that once a person sees no results after repeated effort, they begin to believe that outcomes are out of their control and stop trying. They learn to be *helpless* when they feel their effort is *hopeless*.

Let's face it. We've all confronted a tough problem and after a few moments trying to solve it, our minds automatically ask the question: Is this really worth the effort? How badly do I want this anyway? As a result, young staff need to see their effort produces some kind of positive outcome or they'll stop putting out much effort. Every manager or supervisor has witnessed an employee who lost their passion and work ethic as they lost hope.

HOW TO FOSTER "LEARNED INDUSTRIOUSNESS"

The good news is, leaders can cultivate an opposite effect on their teams. It's called "learned industriousness." This is a behavioral theory from Robert Eisenberger to explain how people exert more effort when they see even the slightest results. Individuals with a history of positive reinforcement for their effort usually transfer this effort to other endeavors. Lab rats that pull a lever twenty times to get food are prone to try harder and longer with another challenge later. They have been conditioned to sustain effort believing it will produce results. Endorphins are released from both the *feeling of hope* and from the *positive outcome*. Every manager or supervisor has witnessed an employee experience the need to see tangible results to motivate them.

> **REFLECT**
> How could you offer tasks and hope that foster learned industriousness in Gen Z?

I watched this work for my son, Jonathan, when he was seven years old. One morning he tried to open a peanut butter jar. The lid was tight, and after several attempts, he began to question how much he wanted that peanut butter. After a while, he gave up and walked away. When he walked out of the kitchen, I unscrewed the lid of that jar, then screwed it back on just tight enough that it would require effort but would be possible for my young son to accomplish his goal. I called him back in the kitchen and asked him to try to open the jar one more time. When he assured me he could not, I told him to work at it for ten full seconds. When he did, he opened the jar. He smiled in triumph, and from that point on, my son was positively challenged to open any jar—pickles, mustard, relish, you name it.

It's learned industriousness. He applied to other areas the belief he developed with one jar: I can achieve difficult goals with extra effort. Both learned helplessness and learned industriousness are *contagious*. Once learned, they spread to other areas of their work.

FROM CANDLES TO BRUSHFIRES

Building resilience is frequently an issue of how we frame a task in their minds. We all have hard projects to complete, but how we look at them often determines our success. It's all a matter of perspective. We must help them choose the right narrative.

One of our new Habitudes images is a favorite of mine: Candles or Brushfires. Consider these two metaphors. Both are flames, but they are fundamentally different based on their size. Candles can be blown out quite easily. You witness this at every birthday party, regardless of how old the celebrant is. A tiny breath can put them out because they're small and fragile. They burn out quickly. Brushfires, on the other hand, not only survive a tiny breath, but they can withstand a huge wind. In fact, they not only survive that huge wind, but the wildfire grows stronger and larger in that wind. I have family in California who endured the January 2025 wildfires. Those fires burned up thousands of acres of land. I heard news reports from Los Angeles residents who begged listeners to "pray against the wind!" The bigger the wind, the bigger the fire.

It is safe to say the marketplace is enduring some harsh winds. Understandably, many are being swept away by the adversity. Their flame goes out. Some say it's felt like going through a hurricane. Many, however, have grown from it all. We've seen these lasting leaders get stronger inside. Their heart's size can be measured by how the harsh wind affects them. These people move from candles to brushfires. *The same wind that extinguishes a candle, extends a brushfire*. The leaders are transformed from fragile to agile amid tough conditions and build young team members into brushfires.

This raises a most important question.

How can we move our young staff from candles to brushfires?

I've observed that people, especially in our day, are one or the other. The narrative they embrace inside prods them to act like a candle with very little perseverance and grit or a brushfire with all kinds of tenacity. How we respond to difficult times has everything to do with the story we tell ourselves. Are we thinking any of the following?

> I'm a victim of my circumstances.
> I have not been able to catch a break in my life and career.
> Someone owes me a better deal, more compensation, perks, or benefits.

Those who refuse to perceive themselves as victims will flourish, even if they are, indeed, victims of a challenging context. These people respond with two qualities that differentiate them from everyone else. I consider these two qualities *metacompetencies* in our day, a skill or quality more important than any other to a flourishing career and team culture. These two competencies are:

1. Resilience
2. Resourcefulness

Just as a brushfire can adapt and display resilience when the wind blows a different direction, these people can maneuver around complicated hardships and navigate unplanned interruptions. Further, just as a brushfire is resourceful, taking advantage of new territory when the wind blows it in that direction, these people find ways to be resourceful and benefit from whatever comes their way. In a very real sense, then:

- Resilience is about adapting to new and harsh realities.
- Resourcefulness is about reversing the effect of those realities.

IT'S ALL ABOUT ADAPTING AND REVERSING

Gene Tunney set a goal as a kid: he wanted to be a professional boxer. At the turn of the twentieth century, boxing was a thrill to watch for many boys, especially in New York. Gene began boxing as a teenager and won several matches as a young man. He joined the Marine Corps during World War I, and while serving in the military, tragedy struck him and threatened to end his career. Gene Tunney broke the fingers in his right hand. As a boxer, you might say he faced his own harsh winds. His coach and trainer both told him he'd have to give up boxing. His bones would be too brittle, preventing him from being a serious contender.

Gene Tunney, however, decided he would not give up on his dream; he would merely change his strategy to achieve it. Although he lacked natural talent, he was an excellent "scientific" boxer who studied his opponents and developed skills to beat them. Gene began to train himself in the art of self-defense before it was popular. He would use the heel of his hand, not his fingers. He trained himself in running backward, knowing if he were to overcome the best boxers, he'd have to run backward a few rounds. And he cultivated patience and grit, knowing it would take time for folks to give him a chance.

Eventually, Gene got that chance to fight the world heavyweight champion.

Jack Dempsey was considered invincible, but Gene's story captured people's imagination. He was a comeback kid and a Cinderella story for boxing fans. Few gave Tunney a chance against Dempsey, but Gene stepped into the ring and stunned the world. He was quick and agile and surprisingly different from before his injury. He beat Jack Dempsey. The victory shocked fans everywhere. It so humiliated Jack Dempsey that Jack challenged him to a rematch. Incredibly, Tunney beat him a second time. He was no fluke. Gene was never defeated again and is now considered one of the greatest boxers of all time. He retired as the heavyweight champion of the world, although few of us have heard of him. Gene's story is a tale of adaptability. He was no candle. He was a brushfire.

Here's the clincher. Fistic experts, who understand boxing, look back on those fights and conclude that there's no way Gene Tunney could have beaten Jack Dempsey had he *not* broken the fingers in his right hand. No one could go toe to toe and head to head with Dempsey and come out alive. It was the hardship, the "harsh wind," he endured that enabled him to reach his goal. He was agile, not fragile.

So, what decisions enabled Gene Tunney to be so agile?

> Resolve. He first decided he would not give up on his original goal. He chose to continue, pushing forward against all odds.

> Adapt. Next, he adjusted how he'd chase his goal. He chose to keep his mission but changed his methods to reach it. He quickly embraced his new normal and shifted.

> Reverse. He leveraged the very problem that could have shut him down to enable him to make his disadvantage an advantage. His obstacle became an opportunity.

BUILDING GRIT AND FOSTERING GROWTH

> Excel. Finally, he didn't just survive the setback, he thrived in it. He accelerated his progress, and his forward movement generated momentum for him.

Living this way makes you a rare breed. In fact, to help you remember these steps above, I want you to notice they spell the word: RARE. The good news is—you can do it too.

Gene Tunney's story is inspiring but not isolated. The pattern we observe in others like him informs our careers today, from Wilma Rudolph and her bout with polio giving her the grit to become the fastest woman in the world as a track star, to Louis Braille, the kid who went blind and later used the very tool that blinded him to help him create a system of reading for the blind worldwide. Resolve. Adapt. Reverse. Excel. It's repeated through history.

Have you spotted this resolve, adapt, reverse, and excel model? How can you teach it?

FOUR STRATEGIES TO BUILD RESILIENCE IN GEN Z

I'll close this chapter by sharing some practical steps you can take to cultivate grit and growth in Generation Z team members. I compiled a list of best practices from leaders and educators I know, especially Hara Estroff Marano, the editor at large for *Psychology Today*.[4] I am a columnist for this periodical and have come to admire Hara's wisdom and scientific approach to the subject of human resilience.[5] The steps below are ones I've taken and encouraged Gen Zers to take to become gritty and resilient.

1. Find a model; be a model.

People do what people see. Not what they hear in a lecture or a motivational speech. Gen Z needs models to follow to know that someone else has faced similar challenges; this mitigates the sense of alienation people feel when they struggle. Don't be afraid to demonstrate how you've struggled through tough times and even show them your battle scars. Also, nothing inspires us to be resilient as much as being a model for someone else who is following us. Encourage Gen Zers to identify a younger or newer staff member they can invest in. Role models are extremely important because they offer a road map to others.

2. Do something scary.
There is something about stepping out of our comfort zones to attempt a risky act—that's unfamiliar and even frightening—that makes us come alive. Our senses are heightened when we take a risk or do something new; we must trust and even rely on one another. Ideally, these initiatives are planned but not scripted. They must include the element of chance. Facing fears is a rite of passage for Gen Z. Doing something that's neither prescribed nor guaranteed unleashes adrenaline and other chemicals in their bodies that awaken them. Fear responses produce endorphins, which can be a natural high. Also, "feel good" chemicals are activated with scary situations, including serotonin and oxytocin. One reason more Gen Zers don't "come alive" is they've been conditioned to be avoiders due to anxiety. We protected them from these rites of passage in the name of safety.

3. Exchange support.
I recall a Stanford experiment that tested how long people could stand barefooted in a bucket of ice water. One outcome was eye-opening: people could remain in the ice water twice as long on average when someone stood near them encouraging them to keep going. People are built for social connection. Gen Zers want it but often don't know how to experience it. Individuals deteriorate mentally without it. Here's the twist. Giving social support to others is as important as getting it. Workplaces can be great spots

to teach Gen Z to exchange social support and encouragement. Place Gen Zers on teams to complete a task and exchange this kind of support. If it helps, pair them up and give them resources to jot notes of encouragement to keep going.

4. Work and wait for results and rewards.
Deliberate exposure to difficult challenges while pursuing a goal deepens our levels of grit. Exposure to moderately tough situations, studies show, alters the hypothalamic-pituitary-adrenal axis in our brains, reducing the hormones that alarm us and helping us to manage stress. Counselors call it "exposure therapy": face a hardship with hope, and you stop being afraid of the hardship.

Stefan is a supervisor who prepares his team for challenging projects, offers a metaphor to illustrate what it will feel like, then tailors the rewards he'll give them to their personalities. Note the three stages: the prep, the metaphor, and the customization of rewards for results.

Jacob Shaidle is a vivid example of a Gen Zer who built fortitude on the job. It wasn't his boss, however, who helped him. It was his parents who practiced the four strategies above. When Jacob was fourteen years old, his mom asked him to clean their outdoor grill. Jacob had seen his parents do it, so he knew what they expected. Jacob surprised her with his work ethic. At that point, Mom and Dad met with Jacob to encourage and challenge him. First, they affirmed him, telling him what they appreciated about his work. Next, they warned him he'd have to pay for college in four years, so he'd better start saving. Then they suggested he go door to door and tell neighbors he'd be willing to clean their barbecue as well. That would be a more lucrative way to save cash than a minimum wage job.

Soon Jacob was an entrepreneur. Not old enough to drive, he walked a half-mile radius to pitch his services, homeowners said yes, and he began making bank that summer. By his second summer, he'd gotten his license and had enough money to buy a car.

Mom and Dad encouraged him to scale the business by adding and training staff. By the third summer Jacob was making six figures, and now, at age twenty, Jacob has a staff of twenty, more than seven hundred customers, and makes $150,000 each summer.[6] He is a picture of grit and growth, thanks to good leadership.

TALK IT OVER

1. Cliff Young's story exemplifies resilience and resourcefulness. How can leaders design workplace challenges or initiatives that help Gen Z employees develop these qualities while maintaining their engagement and motivation?

2. The chapter discusses the impact of "cancel culture" and "binge culture" on reducing grit. What strategies can leaders use to help young professionals overcome these cultural influences and develop a stronger sense of perseverance?

3. The candles or brushfires metaphor highlights the difference between fragility and adaptability in the face of challenges. How can organizations encourage employees to adopt a brushfire mindset and turn obstacles into opportunities for growth?

PART 3

A NEW YOU FOR A NEW TEAM MEMBER

In this final portion of the book, I will land the plane by furnishing a quick summary of how to lead Generation Z as well as the payoff we can expect if we lead them well. Generation Z staff represent a challenge and a choice for us as leaders. We can become frustrated or fascinated with them. We can get furious or get curious about them, as leaders. Here's to a bright future.

14

UPGRADING YOUR LEADERSHIP

If you know anything about college sports, you're aware of terms like *transfer portal* and *name, image, and likeness* (NIL). The portal allows student athletes to jump onto a platform and announce their desire to play for a different school if they're unhappy with their experience on their current team. NIL is about student athletes benefiting financially when their college uses their name or image to earn income. Jerseys, endorsements, ads, and autographs are now a payoff for a student who puts in the time and helps the team generate revenue.

It makes sense. It's so new, however, that the NCAA is still trying to figure the ethics and boundaries of such new rules. The portal is even more complicated. As I watched college football bowl games last year, commentators were admitting the sport is a mess right now, as students are transferring during bowl season, when all eyes are on those games. Many student athletes are selling themselves to the highest bidder. One broadcaster called it the "wild, wild west." Coastal Carolina head coach Tim Beck grieved how different it is to lead today: "You're not building a program anymore. This isn't a program. Each year you just build a team . . . you try to maintain as much culture as you can. . . . We're going to lose our best players every year. That's just part of it."

Coaches and athletic directors have been forced to get used to radically different rules for their industry. It's far more complicated now, with pressure coming from three places: the student athletes, the administration, and the fans. Athletic directors have admitted their job is reduced to putting out fires, not leading. Many forgot their why and chose to quit.

In some ways, this is a picture of our day. Leading in a society that endures a pendulum swinging back and forth between management and labor has become complicated and tiring. The rules seem to be changing. When I began my career, executive-level leaders were clearly calling the shots. Today, it feels like the employees are calling the shots, and it's not always a bad thing. Pay increases and better working conditions needed to happen. Sadly, this democratization of the workforce has caused a rift between managers and Generation Z employees who enter during this power shift. College sports illustrate a new generation of team members entering the workforce. They've been affected negatively and positively by the world in which they grew up.

But if you can get this issue right, you move out of the "red ocean," bloody from the fierce competition that exists in your industry, to a "blue ocean," completely wide open since you changed the rules by which you develop and lead your people.[1] We can either complain about the way things are "today" and wish for "yesterday," or we can adapt and master our new reality. I suggest we do the latter.

The ones that change are the ones that win.

A study by management consultancy McKinsey and Company found Gen Zers to be restless in their jobs, more likely to report hostile work environments and health problems, both mental and physical. Seventy-five percent of Gen Z employees said they were actively seeking other jobs.[2] You may just feel like an NCAA Division I coach with a bunch of your players in the transfer portal. On the brighter side, employers have found that Gen Z staffers show up to work brimming with ideas, ideals, and ambitions.

"Compared to other generations, I find Gen Z to be highly innovative and adaptable," said Adam Garfield, marketing director at Hairbro.[3] "They are not afraid to challenge the status quo and bring new ideas to the table. They also value authenticity and transparency and expect companies to be socially responsible and ethical." Garfield faults the next generation only on interpersonal relations. They need help cultivating emotional intelligence. My question? What if we could capitalize on their strengths and train them in their areas of weakness? That must be our goal.

CHANGING BEFORE IT'S TOO LATE

In 1984, things came to a head at Disney animation. The original "magnificent nine" had mostly retired or passed away. These were the artists who worked on classics like *Lady and the Tramp* and *101 Dalmatians*. Jeffrey Katzenberg was hired to run the studio, and his animation artists split into two factions. The older group of animators desperately tried to control the narrative and cling to the past. They felt holding on to what once succeeded would guarantee new success. The other group included talented twenty-somethings who understood where animation was going and how to make it work for the Disney brand. Katzenberg was thirty years old, positioned in the middle between young and old.

That year, the tenured group worked on a film called *The Black Cauldron*. Roy Disney and Jeffrey Katzenberg were troubled by the violent beginning, the blood, and they felt it wasn't family friendly. The younger group did not like it either. Among them were John Lasseter and Tim Burton, who had recently graduated from CalArts. Katzenberg liked the new artists who saw the future more clearly and knew how to animate with future technology. They seemed to know how to hold on to the timeless values of Walt Disney, yet progress into the future with new animation strategies.

When Katzenberg said *The Black Cauldron* must be edited, the old guard dug their heels in. Producer Joe Hale said, "You can't edit an animation film!" Katzenberg said, "Yes you can, and I will show you." The two groups debated what needed to be changed and reached a stalemate. The film ended up grossing far less than it cost to make. In fact, it was considered a box office bomb.

At this point, Hale and his *Black Cauldron* animators were fired. After the layoffs, Katzenberg began working with the "next gen" team on new projects like *Oliver Twist*, made with dogs. Then *Who Framed Roger Rabbit* and *The Little Mermaid*. Disney animation entered a renaissance. By the 1990s, this renaissance birthed films like *Beauty and the Beast, Aladdin, The Lion King, Hercules, Mulan,* and others. They embraced the family-friendly themes and life lessons yet found new ways to deliver content. This renaissance would not have happened if:

› The older animators stayed around and refused to change.
› A younger generation of animators weren't welcomed into key roles.

Change is often thrust upon us—but when we welcome it, amazing things happen. *While Gen Z may be tougher to lead, they will make us better leaders.* My friend Renee Walter described her leadership saying, "Generation Z is the sandpaper I didn't know I needed." The future will require a new kind of leadership from us, one that assumes a new coaching style that's relationship based, one that believes the best when we don't understand them, and one that continues to learn from anyone, including those who are young. This requires a shift from old-school to new-school styles that work to remain relevant in today's world.

Too many leaders delay making changes until it's too late. Just ask James Keyes, the CEO at Blockbuster Video when it went bankrupt in 2010. Just ask Antonio Perez, the CEO at Eastman Kodak who filed for bankruptcy in 2012. Or just ask Ron Johnson, who failed to navigate changing market conditions at JCPenney. The list goes on and on.

You may have already guessed it, but Generation Z wants fundamental change.

Just before the pandemic, the Barna Research Group surveyed young adults, eighteen to thirty-five years old, in twenty-five countries. This represented a cohort of both millennials and Generation Z. Two of the most important leadership insights from the study were these:

> Understandably, young adults recognize a leadership crisis. They perceive deep and wide systemic problems facing the world's future and feel current leaders are not up to the challenge. Eighty-two percent believe "there are not enough good leaders right now."
> One-third (33 percent) believe that "what it takes to be an effective leader seems to be changing." Those in power are often old and unwilling to adapt to the needs of the world today.[4] (Consider the age of presidential candidates the last three elections.)

Imagine your Gen Z staff. Would they be asking for leadership changes?

In each focus group I've hosted, I hear young adults respectfully *begging* for fundamental change, not incremental change. While employers often propose tweaks to their current systems, today's kids have been exposed to the "dirt" on leaders in nearly all industries, and they want big changes to today's failing systems.

ARE WE READY TO CHANGE?

I'm concerned about the rapid change in culture, namely because business leaders don't seem to keep up with these new norms. We're so obsessed with increased revenue, that we fail to see what it's doing to our ethics and our people. Political agendas change slowly today, but our culture is shifting at warp speed—and not always for the better. After reviewing predictions from futurists and journalists like Ray Kurzweil, Leonard Sweet, Ted Gioia, Nikolas Badminton, and George Friedman, here are my looming questions:

> Everything that can be digitized will be, but what will it do to our people skills and our emotional intelligence?
> Much of our consumer content will be reduced to "free," but will that make us lazy and unwilling to pay a price for something valuable?
> Media and consumer tech will change much faster than legislative initiatives, but are leaders ready to manage the impact?
> AI will disrupt things more than any vote in the Senate, but are we ready to provide ethical guardrails to this technology?
> Dumbed down reality television shows will shape young people's acceptance of cultural norms more than any college class, but is that okay?
> More conflict will happen at educational institutions than in Congress, but are schools willing to change strategies or pedagogies to reach students?
> Manipulative platforms, misleading media reports, and false search engine results will harm us more than a bad governor, but can we spot them?

> Leading with values can make a more meaningful contribution to a healthy future than political rhetoric. Can we embrace this kind of leadership?

We need a new kind of leader.

STARTING WITH THE BASICS

Let's begin with some fundamentals. My surveys of Generation Z employees offered me a snapshot on what they want from their leaders, at the most basic level. After analyzing the research, I've concluded young professionals want three traits from their boss.

1. Neutral—They want employers to be objective and unbiased.
2. Transparent—They want employers to be clear and honest when they speak.
3. Responsive—They want employers to ensure that staff are heard when they speak.

Relevant leaders demonstrate these realities regularly. Keep in mind: *young people do not have the innate need to get their own way, but they do have the innate need to be heard.* Today's workforce is more educated, exposed, and entitled than past generations of employees. Leaders must adjust their approach to lead them. I asked more than three hundred Gen Z employees what qualities they most appreciated in their boss, the ones that enabled that manager to genuinely connect with them. Three qualities topped the list.

THREE QUALITIES THAT WIN THE HEART OF GENERATION Z

1. Humility

Gavin bluntly corrected one of our senior leaders in front of the entire team on a Zoom call. Regardless of the accuracy of Gavin's comment, it divided folks because it was made in an arrogant way. Everyone noticed it but him. The irony is, he expected humility from others but seemed unable to show it. I met with Gavin and attempted to explain the disconnect. The problem wasn't his information; it was his delivery. When people approach a difficult topic or a different generation with humility, it communicates an openness to input, a recognition that they're human and flawed. It says that we know we don't have all the answers. This means I offer ideas, then listen to gain helpful insight myself. Listening screams humility! *I try to speak as if I believe I'm right but listen as if I believe I'm wrong.* More on this later. Gavin never got this and is no longer with our team.

2. Respect

Charlotte had a chip on her shoulder. She was smart and talented enough but began most of her interactions with distrust instead of belief. This twenty-four-year-old even told me when she meets people, she assigns them a grade. They start with an F and must earn an A. She questions everything, which is fine if it's done in a respectful way. I recognize the majority of Gen Z does not trust traditional institutions, but if they hope to make improvements on those institutions, they should know respect can accelerate their progress. Once again, Charlotte demanded respect but didn't offer it to others. We live in a very uncivil, disrespectful era, yet everyone wants to feel respected. Respect communicates your esteem for the other person. Even if you feel you have a better idea, it's good to recall that at one point current ideas were implemented as solutions to problems. Respect begins every interaction with belief.

3. Curiosity

If we enter conversations curious to learn and to see new perspectives, it enables connection between two points of view. When teammates from two generations embody curiosity, they can naturally smooth over rough spots and differences in style. Curiosity trumps conflict and builds a bridge where there might have been a wall. It communicates openness to new ideas and a hunger to grow and improve. Rachel is forty-six and Sam is twenty-two. At first, they butted heads during ideation meetings, but once the need to improve on methods was obvious, both switched gears and became more curious. Those teammates sharpen each other today and now not only overlook their differences but welcome them as an impetus for growth.

> Have you mastered these basics? How successfully have you connected with Gen Z?

When we embody these qualities, we can say almost anything and connect with them.

SIMPLE HABITS TO UPGRADE YOUR LEADERSHIP

1. Start with small and easy habits attached to current ones.
James Clear says, "Your habits are often a byproduct of convenience. Humans are wired to seek the path of least resistance, which means the most convenient option is often the one that wins. Make good choices more convenient and bad choices less so. Behavior will improve naturally."[5] As you see your Gen Z team members needing encouragement or coaching, for instance, set aside time in your calendar to offer it. A few years ago, I inserted

space for "interruption time," margins in my day for disruptions I knew needed my attention but that I had no time for. Bingo. Now I can stop. My stack of empty thank-you notes sits right next to my laptop at my home office, impossible to miss, making a note easier to send. Simple steps can make you a better leader without much trouble.

2. Imagine your team members are volunteers.
This is a step I take on a regular basis. Since Gen Z team members can feel "used" and can see leaders as utilitarian, I walk through our office doors imagining those employees are all volunteers, serving our mission and generating revenue. It changes the way I interact with them, increasing my smiles, gratitude, and grace. It helps me slow down and walk slowly and warmly through the halls. Even though they all get paychecks, I become a better leader by not counting on money to motivate them. Instead, I count on effective, life-giving leadership to do so. When I practice this habit, I lead with higher emotional intelligence, which makes staff serve with better attitudes. They show up because they want to, not because they have to. My improved disposition is contagious.

3. Think: one size fits one.
Each young team member is a unique person with distinct loves, interests, and strengths. The old-school leadership style that shoves everyone into a cookie-cutter mold is outdated. Gen Z wants to be treated as unique and valuable people. They see old-school leaders treating staff like cogs in a wheel, playing a small and often unappreciated role, in a mass of other parts. Gen Z wants to be seen and recognized for who they are. Years ago, we began to assess new team members in their Myers-Briggs profile, their top five strengths, their motivational needs, and their Enneagram results. These were framed and placed in their office. It helped us lead our team like we were playing chess not checkers (which is one of our Habitudes). Each feels valued for who they are.

4. Speak as if you're right, listen as if you're wrong.

Since Gen Zers want to have a voice from day one, I made a change a few years ago when I wrote the book *Eight Paradoxes of Great Leadership*.[6] This decision is a paradoxical one. When I am in meetings, I commit to speak as if I believe I am right (exhibiting confidence), but I listen as if I believe I'm wrong (exhibiting humility). This has been a game changer. Earlier, I had been guilty of finishing their sentences or rolling my eyes at what I assumed I already understood. That wasn't helpful, and it erected a wall instead of a bridge between my young staff member and me. As I listened this way, I found myself saying, "Wow. I had no idea!" Or "I didn't realize that. I appreciate your shedding light on the issue."

5. The people are the point.

Unlike past popular definitions of successful business, which were all about increasing profits for stakeholders, this new leadership paradigm attracts and keeps Gen Zers longer. Employees—more than customers or shareholders—are the most important stakeholders in your organization. I believe taking care of your staff is the critical transaction. I'm sure you've heard the phrase "Happy employees equal happy customers." Starbucks launched a personal growth and leadership training program for young baristas who aspire to management. IBM runs mentorship programs aimed at guiding young employees in tech and leadership. General Electric places a strong focus on leader development and offers rotational programs to learn various parts of the business and mentorship for young staff.

6. Don't argue to win; argue to learn.

Since Gen Z's common narrative is that boomers and Gen Xers are prone to lecture and be stubborn rather than teachable, this leadership habit has transformed the way I debate issues. In meetings, I have typically debated topics to win the argument, which meant I dug my heels in and found new methods to defeat the opposing side of an issue. When I began to argue to learn, I became a more likable leader, and the best idea won, instead of the loudest voice. Our leadership team benefited from inviting two principals (Rick Packer and David Hoyt) from The Table Group to help us with this issue. The power gap was reduced between management and labor, and even between C-suite executive and directors.

7. In trust we grow.
Since Gen Z struggles with trusting authority, this step is valuable. For young staff to discover and contribute their passions—to approach their work as if it were a compelling hobby—leaders must explicitly make trust the foundation of all practices and policies, says Marcus Buckingham, from his *Harvard Business Review* article "Designing Work That People Love." According to the ADP Research Institute, before the pandemic only 18 percent of respondents were fully engaged at work and just 14 percent trusted their senior leaders and team leader.[7] The Centers for Disease Control reported in 2018 that 71 percent of adults had at least one symptom of workplace stress, such as headaches or feeling overwhelmed or anxious.[8] Since the pandemic, it's grown worse. Leaders must host regular check-ins with young staff to ensure lines of trust are strong. Leadership operates on the basis of trust.

What steps could you take to lead Gen Zers more effectively?

FROM GATEKEEPER TO GUIDE

Watching established leaders underperform or misguide people not only leaves a bad taste in Gen Z's mouth, it can be a source of greater anxiety. Only recently have I recognized how poor leaders deepen anxiety and depression in Gen Z team members. Let me illustrate how it works. Author Jonathan Shay wrote a book called *Achilles in Vietnam* in 1994.[9] Shay is a physician and clinical psychiatrist who witnessed so many soldiers return home from Vietnam with PTSD, he chose to study why so many were suffering with deep rage and stress disorders. His findings surprised him. Unlike what he expected, it wasn't the bullets or bombs that were the top reason for their PTSD. Instead, it was the poor leadership displayed by their commanding officers. Many of those officers lacked character, waffled on what the troops should do, and made decisions based on self-interest rather than on values that were in the best interest of the soldiers.

Both on the battlefield and when they returned home, those men were triggered. Shay told stories of friendly fire, in which deaths are a result of weapons being mistakenly directed at one's own side, and of fragging, which is a term used when a fellow soldier deliberately kills their superior on the battlefield out of hatred. Shay, in his work with the veterans, found that many years after their experiences, they are still engulfed in rage. He noted these veterans are the embodiment of the term *walking wounded*. They are unable to access their feelings, often suffer from depression, alcohol, and drug abuse, and suicide. The full title of Shay's book? *Achilles in Vietnam: Combat Trauma and the Undoing of Character.*

While this may sound like an extreme analogy, the point is clear. The problem was the lack of character and connection in their commanding officers. The soldiers didn't feel they could trust them. This uncertainty and angst deepened anxiety in those troops. I believe it does the same thing in a business or on a team.

Many from Generation Z have told me they never served under a healthy, life-giving leader. One of them said, "I haven't seen a good leader yet, so I don't know even what one looks like." These young people recognized the need for good leaders but had no desire to lead. Unfortunately, misconstrued ideas of what leadership looks like have turned many from today's emerging generation away from the responsibility.

In 2021, the Barna Research Group unveiled a study indicating most respondents from Generation Z don't trust traditional institutions in government, education, business, and churches for a couple of reasons.[10] First, every Gen Zer could point to examples of how leaders abused their power in each of these industries. In each case, power appeared to corrupt. The primary reason for this distrust, however, is because those institutions merely perpetuate the old guard, irrelevant ideas (in their minds), and the biases of boomers and Gen Xers.

In the 2016 and 2020 presidential elections, the top candidates in both major parties were old and unappealing to most young voters—Hillary Clinton, Donald Trump, Bernie Sanders, and Joe Biden. In 2024, Kamala Harris was the youngest candidate, and she was sixty. I mean no disrespect, but Generation Z sees these elders as offering "tenure" and "titles," not trust. Many leaders in Washington focused more on holding on to their power than on empowering younger generations to lead. Older leaders have operated more like *gatekeepers* of power, not *guides* who prepare younger generations to lead.

Consider how people became leaders throughout history. We've seen quite an evolution of power over the centuries. How leaders gained the right to exercise authority has changed:

HISTORICAL ERA	LEADERSHIP ROLE	HOW YOU GAINED POWER
1. Autocratic	Dictator/tyrant	Might makes right
2. Tribal	Divine right	God gave it to you
3. Monarchy	Familial right	Family lineage
4. Democratic	Elected right	Popular vote
5. Connection	Earned influence	Relationship/results

Notice the pattern. Thousands of years ago, authority came from power and might. If you could fight and win, you got to lead. Then it moved to divine right, where people felt that leaders gained authority from God. Next, it was about being in the right family—princes came to power when the king died. Centuries ago, reason entered the scenario, when elections were held and the people decided who would lead them. Today, however, while elections still happen, millennials and Generation Z tend to follow a leader who makes connections with them. Someone they believe knows and understands them; someone who does relationships well and gains results through those skills.

When I wrote this, I did a quick self-evaluation. I asked myself: *How do I gain influence with my team? How would they perceive I influence them? How do they think they increase their influence on the team? Is it really about positions or productivity? How do relationships play a role? Do I combine both results and relationships to deepen my influence?*

THE GATEKEEPER ERA IS FADING

As you can see, leadership styles have evolved from one person holding power at the top of a food chain to a more participative style, where others weigh in on decisions and are included in the influence of a team. People today are more savvy, educated, and aware of information in our world and want to be included. The truth is: *people support what they help create.* A person operating as a "gatekeeper" for everyone is an antiquated notion in our day, except in rare situations. Authority has been decentralized in many organizations. Leaders must still run point and own the vision of their organization, but the power gap between followers and leaders is shrinking—and it must continue to shrink. Gen Z has a disdain for leaders who still operate in the style of the

> Have you acted mostly as a gatekeeper leader rather than a guide?

first three eras above. We must move from command and control to connect.

ATTRACTING GENERATION Z BY BECOMING A CORPORATE EXPLORER

We've established that business leaders find it more difficult to work with Generation Z staff than employees from any other generation. Gen Z has overtaken millennials in this category. Managers claim these workers lack technological skills and say Gen Zers are more "easily distracted" and "easily offended." It's enough to frustrate any leader.

Allow me to remind you, however, of one important reality.

Generation Z represents our future. By 2030, three-quarters of the workforce will be made up of millennials and Generation Z teammates, like it or not.[11] Most baby boomers will be gone, and Generation X will be retiring by the thousands every day.

A CORPORATE EXPLORER

As I've said, I benefited when I chose to turn my *frustration* into *fascination* with this emerging generation at work. While their different mindset means they'll need to adapt to collaborate with older teammates, they also bring traits with them that our workplace desperately needs. Once again, seven out of ten Gen Zers want to be an entrepreneur. In short, they want to *start* something more than *join* something. They've come of age during COVID-19 and longed for a job that's "pandemic proof." Many began driving for Uber, learned to code, created content for TikTok, or started a YouTube channel and monetized their ingenuity. Millions in the workforce are working gigs to satisfy their start-up yearnings. Some are making big money. I believe organizations like yours and mine will be more attractive and engaging to them if we take a step in a new direction.

Create an internal "gig economy."

One secret we began to employ at our organization, Growing Leaders, was to create internal teams within the larger team that felt like start-ups. In a word, we started an *intra-preneurship*, which occurs when organizations create an entrepreneurship culture. They have agile teams study and launch innovative products or services (or even internal programs) and give them budget and authority to make something happen. Leaders of these new growth businesses within a larger company are commonly called "corporate explorers." The intra-preneurship culture not only is attractive to Gen Z recruits, but it helps you retain them as well.

> Young team members get the experience of a start-up company.
> Young team members enjoy the security of an established organization.

Why is this important? In a survey from Handshake, an employment site for Generation Z, researchers asked eighteen hundred new graduates what they wanted most from their future employers. The overwhelming majority—85 percent—answered "stability." High pay and benefits also ranked high, but both feel like second cousins to stability. On the other hand, the desire for "a fast-growing company" garnered only 29 percent of the vote.[12] They hesitate in a post-COVID prerecession job market that awaits them. A megatrends report by Accenture recently dubbed this the era of "permacrisis."[13] On the heels of a pandemic in a shaky economy, Gen Zers realize how vital secure financial income is to their peace of mind. This special entrepreneurial zone enables this. Teammates get a *start-up experience* with the *security* of an established organization.

THE FUTURE BEGINS WITH Z

ELEVEN MADISON PARK

Will Guidara did just this with his restaurant in New York City. He wrote a book, *Unreasonable Hospitality,* which is all about offering the kind of service that sets them apart from other eating places. His most famous restaurant is called Eleven Madison Park. He encourages creativity and invites ideas from young waiters and staff. He's unreasonably hospitable to his team as well as his guests.[14] Here are a few of their ideas.

> Wanting customers to feel they were walking into a home, not an establishment, they removed the podium up front. The host memorizes the names of every guest who dines each night and greets them by name as they're shown to their table to enjoy a meal.
> One evening, four guests from out of town talked about all they did while in New York but noted they never had the chance to grab a hot dog from a street vendor. So a team member left, bought a hot dog, and a chef sliced it up and served it to them. They raved the rest of the night about the waiter's creative hospitality.
> Based on young team members' observations, the restaurant decided to give food, drinks, and desserts away based on what they overheard customers talk about. At check time, a waiter arrives with a free bottle of wine and glasses and offers it with the check.
> The restaurant team committed to not wanting any customer to leave the restaurant unhappy. Sometimes this is a tough challenge, but this commitment has drawn out the creativity from

everyone. Each night something different happens that they celebrate.

The best part of this story? Eleven Madison Park was recently voted the best restaurant in the world. Sure, the food and the chef are elite, but Will believes it's about empowering his team, especially the young creatives, to act like enterprisers every day.

This kind of innovation happens all over the world. I want you to meet David Tjokrorahardjo. He started a company called MDCo (Million Dollar Company), and it's all about the next generation. They provide coaching and funding for micro-sized organizations in Indonesia. David attracts Gen Zers by unleashing them. He describes it this way:

> Because over 40 percent of my country, Indonesia, is under twenty-five years old, I wanted to find the best of this population. So, when I interview young people, I ask, "Ten years from now, if money is not an issue and you cannot fail, what do you want to do?" Then I ask, "How can I help you build your dream?" Many join us and stay for three years to prepare. I'm the first investor in their company. If they join us—they work for free the first year, writing a letter to their parents requesting they fund their son or daughter for that preparation year. (They cannot live with parents.) By year's end, I usually invite them to join me as a partner. At this level, they're not given a secure salary but live on dividends they earn. It's a test. We must see if they can do this for two to three years. As this period ends, MDCo finds a leadership role for them in the company, or those young pioneers are turned loose to chase their dream.

Either way, everyone wins because they met in the middle: Gen Zers get a gig experience while being coached, and MDCo gets the best young leaders in the land. David has launched hundreds of companies this way. I'd say he's updated his leadership.

TALK IT OVER

1. The chapter emphasizes that adapting leadership styles to meet Generation Z's expectations is critical for organizational success. What specific changes in leadership approaches do you think are most effective in bridging the generational gap and fostering engagement with Gen Z employees?

2. The concept of creating an internal "gig economy" within organizations to cater to Gen Z's entrepreneurial mindset is introduced. How might implementing this strategy affect workplace culture, and what challenges could arise from its integration?

3. The chapter highlights humility, respect, and curiosity as key traits that resonate with Generation Z. How can leaders actively cultivate and model these qualities in their interactions with younger team members to build trust and collaboration?

15

THE BIG PAYOFF

When I was a young teenager, I was like most boys in our neighborhood. I loved sports, messing around outside, doing well enough in school to go to college, and finding a girlfriend. Something happened at this stage, however, that changed my focus. I loved art class, and my teacher, Mr. Dishon, recognized I had a talent for drawing. He fanned it into flame, influencing me to stay home and design stuff instead of killing time. My friends pleaded with me to play, but I wanted to play at something else—graphic design.

Unbeknownst to me, Mr. Dishon entered one of my pieces in an international art contest, hosted in Japan. Weeks later, I got a phone call with news that I had won first prize in this contest. The following days, my parents got calls from our city newspaper and other media outlets wanting an interview. It was a little surreal for this middle-class fourteen-year-old kid. This milestone led to an art scholarship in college and later a job as an editorial cartoonist for five city newspapers. I was able to monetize my hobby.

I had no idea that investing my time, energy, and talent would pay off this way.

Likewise, you may have the same experience investing in your young team members. Those employees from Generation Z may feel like a misguided investment of time, energy, and talent on your part. You may feel you shouldn't waste too much time; after all, you're busy with important things. Why take time to build a relationship with them when they'll likely leave in a year? What if you train them and they leave? I love Zig Ziglar's response to this question: What if you don't train them, and they stay?

I've found that nine times out of ten, my investment in younger generations has paid off, but only because our leaders became intentional about it. We saw big payoffs.

BIG PAYOFFS

In many ways, I am a classic baby boomer who has transformed the way I approach work and leadership. I have changed because younger generations have forced me to become better. I've attempted to practice what I've preached in this book, and it has improved me on many levels, at home as well as at work. In this final chapter I summarize the takeaways from this book and offer recommendations for you going forward.

Earlier, I mentioned several young team members our organization hired who turned out to be challenging. At the time, I resented all the extra time and effort they required from our department heads. As I reflect on those days, I recognize how much those young staff members drove me to become a clearer communicator, a more inspiring visionary, a more empathetic person, and a more strategic leader. They upset our workplace—darn it—and along the way, they made me better than I was before.

THE BIG PAYOFF

The expense of our improvement was disruption. The payoffs come after the disruption.

Riley joined Don's staff in early 2024. Don had a few internal question marks during Riley's job interview but decided to take a chance on her. She was young and seemed to be an intelligent young lady and a curious learner. She seemed like a good bet.

The next several months were hell for Don and his team. Riley was the epitome of all the rumors we've heard about Generation Z—she was on her phone constantly; she interrupted others in meetings, possessing little emotional intelligence; she was late for meetings; and at times, she called in to say she needed some personal time off. She also needed check-ins with Don every day, asking questions and posing hypothetical situations at work, wondering how they might handle them. Riley's team called them nonsense. Don vacillated on whether to keep her or to let her go. Was she worth the time, effort, and money? His older staff wondered this too and chose to merely tolerate her.

Until Riley barged into Don's office one day with a big smile.

Don told me later he was about to dismiss her, when she posed the question: "What if we could eliminate half of our customer service calls and spend a fraction of what we're spending now on maintenance?" It was a big question that raised Don's eyebrows.

"I'm listening," Don replied.

Riley had been on YouTube and ChatGPT for hours at night, enthralled with solving a problem that Don's team had been unable to solve for years. To make a long story short, Riley had come up with a rudimentary version of a plan to solve this problem that utilized artificial intelligence, cut time and money spent in half, while repositioning employees on tasks that could increase revenue by almost 30 percent. When she finished sharing her epiphany, Don blinked a few times, asked a few probing questions (which she was able to answer due to the tutoring she received on YouTube), then said to her, "Riley, you may be on to something."

She was. At twenty-three years old, Riley was able to revolutionize how Don's team did business. Was it messy? Yes. Did Riley require patience from everyone at work? Yep. But was it worth it all? You bet it was. Riley's disruptive style was tolerable because her ideation and intuition paid off big-time. The payoff was worth the chaos. I predict more of this—if we lead them well.

I CHALLENGE YOU TO MAKE THE CHANGES I MADE

> Don't think GATEKEEPER, think GUIDE. Because we are migrating from the gatekeeper era where bosses command and control everything, Gen Z needs a guide who listens to them, then offers counsel to make the most of their input. They've grown up in a world where gatekeepers, like publishers, record labels, and traditional agents, no longer control content. We must lead with open hands.

> Don't think CORRECT, think CONNECT. Because Gen Zers are young, they prioritize social status on the team and getting respect from others. They'll be highly sensitive to any comments from us that could be interpreted as disrespect. When we threaten status and respect, they lose motivation. A wall goes up between you. When interacting, always begin by connecting with them before you offer correction. We must establish a relationship to gain loyalty.

> Don't just think EXPERIENCE, think EXPERTISE. Because their traditional experience is low, seek the smart-tech experience they have. They may have expertise on some apps or digital strategies

to move your vision forward. Could it be useful? Value and leverage what they bring and watch their engagement increase. When you honor their strengths, you capture their hearts and motivate them.

> **Don't think LOAN the work when they want to OWN the work.** Because Gen Z often quits within two years, we don't let them own the work. Too often, I've led in a traditional fashion: I tell a young staff person what I set out to do as a founder, then give them explicit directions on how to continue this work. This means I am "loaning" my work to them. I learned to share the desired results we sought then let them explore new ideas to reach those goals. We must let them own the work by determining how they do it.

> **Don't think LECTURE, think LISTEN.** I will say it again: we must begin with belief and end with hope. As a leader, I learned to believe the best about them and to always offer hope by the end of our conversation. This means I lay aside my great lecture on the topic we're discussing and start by listening. People do not need to get their own way, but they do need to be heard.

> **Don't think COMMAND, think CONSULT.** Because Gen Zers grew up in a different world than I did, I didn't get much engagement from them at first. I acted like a commanding officer. I realize now: although I'm in charge, I'm no longer a commander, I'm a consultant. I lead with questions. Keep your vision in mind, but begin meetings by posing questions, like a consultant, and see where it goes.

> **Don't think WASTE, think WIKI.** Allowing Gen Zers to weigh in on projects may feel like a waste of time. You'll quickly spot their inexperience and immaturity. But if you'll not worry so much about wasting time and focus on the new "wiki" culture that now exists, you'll see the time you spend as an investment, not a waste. Just like Wikipedia invites input from users all over the world to arrive at definitions and solutions, leaders must let Gen Zers weigh in to get buy-in.

> **Don't think MANAGE, think MENTOR.** Remember, Gen Z staff may disappoint you, since they're inexperienced. When they fail, you'll be tempted to be an "enforcer" (insisting they meet a standard and shaming them for not doing so) or a "protector" (feeling empathy and lowering the standard). Neither are complete. When you stop merely managing them and begin mentoring them, you equip them to reach your standards. You combine high belief with high expectations, saying: "I'm giving you this feedback because I have high expectations of you, and I know you can reach them."

We must begin with belief not suspicion. Actor Denzel Washington put into words how I think life works best:

> The first part of your life you learn.
> The second part of your life you earn.
> The third part of your life you return.

It's time to take our place as mentors, returning the investment someone made in us. Remember—you and I cannot do anything about our ancestors, but we can do something about our descendants. And there are a bunch of them. More than half of our world's population is under the age of thirty.[1] They know a lot, but they need a lot from us as well.

Here is why I have hope. I noticed the interesting parallels the first two generations of the twentieth century have with the first two generations of the twenty-first century.

SENIOR / BUILDER GENERATION KIDS	GEN Z / GENERATION ALPHA KIDS
1. Faced the Spanish flu pandemic	1. Faced the COVID-19 pandemic
2. Grew up in the Roaring '20s	2. Growing up in a new roaring '20s
3. Faced a volatile economic depression	3. Face a volatile economic time

My uncle Gene is nearly 101 years old, and my Aunt Wanda is not far behind him. As I interviewed people who lived during those difficult times of the first four decades of the twentieth century, I asked them what their parents, teachers, and leaders did that enabled them to endure such times with resilience. They all agreed—their leaders didn't let them think like victims. Leaders believed those kids would make it through and thrive as older adults eventually. And that's precisely what happened for millions of them. Tom Brokaw called the World War II population "The Greatest Generation." I wonder: Could we have another "greatest generation," because we've led our young so well today?

THIS COULD GO EITHER WAY

In my introduction to this book, I share the parable of a boy who held a small bird in his hand and, to be clever, asked an older gentleman if he thought the bird was dead or alive. The man reflected for a while and then replied, "This is a trick. If I say it's dead, you'll open your hand to show me it's alive. If I say it's alive, you could crush the bird to show me it's dead. So my response is: the answer is in your hand."

IF WE LEAD THEM WELL	IF WE DON'T LEAD THEM WELL
1. They'll be problem-solvers.	1. They'll be part of the problem.
2. They'll embrace a service mindset.	2. They'll embrace a scarcity mindset.
3. They'll enjoy PTG (posttraumatic growth).	3. They could struggle with stress (PTSD).
4. They'll emerge with a grit narrative.	4. They'll emerge with a victim narrative.
5. They'll see a silver lining.	5. They'll see a dark cloud.
6. They'll be resilient and resourceful.	6. They'll be reactive and regretful.

Whether Gen Z team members flourish or flounder may just be in our hands.

NOTES

Chapter 1
1. Resume Builder, "3 in 4 Managers Find It Difficult to Work with Gen Z," *Resume Builder*, accessed January 29, 2025, https://www.resumebuilder.com/3-in-4-managers-find-it-difficult-to-work-with-genz.
2. Bryan Robinson, "Gen Z Careers: The Worst to Manage? 45% of Hiring Managers Say," *Forbes*, May 26, 2024, https://www.forbes.com/sites/bryanrobinson/2024/05/26/gen-z-careers-the-worst-to-manage-45-of-hiring-managers-say/.
3. CareerBuilder, "How Long Should You Stay in a Job?" *CareerBuilder*, accessed January 29, 2025, https://www.careerbuilder.com/advice/blog/how-long-should-you-stay-in-a-job.
4. Tim Elmore, *Generation iY: Our Last Chance to Save Their Future* (Atlanta, GA: Poet Gardner Publishers, 2010).
5. Tim Elmore, *A New Kind of Diversity: Making the Different Generations on Your Team a Competitive Advantage* (Atlanta, GA: Maxwell Leadership Publishing, 2023).
6. Margaret Mead, *Culture and Commitment: The New Relationships Between Generations in the 1970s* (New York: Natural History Press, 1970).
7. Neil Postman, *The Disappearance of Childhood* (New York: Penguin Random House, 1982).
8. "Gen Z Earns Six Figures as Digital Side Hustlers, New Study Finds," Intuit Credit Karma. Last modified March 4, 2024. Accessed January 29, 2025. https://www.creditkarma.com/about/commentary/gen-z-earns-six-figures-as-digital-side-hustlers-new-study-finds.
9. "Meet Young Scientist Who Created Automated Tourniquet," *Good Morning America*, March 27, 2024, https://www.goodmorningamerica.com/living/video/meet-young-scientist-hannah-herbst-108537503.

NOTES

10. "1 in 4 Gen Zers Brought a Parent to a Job Interview," Resume Templates, April 30, 2024, https://www.resumetemplates.com/1-in-4-gen-zers-brought-a-parent-to-a-job-interview/.

Chapter 2

1. "Gen Z More Likely to Ditch Work for a Mental Health Day—Here's Why That Concerns Job Experts," *New York Post*, February 26, 2024, https://nypost.com/2024/02/26/lifestyle/gen-z-more-likely-to-ditch-work-for-a-mental-health-day-heres-why-that-concerns-job-experts/.
2. "Latest Federal Data Shows That Young People Are More Likely Than Older Adults to be Experiencing Symptoms of Anxiety," Kaiser Family Foundation, accessed September 7, 2023, https://www.kff.org/.
3. *We've Only Just Begun*, Resolution Foundation, February 2024, https://www.resolutionfoundation.org/app/uploads/2024/02/Weve-only-just-begun.pdf.
4. "Gen Z More Likely to Ditch Work for a Mental Health Day—Here's Why That Concerns Job Experts."
5. Anna Lembke, *Dopamine Nation* (New York: Penguin Random House, 2023).
6. "Isolation Among Generation Z in the United States," *Ballard Brief*, accessed February 26, 2024, https://ballardbrief.byu.edu/issue-briefs/isolation-among-generation-z-in-the-united-states/.
7. Tim Elmore, *Artificial Maturity: Helping Kids Meet the Challenge of Becoming Authentic Adults* (Hoboken, NJ: Jossey-Bass Publishers, 2012).
8. "Close Enough: Living Through Others," *Hidden Brain*, accessed February 26, 2024, https://hiddenbrain.org/podcast/close-enough-living-through-others/.
9. "Gen Z: The Complete Guide," *McCrindle*, accessed February 26, 2024, https://mccrindle.com.au/article/topic/generation-z/gen-z-the-complete-guide/.
10. "3 in 4 Managers Find It Difficult to Work with Gen Z," *Resume Builder*, accessed February 26, 2024, https://www.resumebuilder.com/3-in-4-managers-find-it-difficult-to-work-with-genz/.

Chapter 3

1. "Population Change Data Tables," U.S. Census Bureau, accessed January 29, 2025, https://www.census.gov/data/tables/time-series/dec/popchange-data-text.html.
2. Kim Parker and Ruth Igielnik, "On the Cusp of Adulthood and Facing an Uncertain Future: What We Know About Gen Z So Far," *Pew Research Center*, May 14, 2020, https://www.pewresearch.org/social-trends/2020/05/14/on-the-cusp-of-adulthood-and-facing-an-uncertain-future-what-we-know-about-gen-z-so-far/.

NOTES

3. "Generation Z vs. Millennials: How Are They Different?" *Adecco*, accessed January 29, 2025, https://www.adecco.com/en-us/employers/resources/article/generation-z-vs-millennials-infographic.
4. Kim Parker and Ruth Igielnik, "On the Cusp of Adulthood and Facing an Uncertain Future: What We Know About Gen Z So Far," *Pew Research Center*, May 14, 2020, https://www.pewresearch.org/social-trends/2020/05/14/on-the-cusp-of-adulthood-and-facing-an-uncertain-future-what-we-know-about-gen-z-so-far/.
5. Richard V. Reeves and Ember Smith, "The Growing Gender Gap Among Young People," *Brookings Institution*, accessed January 29, 2025, https://www.brookings.edu/articles/the-growing-gender-gap-among-young-people/.
6. "LinkedIn Economic Graph," *LinkedIn*, accessed January 29, 2025, https://www.linkedin.com/showcase/linkedin-economic-graph/.
7. "New ZenBusiness Research Finds Class of 2023 Sees Neurodiversity as an Asset in Leadership, Is Primed to Be the Most Entrepreneurial," *BusinessWire*, June 14, 2023, https://www.businesswire.com/news/home/20230614082058/en/New-ZenBusiness-Research-Finds-Class-of-2023-Sees-Neurodiversity-as-an-Asset-in-Leadership-is-Primed-to-be-the-Most-Entrepreneurial.
8. "Deloitte Gen Z and Millennial Survey," *Deloitte*, accessed January 29, 2025, https://www.deloitte.com/global/en/issues/work/content/genz-millennialsurvey.html.
9. "Gen Z Activism Survey," *United Way NCA*, accessed January 29, 2025, https://unitedwaynca.org/blog/gen-z-activism-survey/.
10. "UK Students Rankings 2023," *Universum Global*, accessed January 29, 2025, https://universumglobal.com/resources/news-press/uk-students-rankings-2023/.
11. "John Parsons," *McKinsey & Company*, accessed January 29, 2025, https://www.mckinsey.com/our-people/john-parsons.

Chapter 4

1. Ryan Jenkins and Steven Van Cohen, *Connectable: How Leaders Can Move Teams From Isolated to All In* (New York, NY: McGraw Hill, 2022).
2. "Sleepunders and Lateovers: The New Alternative to Sleepovers," *New York Times*, January 11, 2024, https://www.nytimes.com/2024/01/11/style/sleepunders-lateovers-sleepovers.html.
3. Edison Research, *Gig Economy 2018: Marketplace Edison Research Poll*, January 2019, https://www.edisonresearch.com/wp-content/uploads/2019/01/Gig-Economy-2018-Marketplace-Edison-Research-Poll-FINAL.pdf.
4. David Yeager, *10 to 25* (New York, NY: Simon and Schuster, 2024).
5. Fuller Youth Institute, accessed January 29, 2025, https://fulleryouthinstitute.org/.

6. Jennifer Gerhardt, "Who You Gonna Call? Crossing the Streams of Gen Z and the Boomers at Work," *Prof Gerhardt*, accessed January 29, 2025, https://profgerhardt.com/who-you-gonna-call-crossing-the-streams-of-gen-z-and-the-boomers-at-work/.

Chapter 5

1. "How Long Should You Stay in a Job?" *CareerBuilder*, accessed January 29, 2025, https://www.careerbuilder.com/advice/blog/how-long-should-you-stay-in-a-job.
2. "A Generation Disconnected: The Data on Gen Z in the Workplace," *Gallup*, accessed January 29, 2025, https://www.gallup.com/workplace/404693/generation-disconnected-data-gen-workplace.aspx.
3. David Yeager, *10 to 25*, 246.
4. "Deloitte Gen Z and Millennial Survey."
5. "Most QSR Employees Worked 90 Days Before Quitting in 2022," *HR Dive*, accessed January 29, 2025, https://www.hrdive.com/news/most-qsr-employees-worked-90-days-before-quitting-2022/641061/.
6. "Chick-fil-A Retention Data," *Comparably*, accessed January 29, 2025, https://www.comparably.com/companies/chick-fil-a/retention.
7. *Your Game Plan for Winning Early Talent*, Handshake, March 2022, https://joinhandshake.com/employers/resources/your-game-plan-for-winning-early-talent/.
8. Chip Heath and Dan Heath, *The Power of Moments: Why Certain Experiences Have Extraordinary Impact* (New York, NY: Simon and Schuster, 2017).
9. "Workers Feel Undervalued," *HR Dive*, accessed January 29, 2025, https://www.hrdive.com/news/workers-feel-undervalued-workhuman/639999/.
10. "Workers Feel Undervalued."

Chapter 6

1. Anna Russell, "Why So Many People Are Going 'No Contact' with Their Parents," *The New Yorker*, August 30, 2024, https://www.newyorker.com/culture/annals-of-inquiry/why-so-many-people-are-going-no-contact-with-their-parents.
2. David Yeager, *10 to 25* (New York, NY: Simon and Schuster, 2024), 81.
3. Désirée Nießen, Isabelle Schmidt, Katharina Groskurth, Beatrice Rammstedt, and Clemens M. Lechner, "The Internal-External Locus of Control Short Scale-4 (IE-4): A Comprehensive Validation of the English-Language Adaptation," *PLoS One* 17, no. 7 (2022): e0271289, https://doi.org/10.1371/journal.pone.0271289.
4. Peter Gray, *Free to Learn: Why Unleashing the Instinct to Play Will Make Our Children Happier, More Self-Reliant, and Better Students for Life* (New York, NY: Hachette Book Group, 2013).

NOTES

5. *2019 Retention Report*, Work Institute, accessed January 29, 2025, https://info.workinstitute.com/hubfs/2019%20Retention%20Report/Work%20Institute%202019%20Retention%20Report%20final-1.pdf.
6. "Best Grocery Store in America," *Reader's Digest*, accessed January 29, 2025, https://www.rd.com/article/best-grocery-store-america/.

Chapter 7

1. Jean Twenge, *iGen: Why Today's Super-Connected Kids Are Growing Up Less Rebellious, More Tolerant, Less Happy and Completely Unprepared for Adulthood* (New York, NY: Atria Books, 2017).
2. Jonathan Haidt, *The Anxious Generation* (New York, NY: Penguin Press, 2024).
3. Greg Lukianoff and Jonathan Haidt, *The Coddling of the American Mind: How Good Intentions and Bad Ideas Are Setting Up a Generation for Failure* (New York, NY: Penguin Publishing House, 2019).
4. Jeff Hancher, *Firm Feedback in a Fragile World* (Atlanta, GA: Maxwell Leadership Publishing, 2025).
5. "Alabama Football: Everything Nick Saban, Players Said After 27–6 Win Over Cincinnati," *247Sports*, accessed January 29, 2025, https://247sports.com/college/alabama/LongFormArticle/Alabama-Football-Everything-Nick-Saban-players-said-after-27-6-win-over-Cincinnati-Bearcats-Brian-Robinson-Will-Anderson-Bryce-Young-179525506/#179525506_6.
6. "3 in 4 Managers Find It Difficult to Work with Gen Z," *Resume Builder*, accessed January 29, 2025, https://www.resumebuilder.com/3-in-4-managers-find-it-difficult-to-work-with-genz/.
7. David Scott Yeager, Julio Garcia, Patti Brzustoski, William T. Hessert, Valerie Purdie-Vaughns, Nancy Apfel, Allison Master, Matthew E. Williams, and Geoffrey L. Cohen, "Breaking the Cycle of Mistrust: Wise Interventions to Provide Critical Feedback Across the Racial Divide," *Journal of Experimental Psychology* 143, no. 2 (2014): 804–824, accessed January 29, 2025, https://www.apa.org/pubs/journals/releases/xge-a0033906.pdf.
8. "The 4 Baumrind Parenting Styles," *Parenting for Brain*, accessed January 29, 2025, https://www.parentingforbrain.com/4-baumrind-parenting-styles/.
9. Jeremy Sutton, "Growth Mindset vs. Fixed Mindset," *Positive Psychology*, October 27, 2021, accessed January 29, 2025, https://positivepsychology.com/growth-mindset-vs-fixed-mindset/.

Chapter 8

1. "How Does Gen Z See Its Place in the Working World? With Trepidation," *McKinsey & Company*, accessed January 29, 2025, https://www.mckinsey

NOTES

.com/featured-insights/sustainable-inclusive-growth/future-of-america/how-does-gen-z-see-its-place-in-the-working-world-with-trepidation.

2. Tim Elmore, *The Pandemic Population: Eight Strategies to Help Generation Z Rediscover Hope After Coronavirus* (Atlanta, GA: Poet-Gardener Publishing, 2020).
3. "Gen Z Mental Health: The Impact of Tech and Social Media," *McKinsey & Company*, accessed January 29, 2025, https://www.mckinsey.com/mhi/our-insights/gen-z-mental-health-the-impact-of-tech-and-social-media.
4. Jean M. Twenge and W. Keith Campbell, "Associations Between Screen Time and Lower Psychological Well-Being Among Children and Adolescents: Evidence from a Population-Based Study," *Preventive Medicine Reports* 12 (2018): 271–283, https://doi.org/10.1016/j.pmedr.2018.10.003.
5. "Employee Wellness Statistics," *Zippia*, accessed January 29, 2025, https://www.zippia.com/advice/employee-wellness-statistics/.
6. Mark McDonald, *United States of Fear: How America Fell Victim to a Mass Delusional Psychosis* (Bombardier Books, 2021).
7. *State of Gen Z 2020: The Impact of Covid-19 on Gen Z and Future*, Center for Generational Kinetics, accessed January 29, 2025, https://www.msjc.edu/careereducation/documents/fow/State-of-Gen-Z-2020-by-CGK-Impact-of-Covid-19-on-Gen-Z-and-Future-3-of-3-in-Study-Series.pdf.
8. Tim Elmore, *Stressed Out: Five Research-Based Methods to Help Teens Beat Stress and Anxiety* (Growing Leaders, free publication).
9. *Healthy Consulting*, accessed January 29, 2025, www.healthyconsulting.com.
10. "How Big of a Problem Is Anxiety?" *Psychology Today*, accessed January 29, 2025, https://www.psychologytoday.com/us/blog/anxiety-files/200804/how-big-problem-is-anxiety.
11. Bessel van der Kolk, "Posttraumatic Stress Disorder and the Nature of Trauma," *Dialogues in Clinical Neuroscience* 2, no. 1 (2000): 7–22, https://doi.org/10.31887/DCNS.2000.2.1/bvdkolk.
12. John Tierney and Roy Baumeister, *The Power of Bad: How the Negativity Rule Affects Us and How We Can Rule It* (New York, NY: Penguin Random House, 2019).
13. Charles Duhigg, *Supercommunicators: How to Unlock the Secret Language of Connection* (New York, NY: Random House Publishers, 2024).
14. Dana L. Helmreich, J. Paul Bolam, and John J. Foxe, "The European Journal of Neuroscience's Mission to Increase the Visibility and Recognition of Women in Science," *European Journal of Neuroscience* 46, no. 9 (2017): 2427–2428. https://doi.org/10.1111/ejn.13728.

Chapter 9

1. "The Fundamental Attribution Error," *Harvard Business School Online*, accessed January 29, 2025, https://online.hbs.edu/blog/post/the-fundamental-attribution-error.

NOTES

2. Noah Sheidlower, "Managers Say Gen Z Is Easily Offended—It's the Top Cause of Firing, Survey Finds," *Business Insider*, April 2023, https://www.businessinsider.com/managers-say-gen-z-easily-offended-top-cause-firing-survey-2023-4.
3. Noah Sheidlower, "The Roadmap Generation: Gen Z Prioritizes Long-Term Career Plans." *Business Insider*, June 2024. https://www.businessinsider.com/the-roadmap-generation-gen-z-prioritizes-long-term-career-plans-2024-6.
4. "Gen What? Debunking Age-Based Myths About Worker Preferences," *McKinsey & Company*, accessed January 29, 2025, https://www.mckinsey.com/capabilities/people-and-organizational-performance/our-insights/gen-what-debunking-age-based-myths-about-worker-preferences.
5. *Noba Project*, "The Psychology of Groups," accessed January 29, 2025, https://nobaproject.com/modules/the-psychology-of-groups.

Chapter 10

1. Daniel H. Pink, *Drive: The Surprising Truth About What Motivates Us* (New York: Penguin Random House, 2009).
2. "Gen Z in the Workplace: How Should Companies Adapt?" *Imagine*, Johns Hopkins University, April 18, 2023, https://imagine.jhu.edu/blog/2023/04/18/gen-z-in-the-workplace-how-should-companies-adapt/.
3. Adam Grant, *Hidden Potential: The Science of Achieving Greater Things* (New York: Penguin Random House, 2023), 89.
4. Adam Grant, *Hidden Potential*, 91.
5. Bibb Latané, Kipling Williams, and Stephen Harkins, "Many Hands Make Light the Work: The Causes and Consequences of Social Loafing," *Journal of Personality and Social Psychology* 37, no. 6 (1979): 822–832, https://doi.org/10.1037/0022-3514.37.6.822.
6. James A. Shepperd, "Productivity Loss in Performance Groups: A Motivation Analysis," *Psychological Bulletin* 113, no. 1 (1993): 67–81. https://doi.org/10.1037/0033-2909.113.1.67.

Chapter 11

1. Chip Heath and Dan Heath, *Made to Stick: Why Some Ideas Survive and Others Die* (New York: Random House, 2007), 19–20.
2. "Distinguishing Between Your 'What' and 'Why' Can Greatly Impact Your Brand," *Forbes*, March 9, 2020, https://www.forbes.com/councils/forbescommunicationscouncil/2020/03/09/distinguishing-between-your-what-and-why-can-greatly-impact-your-brand/.
3. "Mehrabian's 7-38-55 Communication Model," *World of Work Project*, accessed January 29, 2025, https://worldofwork.io/2019/07/mehrabians-7-38-55-communication-model/.

NOTES

4. "September 2023 Message from Dr. Carol R. Bradford," *Ohio State Medicine*, accessed January 29, 2025, https://medicine.osu.edu/ohio-state-medicine-dr-bradford-message/september-2023.
5. "Gen Z in the Workplace: How Should Companies Adapt?" *Imagine*, Johns Hopkins University, April 18, 2023, accessed January 29, 2025, https://imagine.jhu.edu/blog/2023/04/18/gen-z-in-the-workplace-how-should-companies-adapt/.
6. Kevin Eikenberry, "Keychain Leadership," *Outcomes Magazine*, accessed January 29, 2025, https://outcomesmagazine.com/keychain-leadership/.

Chapter 12

1. "United States Army," *Wikipedia*, last modified December 29, 2024, accessed January 29, 2025, https://en.wikipedia.org/wiki/United_States_Army.
2. "Nicholas Humphrey," *Wikipedia*, last modified October 26, 2024, accessed January 29, 2025, https://en.wikipedia.org/wiki/Nicholas_Humphrey.
3. Chiara Succi, "Soft Skills for the Next Generation: Toward a Comparison between Employers and Graduate Students' Perceptions," *Sociologia del Lavoro* 137 (2015): 244–256.
4. Chiara Succi, "Soft Skills for the Next Generation," 244–256.
5. Kartic Narayan, "Is AI a Job Killer or a Job Creator? What History Tells Us," *The Economic Times*, October 26, 2023, https://economictimes.indiatimes.com/jobs/hr-policies-trends/is-ai-a-job-killer-or-a-job-creator-what-history-tells-us/articleshow/104728338.cms.
6. "Leadership Skills That Are Still Relevant in the AI Age," *Forbes Business Development Council*, accessed January 29, 2025, https://councils.forbes.com/forbesbizdevcouncil.
7. Janna Anderson, Lee Rainie, and Alex Luchsinger, "Artificial Intelligence and the Future of Humans," Pew Research Center, December 10, 2018, https://www.pewresearch.org/internet/2018/12/10/artificial-intelligence-and-the-future-of-humans/.

Chapter 13

1. Angela Duckworth, *Grit: The Power of Passion and Perseverance*, accessed January 29, 2025, https://angeladuckworth.com/grit-book/.
2. Ted Gioia, "The State of the Culture 2024," *The Honest Broker*, accessed January 29, 2025, https://www.honest-broker.com/p/the-state-of-the-culture-2024.
3. Martin E. Seligman and Steven F. Maier, "Failure to Escape Traumatic Shock," *Journal of Experimental Psychology* 74, no. 1 (1967): 1.
4. Hara Estroff Marano, contributor page, *Psychology Today*, accessed January 29, 2025, https://www.psychologytoday.com/us/contributors/hara-estroff-marano.

NOTES

5. "9 Ways to Overcome Adversity," *Psychology Today*, November 2024, accessed January 29, 2025, https://www.psychologytoday.com/us/articles/202411/9-ways-to-overcome-adversity.
6. "This 20-Year-Old's Summer Side Hustle Earned $150,000," *Entrepreneur*, accessed January 29, 2025, https://www.entrepreneur.com/starting-a-business/this-20-year-olds-summer-side-hustle-earned-150000/480636.

Chapter 14

1. Chan W. Kim and Renée Mauborgne, *Blue Ocean Strategy: How to Create Uncontested Market Space and Make the Competition Irrelevant* (Brighton, MA: Harvard Business Review Press, 2005).
2. "How Does Gen Z See Its Place in the Working World? With Trepidation."
3. "Gen Z Is the Most Difficult Generation in the Workplace: Poll," *New York Post*, April 21, 2023, accessed January 29, 2025, https://nypost.com/2023/04/21/gen-z-is-the-most-difficult-generation-in-the-workplace-poll/.
4. "Reviewing Global Young Adults," *Barna Group*, accessed January 29, 2025, https://www.barna.com/research/reviewing-global-young-adults/.
5. James Clear, *Atomic Habits: An Easy & Proven Way to Build Good Habits & Break Bad Ones* (New York, NY: Random House Business, 2018).
6. Tim Elmore, *Eight Paradoxes of Great Leadership: Embracing the Conflicting Demands of Today's Workplace* (Nashville, TN: HarperCollins Leadership, 2021).
7. "Designing Work That People Love," *Harvard Business Review*, May 2022, accessed January 29, 2025, https://hbr.org/2022/05/designing-work-that-people-love.
8. Donna Pickett, "Mental Health in the Workplace," Centers for Disease Control and Prevention, July 2018, accessed January 29, 2025, https://stacks.cdc.gov/view/cdc/152725.
9. Jonathan Shay, *Achilles in Vietnam* (New York, NY: Simon & Schuster, 1994).
10. "Gen Z Questions Answered," *Barna Group*, accessed January 29, 2025, https://www.barna.com/research/gen-z-questions-answered/.
11. "Gen Z in the Workplace: How Should Companies Adapt?" *Imagine*, Johns Hopkins University, April 18, 2023, accessed January 29, 2025, https://imagine.jhu.edu/blog/2023/04/18/gen-z-in-the-workplace-how-should-companies-adapt/.
12. "6 Things Gen Z Wants from Their Job," *Handshake Blog*, accessed January 29, 2025, https://joinhandshake.com/blog/employers/6-things-gen-z-wants-from-their-job/.
13. *Accenture Life Trends 2023 - Full Report*, accessed January 29, 2025, https://www.accenture.com/content/dam/accenture/final/capabilities/song/marketing-transformation/document/Accenture-Life-Trends-2023-Full-Report.pdf.

NOTES

14. Will Guidara, *Unreasonable Hospitality: The Remarkable Power of Giving People More Than They Expect* (New York, NY: Penguin Random House, 2022).

Chapter 15
1. Ameena Razzaque, "Are We Prepared to Serve the Youngest Half of the Global Population?" *Collaborative on Global Children's Issues*, Georgetown University, July 16, 2023, accessed January 29, 2025, https://globalchildren.georgetown.edu/posts/are-we-prepared-to-serve-the-youngest-half-of-the-global-population.

ACKNOWLEDGMENTS

Melissa Dill, who is by my side every step I take, doing whatever must be done, from proofreading chapters, to offering suggestions, to scheduling focus groups, to furnishing encouragement along the way—I could never repay you, my friend. You not only serve me well—you spoil me. I don't want to do any projects without you, Melissa!

Matt Litton, who met for hours with me to map out this book and ensure it includes the big ideas it contains. Matt—you are the king of the big picture. You're a master craftsman. I consider you not just a colleague but a friend.

Zach Thomas, Mike Wade, Andrew Johnson, Terese Fogleman, Nick Westbrook, and John and Cristina Crays, who assembled Generation Z employees for focus groups. I appreciate your friendship, your collaboration, and your belief in the next generation.

Tim Burgard and the HarperCollins Leadership team, who quickly agreed to do this book, believing it was an important message for leaders (and other readers) to hear. Thanks for the care you take to create and promote resources at HCL!

Mark Cole, Jared Cagle, and the rest of my dear friends at Maxwell Leadership, who took this book on as a Maxwell Imprint and are letting their world know about it. You are family to me. I love the energy you bring to leader development and your belief in younger generations.

ACKNOWLEDGMENTS

My man Cam Turner, who did some early research, collecting trends among Generation Z members. Thanks, Cam, for caring deeply about today's youngest generations. You are both a teacher and a learner, as a "next gen" leader yourself.

Our team at Growing Leaders, who works each day investing in the "next generation." Over the years, you have influenced millions of educators and students, and we've only scratched the surface. Thanks for believing in Generation Z.

Chris Carneal, whose energy never wanes when it comes to leadership and the next generation. Chris, you and your team at Booster Enterprises offered to host two launch events to get this book off the ground. I am forever grateful.

Jonathan Elmore, my son, who helped me find great Generation Z interviews and who had endless conversations with me about this younger population right behind his. I love our reverse mentoring relationship we've enjoyed for three decades, my buddy.

Pam Elmore, my bride of forty-four years, who not only believes in me but assumes that what I create will be good, every time. Sometimes to a fault. Thanks, babe, for not only being my wife for decades but for being my balcony person all these years.

INDEX

absenteeism, 23–24, 26–27
adaptability, 250–251, 267–269
affiliation as teamwork trigger, 209
affirmation, 102–103
agency, 48, 57–58, 111
agility, 250–251
Ahrendts, Angela, 200–201
AI (artificial intelligence), 53, 248–251
"A LEG" (Ask, Listen, Empathize, Guide), 139–142
Allen, Sam, 101
ambition. *See* motivation and ambition
ambivalence, 262–263
Ambroza, Tony, 250
anxiety, 26, 48, 157, 166, 286–287. *See also* mental health
Apartments or Homes, 245
Apollo 11 mission, 20–22
application, 221, 242
appreciation, 102
arguing to learn, 285–286
Aristotle, 224
Augsburger, David, 141, 182
authenticity, 34–35, 249
authority
    culture of distrust of, 28
    democratization of the workforce, 24–25
    evolution of, 287–288
    falling age of, 8–11

    generational change in sense of, 110–112
    intuitive vs. positional, 13
    myth on distrust of, 72
    Toyota's "Andon Cord," 98
autonomy, 7, 122, 173, 182, 193
AutoTQ, 13–14

Baby Boom Generation, 30, 33, 39, 110, 195–196
Barra, Mary, 4–5
Baumrind, Diana, 146
belief
    expectations and, 143–144, 300
    feedback from a context of, 135
    hope and, 221
    mentor mindset and, 78, 114–115
    myths about Gen Z vs., 82–83
    respect and, 82, 282–283
    surgeon leaders and, 143
    velvet-covered bricks, 144–146
belonging needs, 79–80, 184–185
binge culture, 33–34, 260–261
Boldt, George, 205–206
Brief, Ballard, 36
Brokaw, Tom, 301
Brooks, Arthur, 101, 163–164
Brower, Tracy, 54
Brown, Brené, 79–80, 185
Buber, Martin, 246
Buckingham, Marcus, 286
Burberry Coats, 200–201

INDEX

CAB (context, applications, belief), 220–221
Campbell Soup Company, 230–231
cancel culture, 29, 73, 95, 129, 259–260
Candles to Brushfires, 265–267
Cathy, Truett, 103
Chess and Checkers, 204–205
Chick-fil-A, 91, 177–178, 252
Churchill, Winston, 136
Clear, James, 283
coaching, 6–7, 19–20, 43, 93
Coffee Meetings, 101–102
Coffee Step, 243
cofigurative society, 12
command vs. consult, 299–300
commitment, 74, 88, 117, 178–179
commodification of employees, 62–63
communication. *See also* conversations; feedback and tough conversations; listening
  comfort zones and preferred zones, 219–220
  in emotional contexts, 69–70, 161–163
  EPIC approach, 222–227
  hooks for, 217–218
  information vs., 216
  in interviews, 93
  point, picture, and practice, 230–231
  preferences by generation, 30–31
  problem and challenge, 214–217
  seven principles, 227–229
  Tappers and Listeners experiment, 213–214
  in times of disruption, 220–221
  velvet-covered bricks and, 144
  warm, clear, and simple, 93
community, 36, 79–80, 184–186. *See also* connection
compassion, 56, 163–166
Conant, Doug, 230–231
connection. *See also* community
  communication and, 225–226
  before correction, 134, 298
  establishing early, 101–102
  feedback and, 134
  in-person commerce, return of, 51
  open workplaces, 98–99
  post-interview, 95
  right to influence and, 112
  superficial, 36
  trust and, 42
consult vs. command, 299–300
conversations. *See also* feedback and tough conversations
  emotional, 162
  napkin, 119
  practical, 162
  slide deck, 120
  social, 162
  soft skills and, 241, 242–246
  white board, 119–120
corporate explorers, 290–291
Counselor posture, 247
COVID pandemic, 152–153
Crockpots and Microwaves, 177–178, 243–244
curiosity, 283
currency, 63–65
cynicism, 28, 40, 43

Dahl, Ron, 77
dance, 169–171
Dearstyne, Jacob, 251
Dechter, Ernest, 119
decision-making, 178–179, 251
Deep Work Wednesdays, 113
Deloitte, 239–240
demands, 96, 175
democratization of the workforce, 24–25, 93, 94, 112, 276
demonstration, 241
Dentists and Cavities, 176–177
depression, 26, 154, 261, 263, 286–287. *See also* mental health
Disney animation, 277–278
dispensability, perception of, 207–208
Doctor posture, 247
dopamine culture, 33–34, 261–262

INDEX

Duckworth, Angela, 257–258
Duhigg, Charles, 161–162, 226
Dupree, Max, 220
duty, 186–187, 203
Dweck, Carol, 146

Early Birds and Mockingbirds, 244
Eastman Kodak, 59–61, 279
Eight Paradoxes of Great Leadership (Elmore), 285
Eisenberger, Robert, 264
Eleven Madison Park, 292–293
Elliott, T. S., 176–177
emotional intelligence, 57, 158–159, 249–250, 251, 284
empathy, 56, 141, 163–166
employment statistics, 5
encouragement, 102–103
enforcer mindset, 114–115
engagement, 214–215, 241, 299
Enterprise Car Rental, 87–88, 90
entitlement, 71–72
entrepreneurialism, 6, 10, 55–56, 76, 121, 192, 290–291
equity, 203–204
evaluation, 242
expectations
 big picture, value of, 187–188
 disconnect, metaphors of, 176–179
 feedback and, 135, 143–144
 of how work works, 172–173
 lowered, 145
 natural laws of the workplace, 173–175
 ownership and responsibility, 180–181
 PERKS template, 96, 175
 pros and cons of Gen Z, 171–172
 steps to meet in the middle, 181–183
 team players, 183–187
 velvet-covered bricks, 144–146
 want vs. need, 184–185
experience
 antiquated, 81
 evaluation and, 242

experiments vs., 8
expertise vs., 298–299
generational perspective on, 13
hacked, 121
information masquerading as, 35–36, 38
intra-preneurship and, 291
lack of, 6, 18, 64, 171, 214, 300
NASA story and, 21
virtual, 37–38, 60
voice and, 179–180
expertise vs. experience, 298–299
external locus of control, 117–118

Faded Flag principle, 229
feedback and tough conversations
 action steps for fragile generation, 134–136
 "A LEG" approach, 139–142
 fragility culture and, 127–129, 133–134
 impasses, 138–139
 instinctual mode of operation, 142
 responses under pressure, 158–159
 Surgeons and Vampires, 142–144
 velvet-covered bricks, 144–146
 when to be silent, 130–132
financial uncertainty, 55
fitting in vs. belonging, 80, 185
fixed mindset, 146
flexibility, 122
fluidity, 99
food in the workplace, 53–54
Forbes, Ron, 199
four-day workweek, 51
fragility, 73–74, 127–129, 133–136
Friedman, Milton, 63
Frost, Carolyn, 158–159
Frost, Maxwell, 59
fun and play, 99
fundamental attribution error, 68, 172
future predictions, 50–54

Garfield, Adam, 277

INDEX

Garman, Jack, 22
gaslighting, 124, 140
gatekeepers, 71, 93, 286–290, 298
General Mills, 119, 231
General Motors, 3–5
generational comparison, 30–33, 39
Generation Alpha, 48, 56
generation gap, 108
Generation iY (Elmore), 8
Gen X, 31, 33, 39, 110, 196
Gen Z
   as advanced and behind, 17–18
   authority, falling age of, 8–11
   characteristics of, 39–42, 48–49
   cognitive abilities, 11
   delayed maturity, 14–17
   as difficult to work with, 5
   generational comparison, 30–33, 39
   identity, belonging, and purpose needs, 78–81
   masquerades and, 35–38
   Peter Pan Paradox, 7–8
   postfigurative society and rookie smarts, 11–14
   pros and cons of, 171–172
   reality vs. facsimile and, 34–35
   seasoned veterans vs. young rookies, 6
   status, respect, and value recognition, need for, 76–78
   world of, 27–30, 32
gig economy, 76, 89, 121, 290–291
Giola, Ted, 226, 261–262, 280
Glennie, Evelyn, 199–200
global leadership, 59–60
Golden Buddha, 237–238
Goodell, Roger, 115
Google, 240
Grant, Adam, 9, 24, 77, 93, 112, 199–200, 226
Gray, Peter, 118
Grindley, Trey, 78–79
grit and resilience
   adapting and reversing, 267–269
   ambivalence and, 262–263
   background, 255–257
   from Candles to Brushfires, 265–267
   cultural factors, 259–262
   Grit Scale, 257–258
   learned helplessness, 263–264
   learned industriousness, 264–265
   strategies for building, 269–272
Grout, Maggie, 9–10
Growing Leaders, 8–9, 58–59, 113, 227
growth mindset, 146
growth needs, 100, 123, 250. *See also* grit
grunt work, 74–75
guide approach, 93, 141–142, 286–290, 298
Guidera, Will, 292–293

Habitudes
   books, 245–246
   in Brazil, 227
   Candles to Brushfires, 265–267
   Chess and Checkers, 204–205
   Crockpots and Microwaves, 177–178, 243–244
   Dentists and Cavities, 176–177
   five big conversations, 242–245
   Golden Buddha, 237–238
   Half-Hearted Mountain Climber, 178–179
   images and, 224–225
   online, 9
   seven principles for getting through, 227–229
   sports teams and, 29
   The Starving Baker, 223
   Surgeons and Vampires, 142–144
   Thermostats and Thermometers, 225
   the Waldorf principle, 205–206
Habitudes for Communicators (Elmore), 227–229
hacking, 58–59
Haidt, Jonathan, 11, 73, 129
Hale, Joe, 278
Half-Hearted Mountain Climber, 178–179

INDEX

Hancher, Jeff, 136
Harris, Sydney, 216
Hastings, Reed, 60
Heckman, James, 239
help, asking for, 186
Herbst, Hannah, 13–14
Hidayat, Farhand, 11
hobby, job as, 197–198, 201–202
hope, 43–44
Host posture, 247
Hough, Derek, 169–170, 188
House on Fire principle, 228
human touch, 252
humility, 251, 282
Humphrey, Nicholas, 239
Hy-Vee, 125

identity needs, 78–79, 184–185
influence, 59–60, 112, 141, 209
influencers, 51–52, 174–175
information, 35–36, 216
intelligence, 13, 37–38, 81–83. *See also* emotional intelligence
internal locus of control, 117–118
internships, 52–53
interviewing, 92–97, 175

Jenkins, Ryan, 68
job hopping, 88–91
John Deere, 100–101
Johnson, Derric, 13
Juhl, Sam, 59–60

Katzenberger, Jeffrey, 277–278

laziness, myth of, 71–72
leadership. *See also* feedback
  cultural change and, 275–281
  descriptive, 123–124
  gatekeeper vs. guide, 286–290
  habits to upgrade, 283–286
  humility, respect, and curiosity, 282–283
  interest in, 59–60
  intra-preneurship, 290–294
  neutral, transparent, responsive, 281
  new type of leader, 52
  with permission vs. position, 113
  prescriptive, 118, 123–124
  Surgeons and Vampires, 142–144
  visibility or invisibility, 131
Leahy, Robert, 159
learned helplessness, 263–264
learned industriousness, 264–265
Lembke, Anna, 33–34, 260
Lincoln, Abraham, 124
listening
  authority and, 112
  feedback and, 140–141
  humility and, 282
  as if you're wrong, 122–123, 182–183, 282
  lecturing vs., 130, 142, 299
  more, need for, 6–7, 19
  myth on not caring and, 70–71
  Toyota's "Andon Cord," 98
  when to be silent, 130–132
loyalty, 74–75
Lukianoff, Greg, 73, 134

Mackey, John, 113, 115
Makosinski, Ann, 55–56
Marano, Hara Estroff, 269
margin, 156
masquerades, 35–38
mastery, 193
maturity, 14–18, 37–38
Maxwell, John, 75, 103, 174, 251, 263
May, Rollo, 217
McCrindle, Mark, 42
McDonald, Mark, 152–153
MDCo, 293–294
Mead, Margaret, 11–12
meaning, 99, 122
Mehrabian, Albert, 217
mental health. *See also* fragility
  common mental disorders, 26–27
  communication and, 161–163
  company wellness programs, 152
  compassion and, 163–166
  culture of uncertainty and, 28
  margin, movement, mindfulness, and management, 156–158

INDEX

mental health (cont'd)
  pandemic + smartphone and, 152–153
  rates of mental illness, 26, 150
  real challenges, 150–152
  tensions and vulnerabilities, 153–156
  tough conversations, responses in, 158–159
  trauma, 159–161
mentoring. *See also* coaching; soft skills
  desire for, 43
  managing vs., 43, 79, 300
  mentor mindset, 78, 114–117
  NASA story, 20, 81
  programs, 239–240, 285
  reverse, 53, 59, 124
  Sherpa guides, 103–105
  vocation rotation, 115–116
metaphors. *See* Habitudes
Millennial Generation, 31, 33, 39, 88, 111, 196–197
mindfulness, 157
mission, 79–81, 99, 122, 182, 193, 208
Mitchell, Shawn, 104
Moore, Alaina, 193–194
Moore, Ashley Rae, 210
Moore, Dayton, 116–117, 166
Moore, Josiah, 191–192
motivation and ambition
  appealing to significance, equity, and benefit, 202–204
  autonomy, mastery, and purpose, 192–194
  background, 191–192
  building, 42
  dispensability, perception of, 207–208
  from external to internal, 209–210
  by generation, 194–197
  job as hobby, 197–198, 201–202
  metaphors for conversations, 204–206
  pulling of triggers, 208–209

  teamwork as social dilemma, 206–207
  turning work into play, 199–201
myths about Gen Z
  background, 66–70
  belief vs., 82–83
  disloyalty and no grunt work, 74–75
  distrust and fake news, 72
  don't listen and don't care, 70–71
  fragileness and social media, 73–74
  laziness, entitlement, and cluelessness, 71–72
  not serious about work, 75–76

NASA, 20–22, 81
Nast, Thomas, 229
need vs. want, 184–185
neurobiological-incompetence model, 89
new-collar jobs, 122
New Kind of Diversity, A (Elmore), 10
Newton, Elizabeth, 213–214
Nikols, Jonathan, 251
Nishimura, Jorge, 227
no-collar jobs, 122
nuance, 41
Number Three Pencil principle, 228–229
nurturing, 136–137

office influencer role, 51–52
onboarding and welcoming
  background, 87–90
  encouragement and affirmation, 102–103
  ideal workplace for Gen Z, 98–100
  interviewing, 92–97
  personal connections, 101–102
  Sherpa guides, 103–105
  Toyota example, 97–98
  unforgettable first day, 100–101
open workplaces, 98–99
Orange Leaf Frozen Yogurt, 115
outcome motivation, 209

INDEX

overwhelm, 40
ownership, 43, 117–119, 180–181, 299

passion, 200
PERKS template, 95–97, 175
personal time off (PTO), 26–27, 113
persuasion motivation, 209
Peter Pan Paradox, 7–8
Peters, Tom, 230
Piloseno, Tony, 10–11
Pink, Daniel, 193
portable devices, 28, 36
postfigurative society, 11–12
Postman, Neil, 12
Powell, Kara, 223
power, 54, 64, 141, 287–288
pragmatism, 40–41
preferences, 96, 175
prefigurative society, 12
PricewaterhouseCoopers, 240
professionalism, 139, 214–215
promotion, 173–174
protector mindset, 114–115
psychological contract, new, 24–25
PTSD and PTG, 159–161, 287
purpose needs, 80–81, 193
Putnam, Robert, 36
Pyrrhic victories, 187

Rao, Gitanjali, 57
RARE (Resolve, Adapt, Reverse, Excel), 267–269
relationships, 95, 101, 134, 141. *See also* connection
remote work, 122, 155, 173, 219, 221
requests, levels of, 175
resilience. *See* grit and resilience
resourcefulness, 250–251, 257–259, 266–267
respect, 76–78, 80, 82, 89–90, 122, 282–283
responsibility, 92, 117–118, 180–181
results, 174, 209
reversing, 267–269
road map generation, 182–183
robots, 53

rookie smarts, 13, 21, 81–83
Rotter, Julian, 117–118

Saban, Nick, 136–137
safety, psychological, 124
salary discussions, 97
Salyers, David, 177–178
Sandberg, Sheryl, 44, 172
Sasson, Steven, 59–60
Sauce Pricing, 4
School Yearbook principle, 229
self-esteem, 236–237
Seligman, Martin, 263
Sessions, Michael, 59
Shaidle, Jacob, 271–272
Shay, Jonathan, 286–287
Sherpa guides, 103–105
sick leave, 26–27
Silent Generation, 30, 33, 39, 110
Simulation Supervisors (SimSups), 20, 22, 81
Sinek, Simon, 141
Smith, Jaylen, 59
social contract, 186
social identity theory, 185
social intelligence, 239
social justice, 56
social loafing, 207
social media, 26, 36, 72–74, 151–152, 179–180, 228
social media influencers, 51–52
social motivation, 209
Socratic method, 226
soft skills
  for the AI age, 248–251
  big conversations, 242–246
  building blocks, 241–242
  host, doctor, counselor, and tour guide postures, 246–248
  human touch, 252
  the self-esteem problem, 235–238
  the soft skill problem, 238–240
Stanley, Andy, 221
status, 76–77, 79, 89–90
stereotyping, 68, 172
Stressed Out (Elmore), 156
superpowers, 123

INDEX

surgeon-style leadership, 142–144
Sweet, Leonard, 222, 224, 280
systems, disruption of, 112

Tanner, Don, 43–44
Tappers and Listeners experiment, 213–214
Tassopoulos, Alex, 252
team awareness, 251
team players, 183–187
teamwork, 206–209
Teirney, John, 160
Thinking Huts, 9–10
Thomas, Zach, 43–44, 91
Thomas Nast principle, 229
Thompson, Brian, 54
Three Levels of Planning, 119
Tjokrorahardjo, David, 293
Tour Guide posture, 248
Toyota, 97–98
Trains and Tracks, 244
transparency, 249
Trapp, Brett, 142
trauma, 159–161, 287
triggers for teamwork, 208–209
trust, 42, 72, 82, 113, 136–138, 286
Tunney, Gene, 267–269
turnover, 90–91
Twenge, Jean, 129, 151–152

Vajre, Sangram, 15
value of Gen Z
    age of influence, 59–60
    as currency, 63–65
    more than commodity, 62–63
    painting analogy, 46–48
    positive traits, 54–60
    predictions on future of work, 50–54
    quick read on Gen Z, 48–50
    recognition of, 77–78
vampire-style leadership, 142–144
Varney, Stuart, 138–139
velvet-covered bricks, 144–146
virtual reality, 37–38, 53
vocation rotation, 115–116
voice, 179–183

Waldorf principle, 205–206
Walsh, John, 128
Walter, Renee, 278
want vs. need, 184–185
Washington, Denzel, 300
waste vs. wiki, 300
Webb, Colin, 3–4
welcoming. *See* onboarding and welcoming
Welles, Orson, 66–67
Whole Foods, 113–114
wiki culture, 109–110, 300
Windows and Mirrors principle, 228
women, role of, 52
work ethic of future, 50

Yeager, David, 76–78, 89, 114
Young, Cliff, 255–257

Ziglar, Zig, 296
zillenials (tweeners), 27

ABOUT THE AUTHOR

TIM ELMORE is first and foremost a family man. He has been married to Pam for forty-four years, and they have two adult children, both married and in their careers. His other loves include their dog Sadie (CEO of their home), reading, sports, and popcorn, not necessarily in that order. He not only leads Tim Elmore, Inc., as he speaks to businesses, sports teams, and nonprofits, but is also the founder of Growing Leaders, a nonprofit organization created to develop emerging leaders. His passion for leader development and for the emerging generation grew out of his work alongside bestselling author Dr. John C. Maxwell since 1983. Growing Leaders and the Maxwell Leadership Foundation merged in 2023.

Over the last decade, Tim has spoken to more than five hundred thousand leaders in corporations nationwide, such as Chick-fil-A, the Home Depot, Ford Motor Company, Cox Communications, Cicis Pizza, Coca-Cola Bottlers Association, and Delta Global. His curriculum has been used by sports teams like the Kansas City Royals, New York Giants, Buffalo Bills, Tampa Bay Buccaneers, Houston Rockets, and San Francisco Giants, as well as by athletic departments at the University of Alabama, Ohio State University, Stanford University, and Duke University. He is committed to building the next generation of leaders all over the globe.

Dr. Elmore's expertise on the emerging generation and generational diversity in the workplace has led to national media coverage

ABOUT THE AUTHOR

on CNN Headline News, Fox Business, Newsmax, and *Fox & Friends*. A TEDx speaker, his blog is read by more than one hundred thousand people weekly. Tim writes columns for *Psychology Today* and *Inc.*, and he was listed as one of the Top 100 Leadership Speakers in America by *Inc.* magazine.

Tim has written forty books, including the bestselling *Generation iY: Our Last Chance to Save Their Future*, *Habitudes®: Images that Form Leadership Habits and Attitudes*, *The Eight Paradoxes of Great Leadership*, and *A New Kind of Diversity: Making the Different Generations on Your Team a Competitive Advantage*. For information or to explore a speaking event, visit: timelmore.com.

LEAD GEN

Z

WITH CLARITY AND CONFIDENCE

You've read the insights—now bring them to life.

Tim Elmore's full video series *The Future Begins with Z* is now on LeaderPass. With over **50 short, high-impact lessons**, it's split into two powerful tracks: **Foundation** (to understand Gen Z) and **Strategy** (to lead them well).

- ✓ Watch lessons that match your current challenge
- ✓ Use it with your team to guide conversations
- ✓ Each session is just minutes long—easy to fit into real life
- ✓ Lifetime access, with new content added throughout the year

Start now at:

Clear, practical, and ready when you are.